THE EASTER BUNNY AND HIS FRIENDS

TOM WOLFE

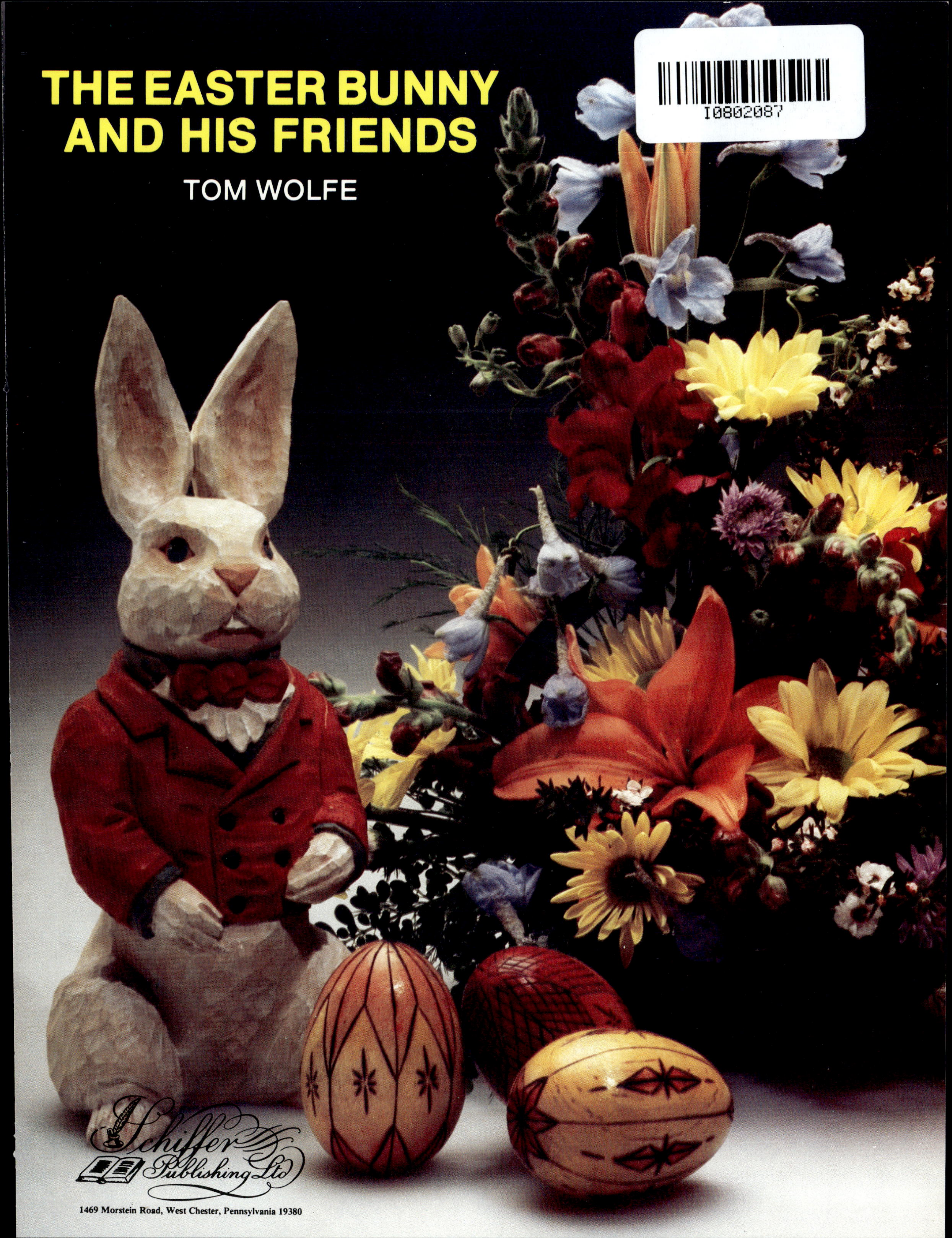

Schiffer Publishing Ltd

1469 Morstein Road, West Chester, Pennsylvania 19380

Contents

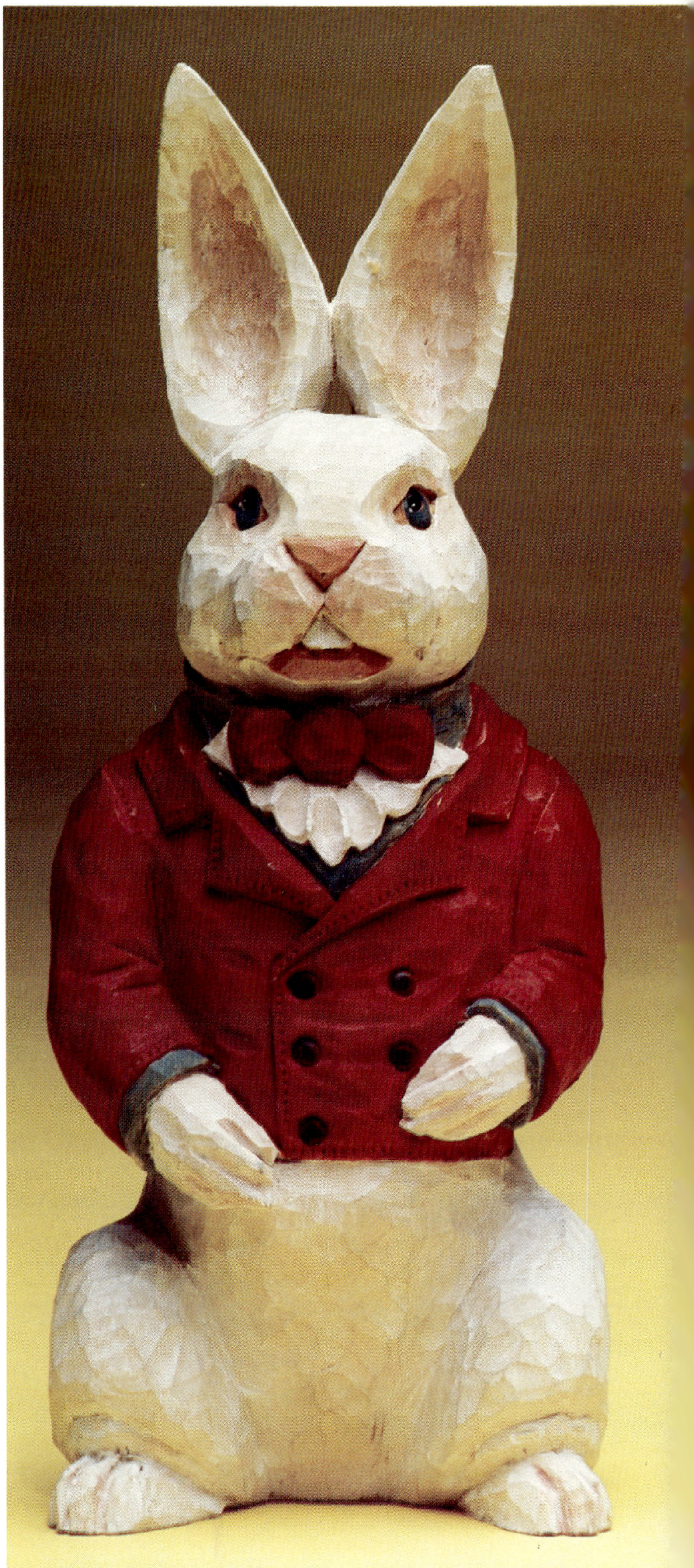

Published by Schiffer Publishing, Ltd.
1469 Morstein Road
West Chester, Pennsylvania 19380
Please write for a free catalog.
This book may be purchased from the publisher.
Please include $2.00 postage.
Try your bookstore first.

We are interested in hearing from authors
with book ideas on related subjects.

Library of Congress Catalog Number: 91-67010.

Printed in the United States of America.
ISBN: 0-88740-381-6

Introduction

The origins of the Easter Bunny are lost in the murky recesses of history and mythology. In the ancient tribes of Germany, the pagan goddess of Spring was known as Eastre, Eostre, or Ostara. Her name was given to the month that we now know as April and the spring festivals that were celebrated then. In the eighth or ninth century, the Christian celebration of Christ's resurrection became associated with the name Easter.

The legend has it that the hare was sacred to Eastre. And with the mythological equivalent of genetic engineering, she endowed it with the power to lay eggs. Both the rabbit and the egg, of course, are ancient symbols of fertility, for obvious reasons. For its part the hare reproduces rapidly. Beginning when they are very young, a hare can give birth to several litters in a year.

The Easter Bunny grows out of this ancient tradition. The first written reference to it is in a German book of the sixteenth century. The idea spread, although some people thought it silly and dangerous to the faith.

In her interesting book, *An Egg at Easter* (Indiana University Press, 1971), Venetia Newall recounts some of the traditions surrounding the Easter Bunny and his eggs. Children in Germany built nests of hay and flowers for the Easter Bunny to leave his eggs. In Odenberg they built little moss covered houses.

In Denmark eggs with the children's names on them, called *hareaegs*, are hidden in the garden for them to find. In Yugoslavia they are hidden in a stable. In Harz the Easter Bunny puts decorated eggs in shoes which the children have placed outside their bedroom doors.

The tradition was brought to America by the Pennsylvania Dutch. According to Newall, the children must search everywhere for the eggs for the *Oester Haws* may leave them anywhere, inside or out. Others put a nest or Easter basket out for the eggs, but if they do, they had better be confident that they have been well-behaved. If they have misbehaved, they are liable to find the nest full of rabbit dung in the morning.

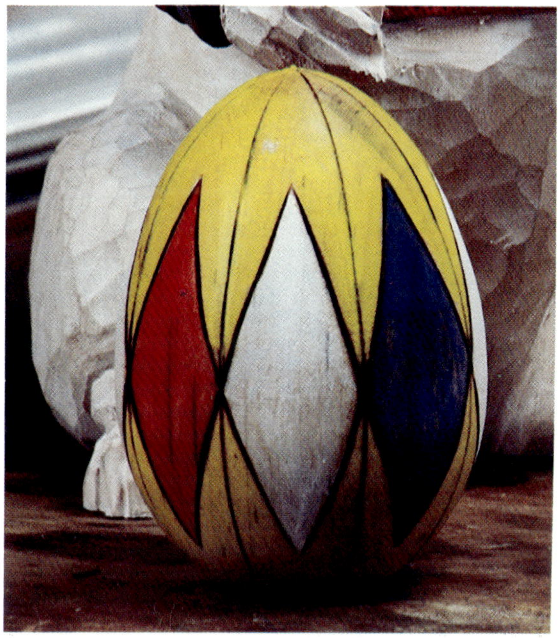

Today the Easter Bunny is awaited by most American children, who are completely, and blissfully ignorant of its origins. All they know is that the Bunny brings them wonderful treasures to welcome Spring and resurrection.

The Easter egg's history is probably more ancient than the Bunny's. The egg, too, was a widely used symbol for fertility and birth, and plays a vital part in many peoples' creation myths. As early as the first century A.D. the symbol of the Phoenix and the egg from which it arose became identified with the resurrection of Jesus.

The earliest recorded decorated eggs were in eleventh century Poland, and the practice continued to grow in eastern Europe and Germany. Royalty painted and gilded eggs to give to members of their courts, while common people offered Easter eggs as signs of friendship, esteem, or romantic love.

One Polish legend traces the origin of the Easter egg to Mary, the mother of Jesus, who was said to have painted eggs to please the Christ child. Another story tells how Mary Magdalene took a basketful of eggs to the tomb of Jesus, to eat while she anointed his body. When she arrived the eggs miraculously took on beautiful, brilliant colors (Newall, page 268).

Whatever the true origins of the Easter egg, they have been the object of creativity for many cultures across the years. From simple scratch patterns on dyed eggs, to the magnificent Fabergé eggs that found their way into the collections of royalty, the form lends itself to self-expression and imagination.

While most of the decorated eggs used actual shells, some were of porcelain or glass, and some were of wood. Particularly in the late part of the 1800s many people shared the hobby of carving wood. We are in good company!

So you are about to enter into a great tradition. I hope you enjoy and have fun with the projects in this book. I spend a lot of time carving "humanimals," animals in human clothing or situations. They are able to carry a great deal of the emotion and humor of the human creature. But when carving "humanimals" it is important to study the animal's anatomy. Even though they are humanized, they must also be believable as the creatures. You don't want an arm coming out in the wrong place, or a leg at an impossible angle.

So good carving and good luck!

The Patterns

The Tools and Patterns

The tools needed for the Easter Bunny project include a simple set of palm gouges, a turned-down blade and a turned-up blade, and some eye punches or nailsets for the eyes and buttons. The wood I use is bass, and it is probably the best for these figures. It carves and takes the paint nicely. The eggs are standard maple forms available at most craft stores. The patterns are applied with a woodburning tool.

The patterns are reproduced at their actual size. You may use them as they appear or enlarge or reduce them on a photocopying machine. While you are at the copying machine, print several copies so you can cut them apart as needed to help in the drawing of the various parts.

I do not use a full-frontal pattern because I find it leads to more trouble than its worth. People tend to try to follow it too exactly and find that at some point they have cut off something they're going to need later. Besides, if everything is laid out too completely it limits the creativity that comes in the carving. The photographs in the book are designed to give plenty of guidance without overdoing it.

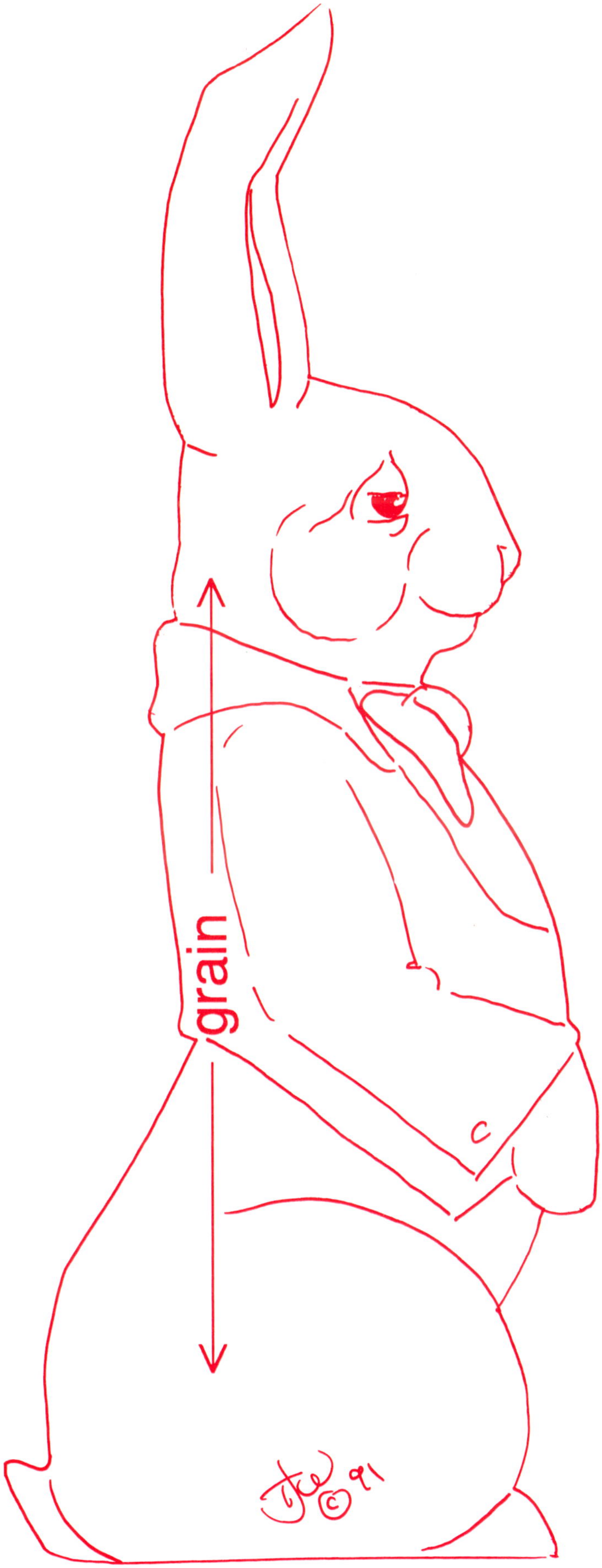
grain

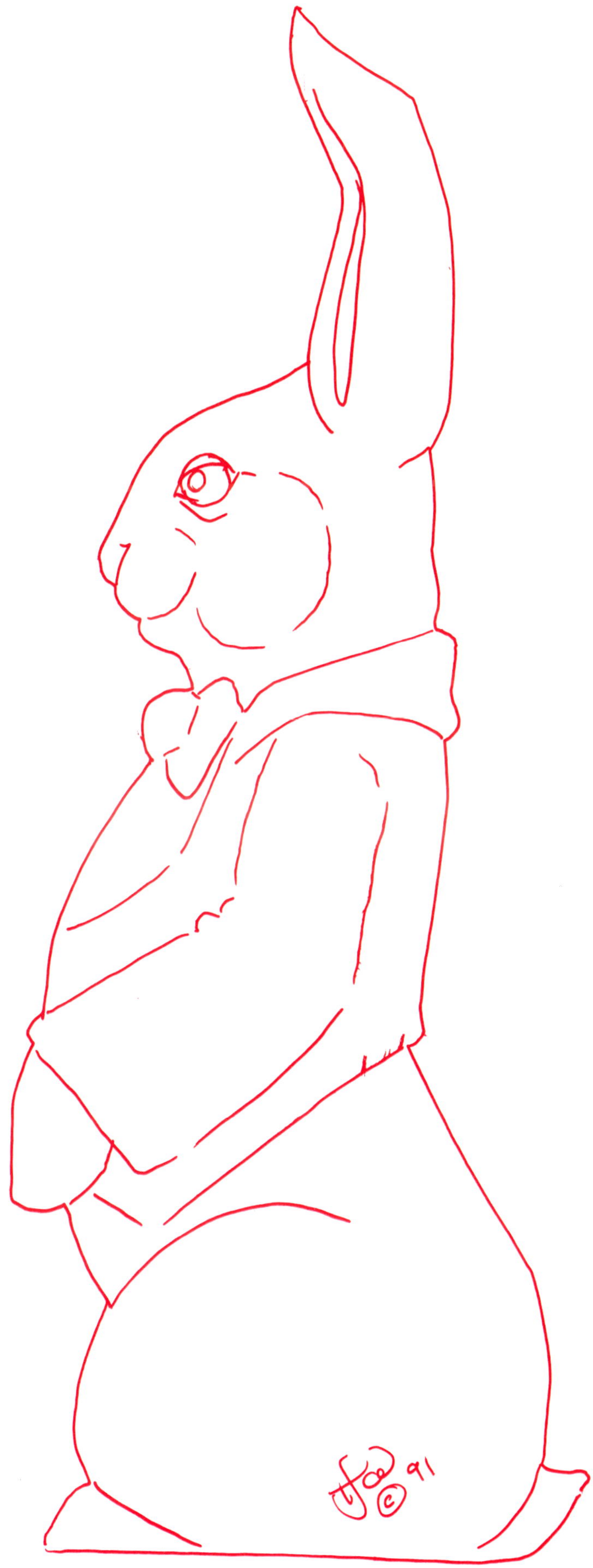

Carving the Easter Bunny

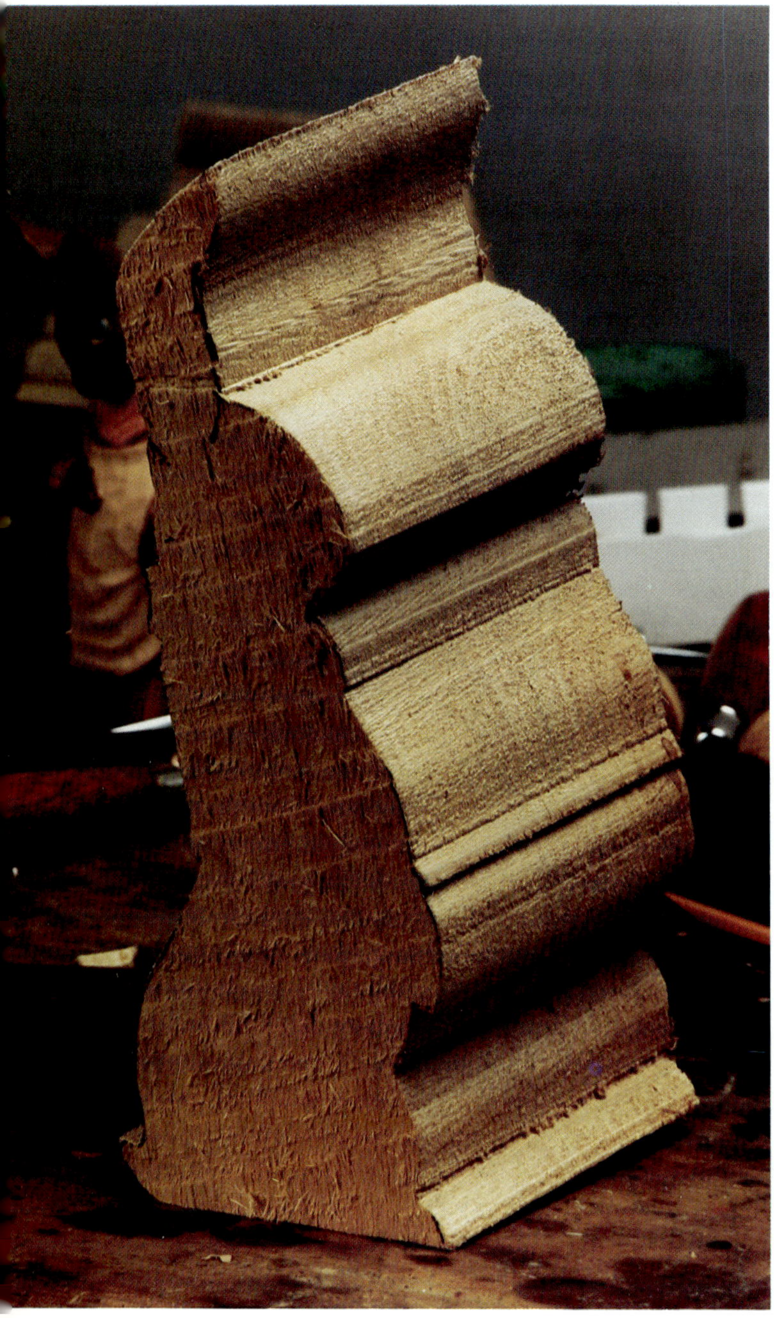

Cut the blank from bass wood on a bandsaw.

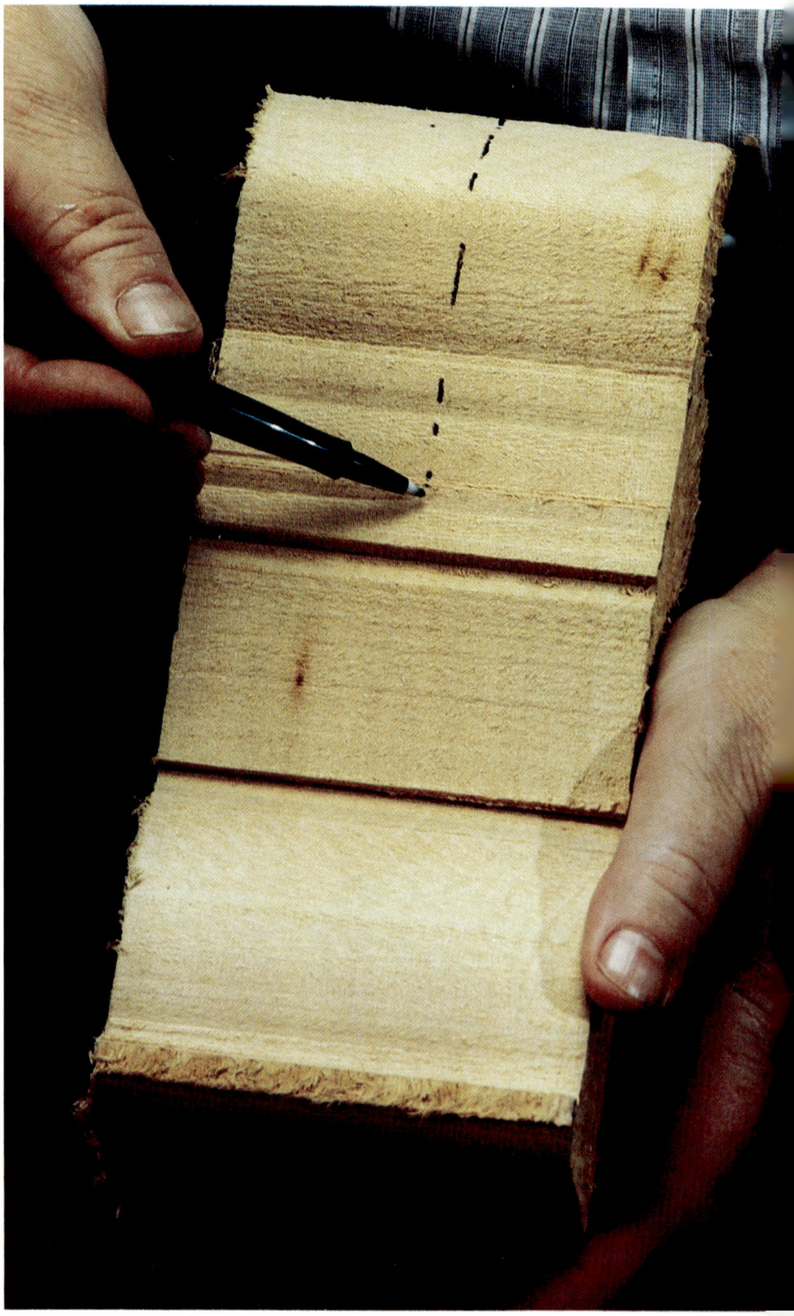

Draw a center line around the back...

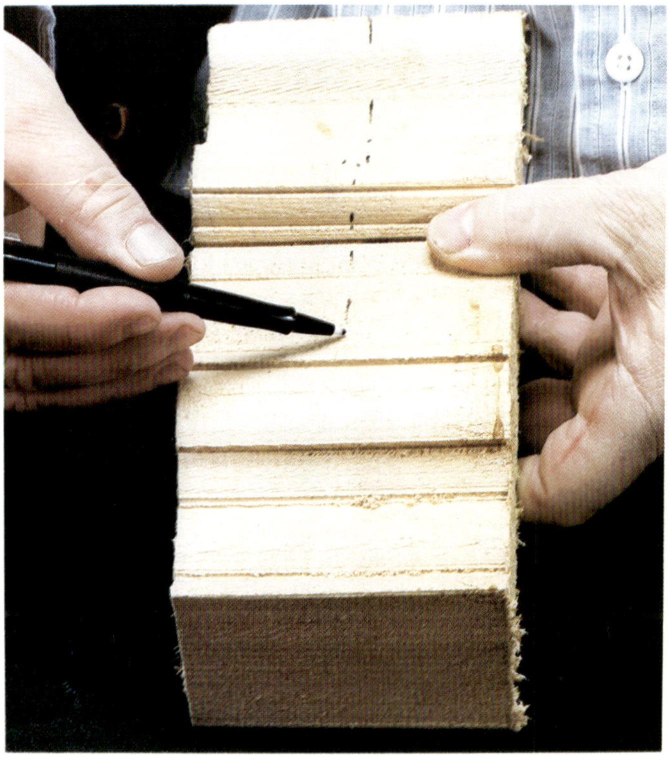

and the front of the blank.

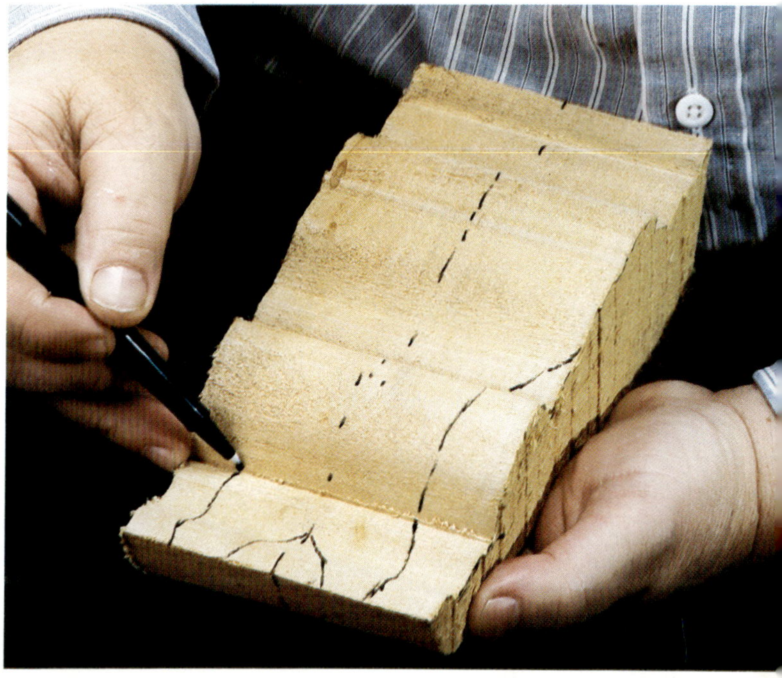

Draw in the front view. I generally do this freehand, because using a pattern over these contours leads to distortions.

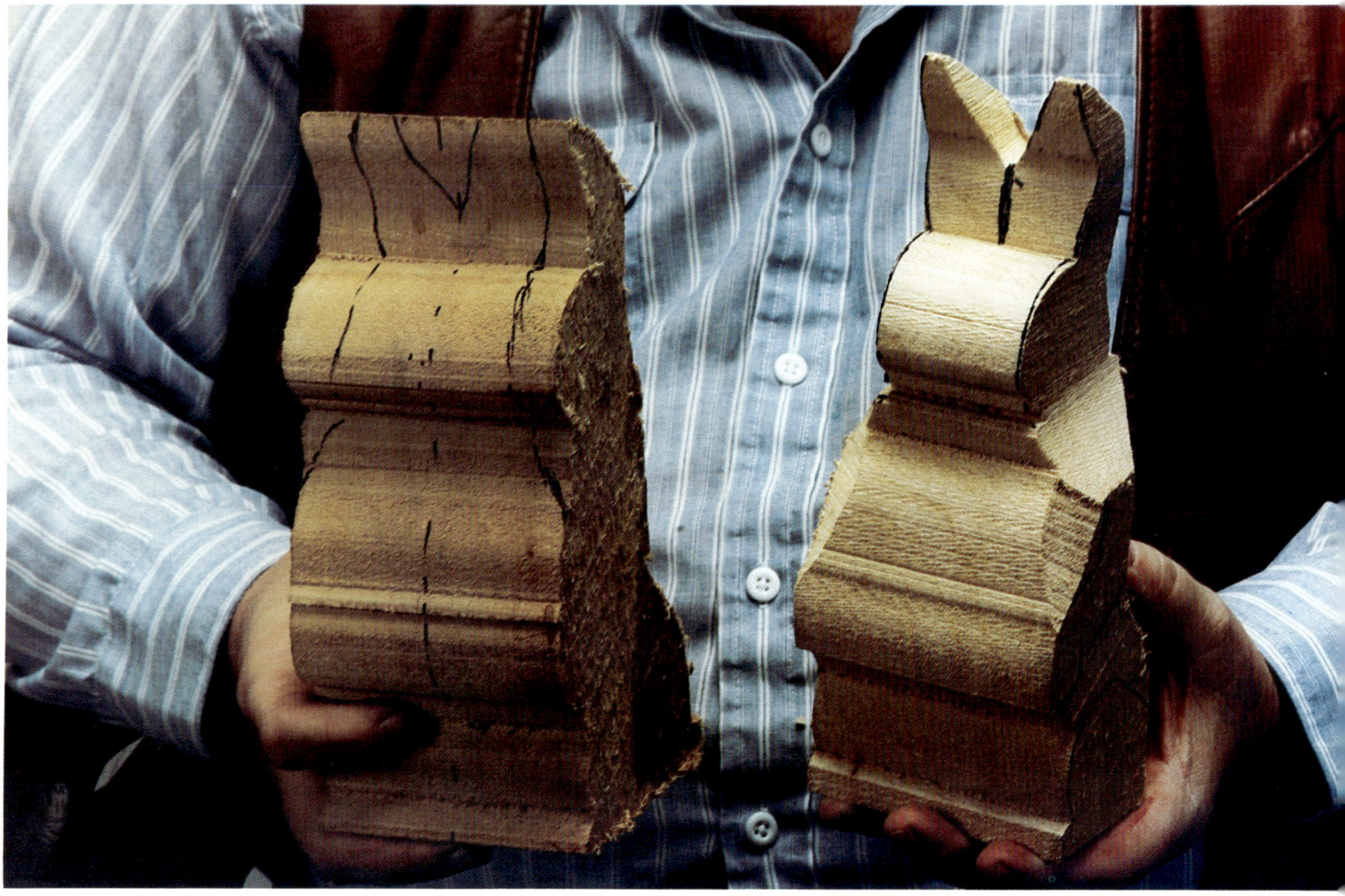

Return to the bandsaw and cut the head-on pattern.

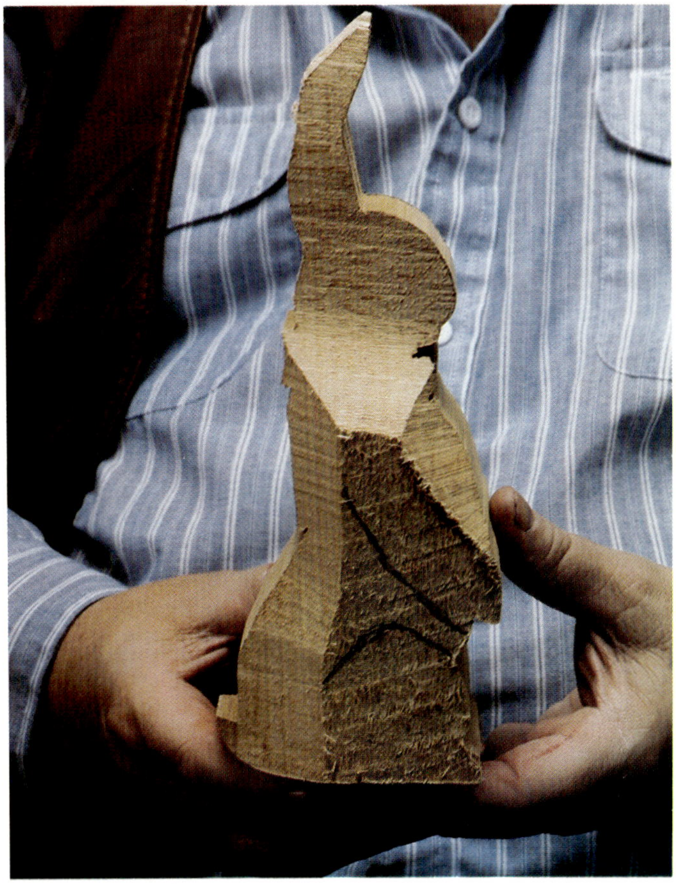

Also use the bandsaw to make 45 degree cuts on the front shoulders and the back corners.

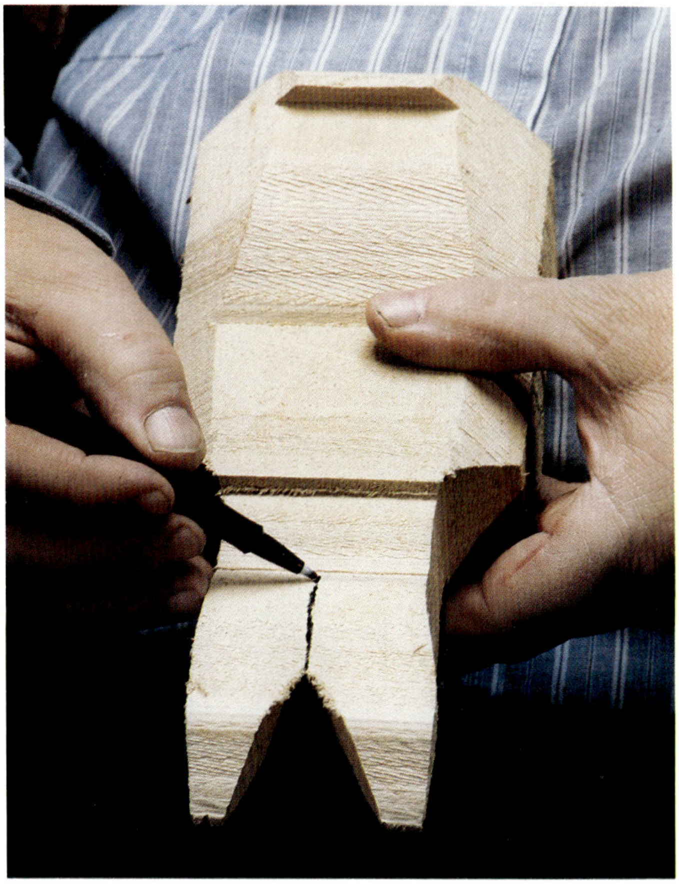

Mark between the ears.

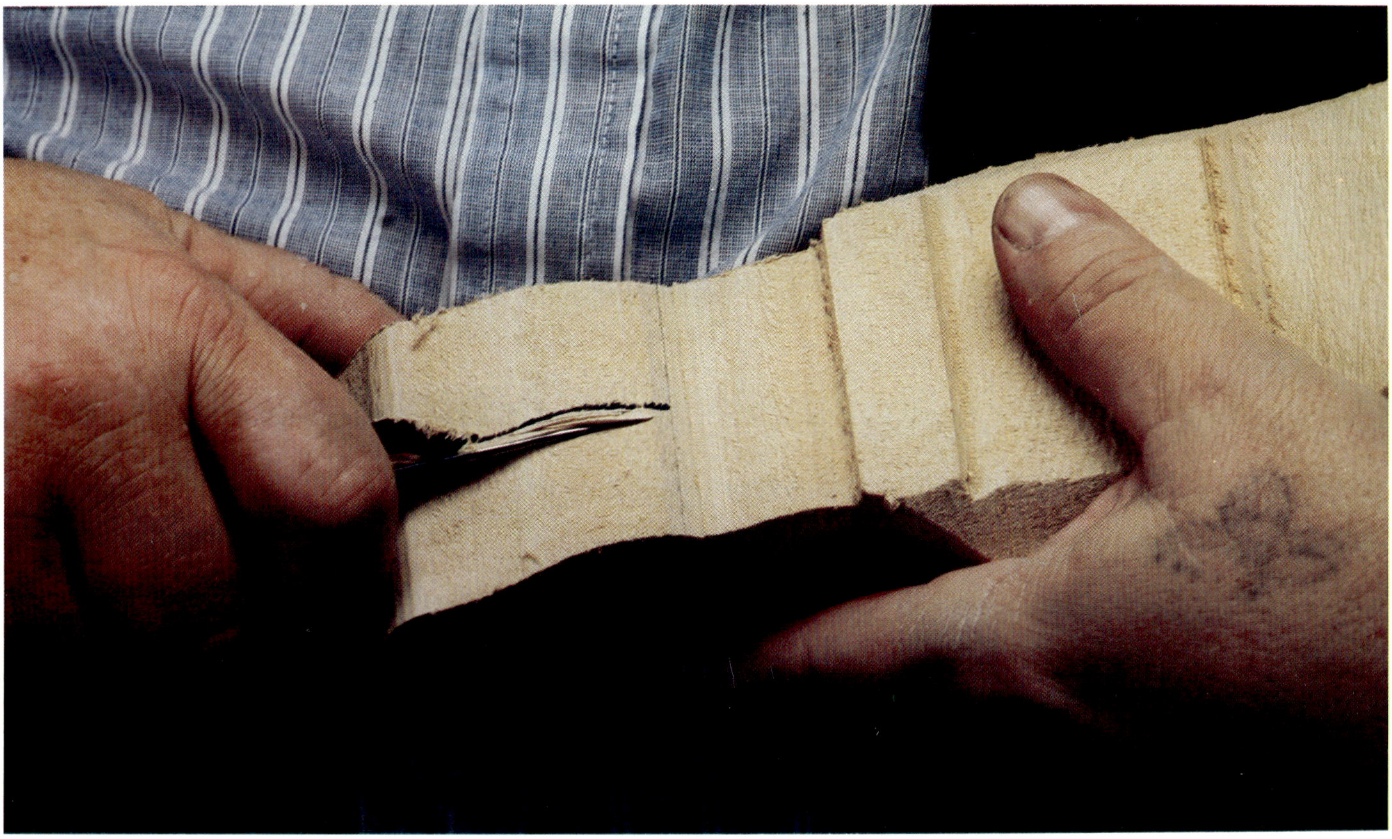

Use a knife to cut a v-line between the backs of the ears.

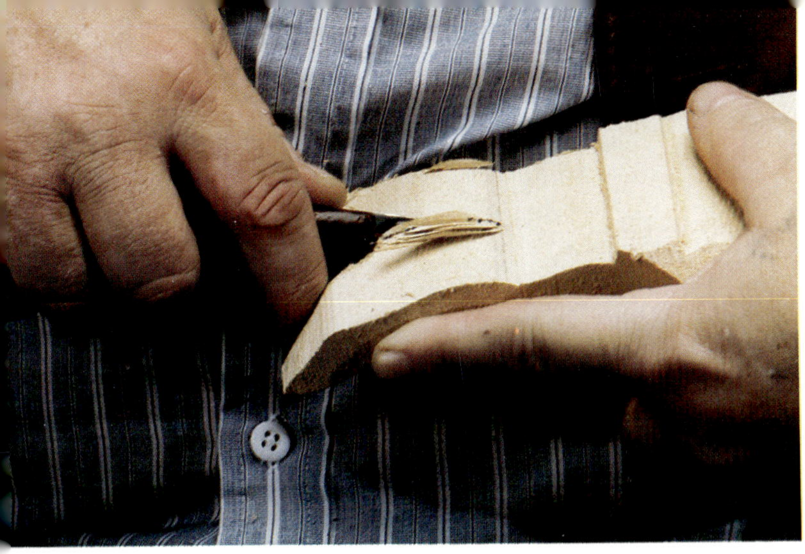

Cut from both sides and pop out the excess between.

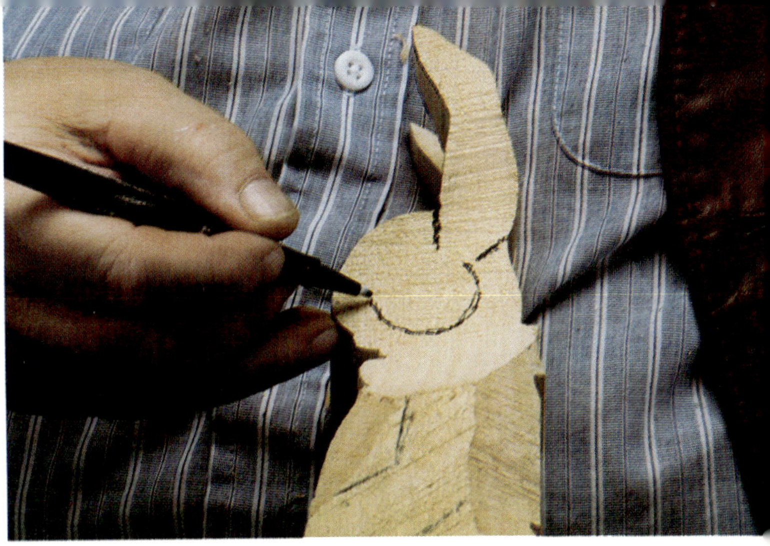

Mark the jaw line and ear lines on the sides of the head.

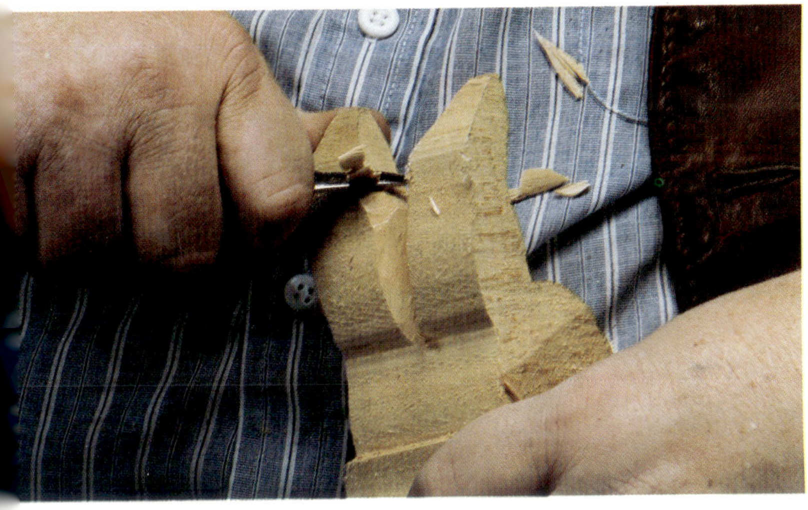

Deepen the space between the ears and round off the back of the ears starting on the inside edges. Keep your thumbs hidden to avoid injury.

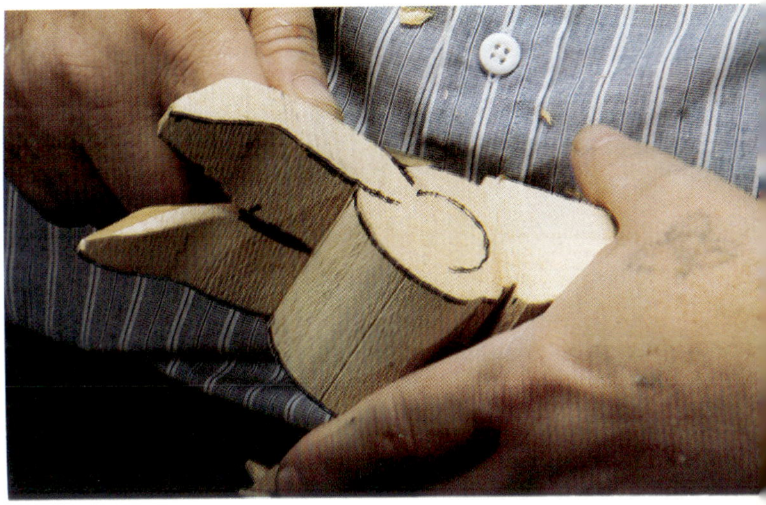

Cut a stop on the line at the back of the ear by pushing your knife into it and rocking it back and forth.

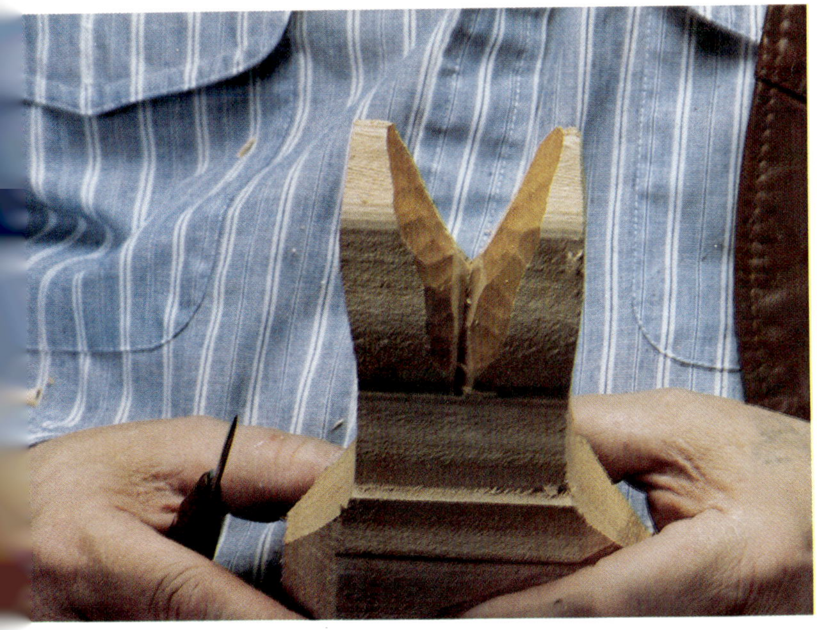

Carve until you get to this position.

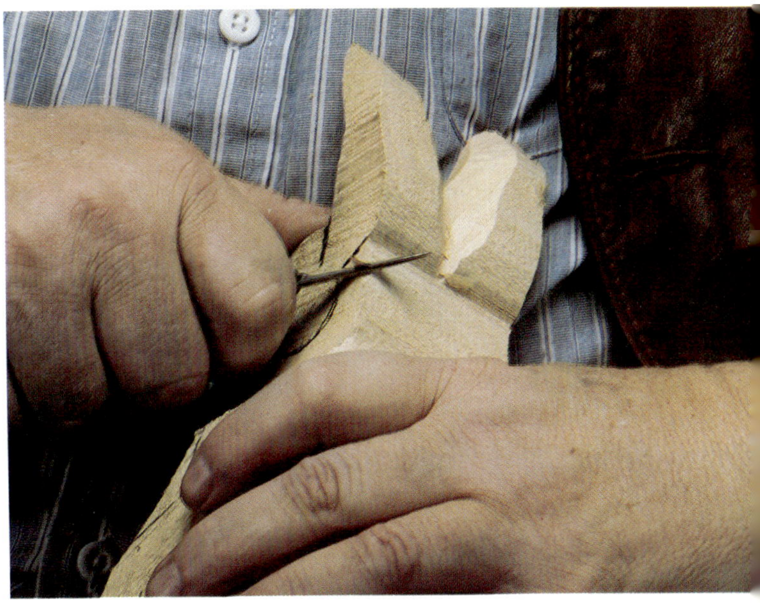

Cut back to the stop from the neck, rounding the head under the ears.

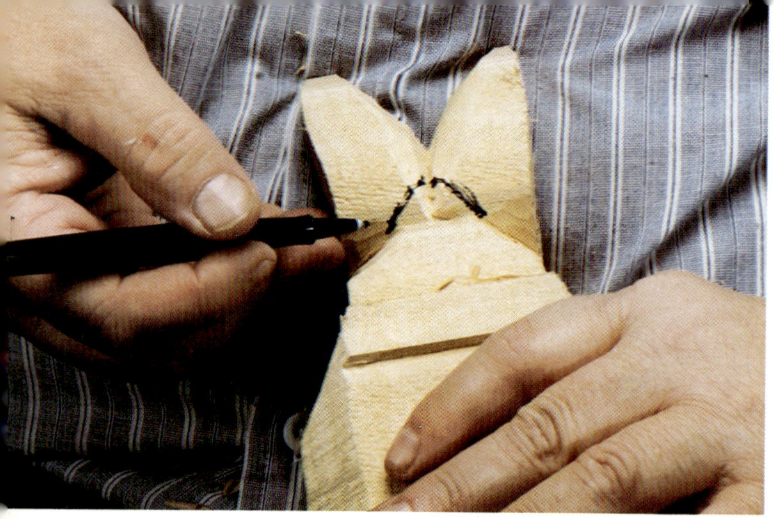

Nitches at the base of ears will give the illusion of them being separated while they are still together for strength. They go here.

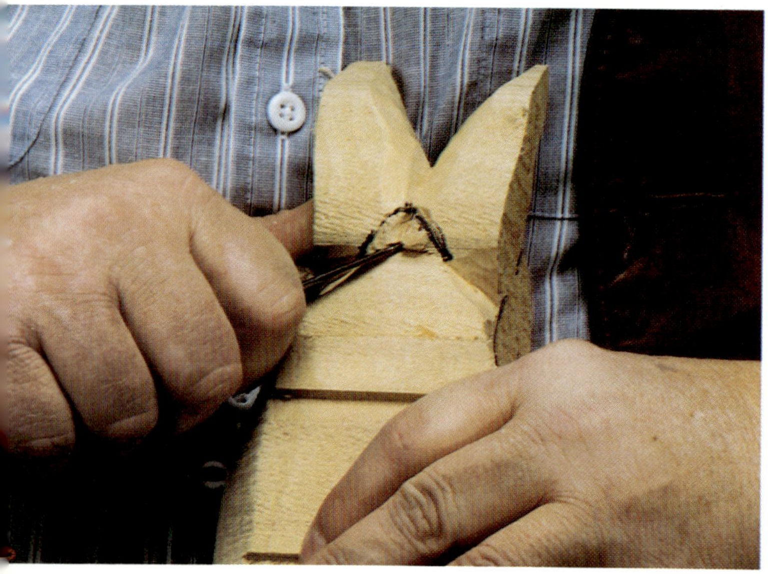

Cut stops along these lines and cut back to them from the head, popping out the excess.

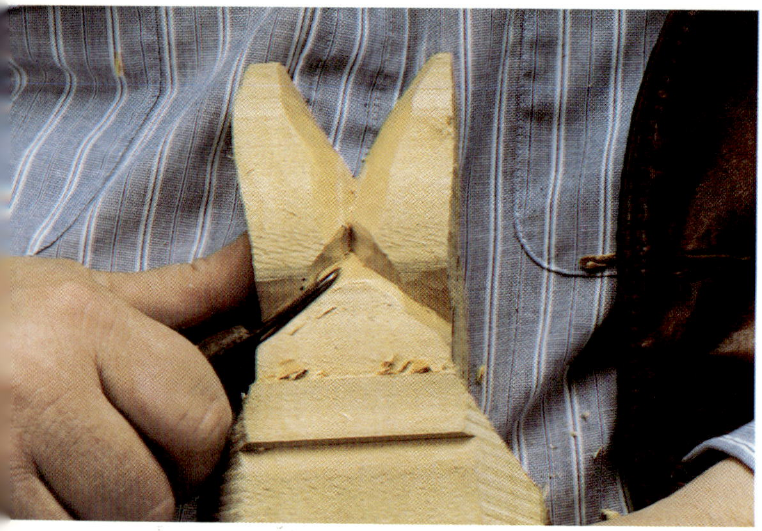

When the nitch is cleaned out, the ears become nicely defined.

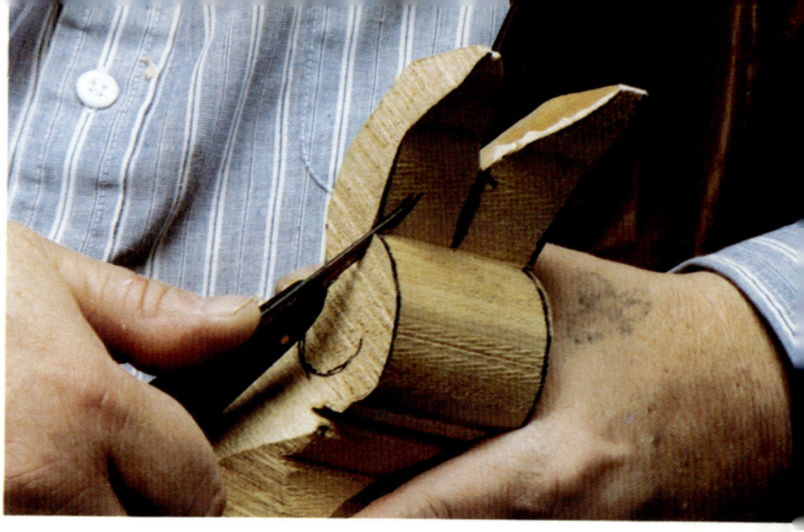

Cut a stop on the line at the front of the ear...

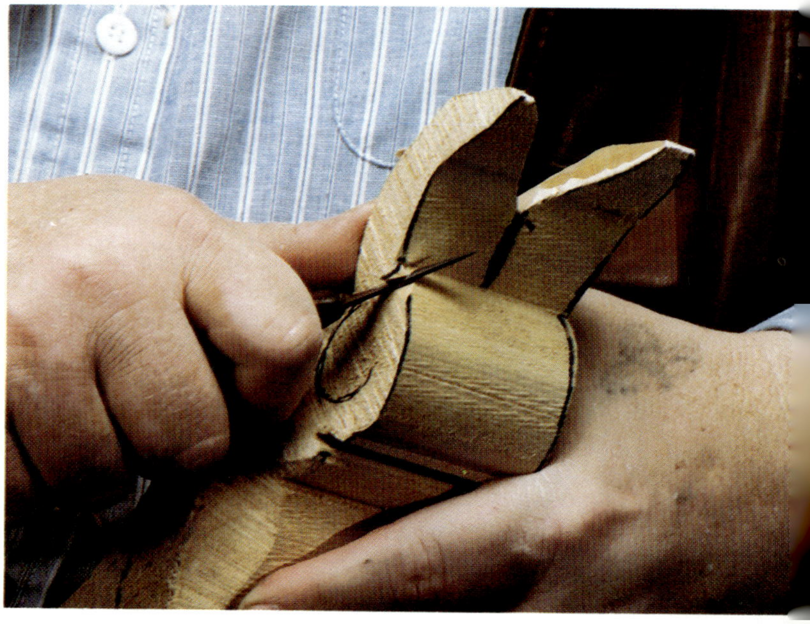

and cut back to it from the top of the head.

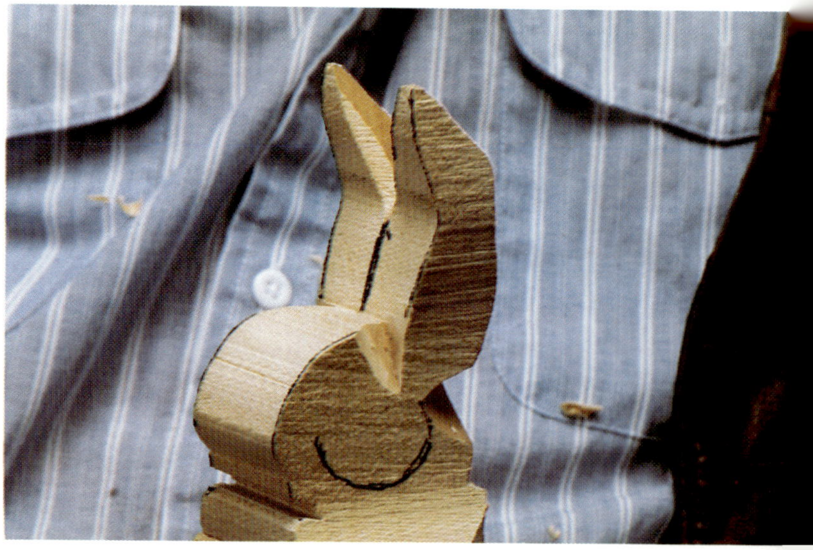

The result is a notch in front of the ears that separates and defines them even more.

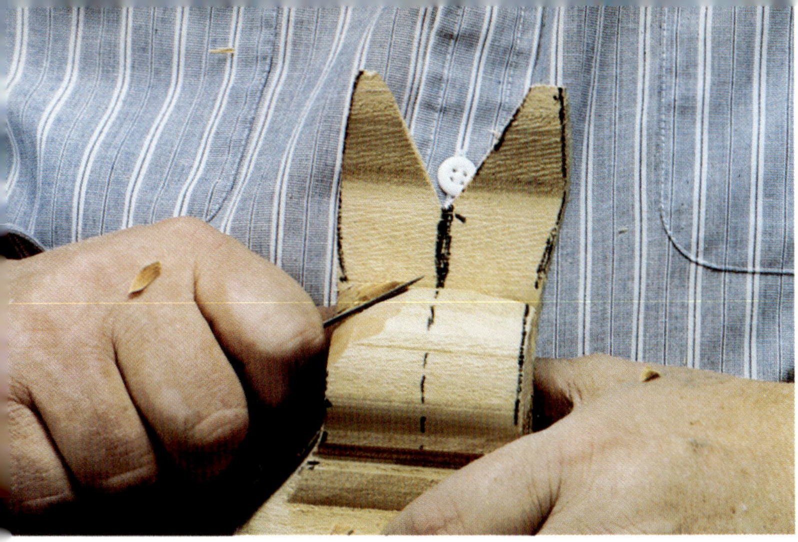

Round the forehead over to the center line.

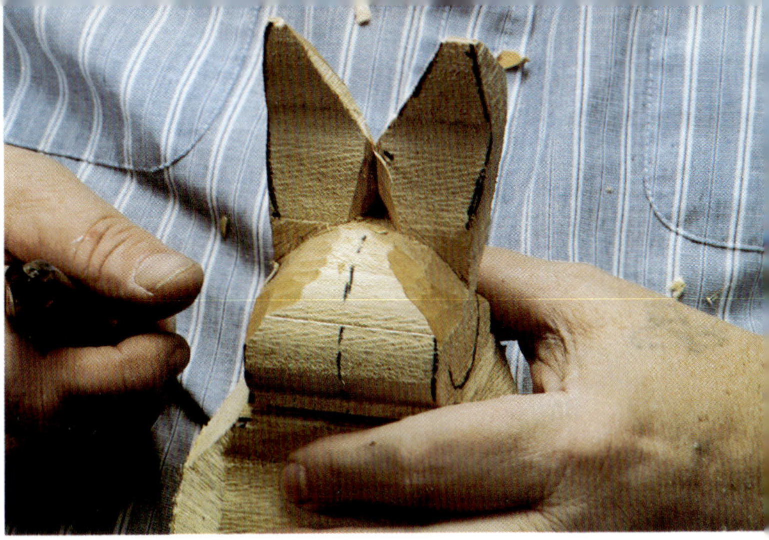

Open up the slice at the base of the ears...

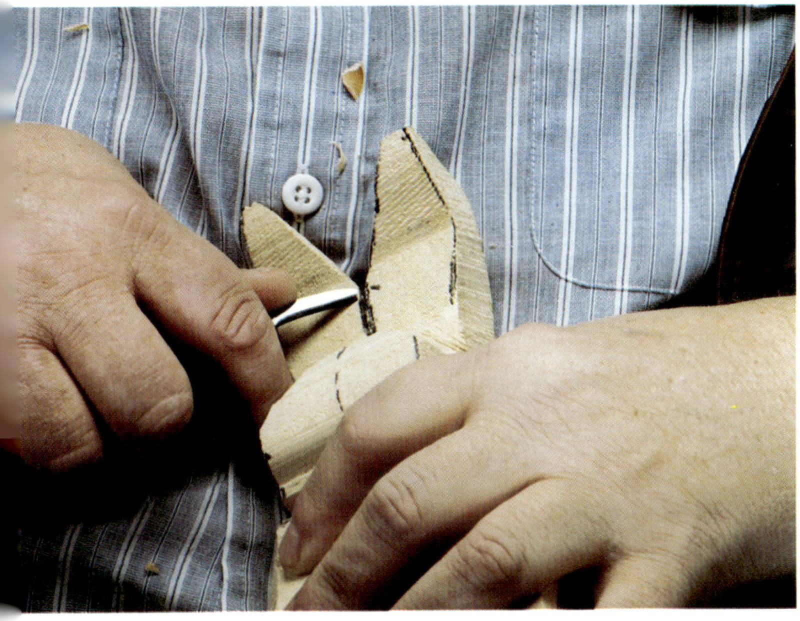

Slice down both sides of the line between ears to create a shallow v-line.

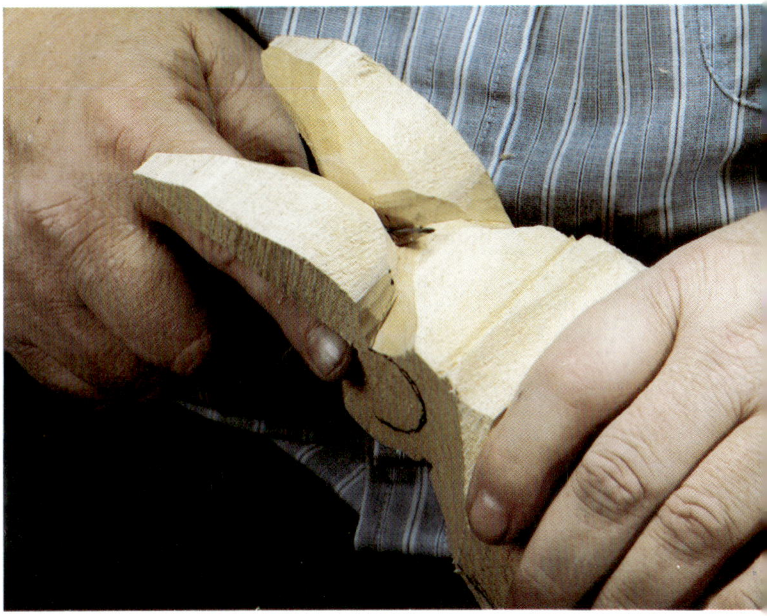

until you get through to the back.

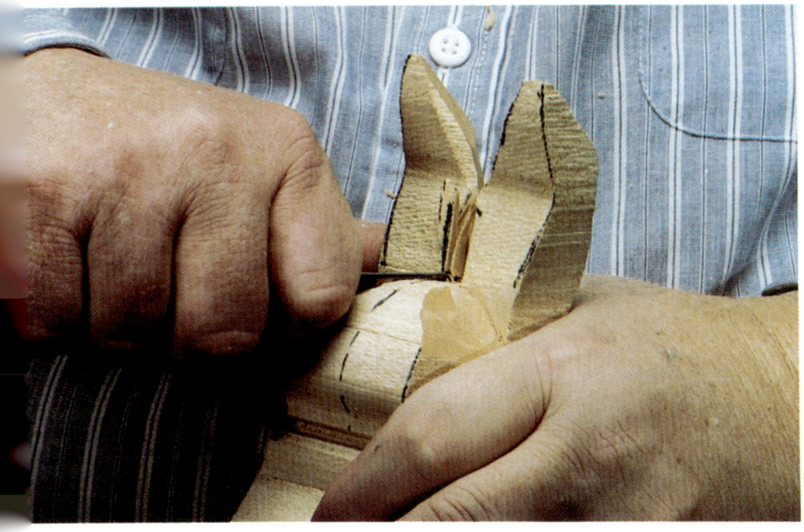

Clipping the slice at its end will allow it to come out easily and cleanly.

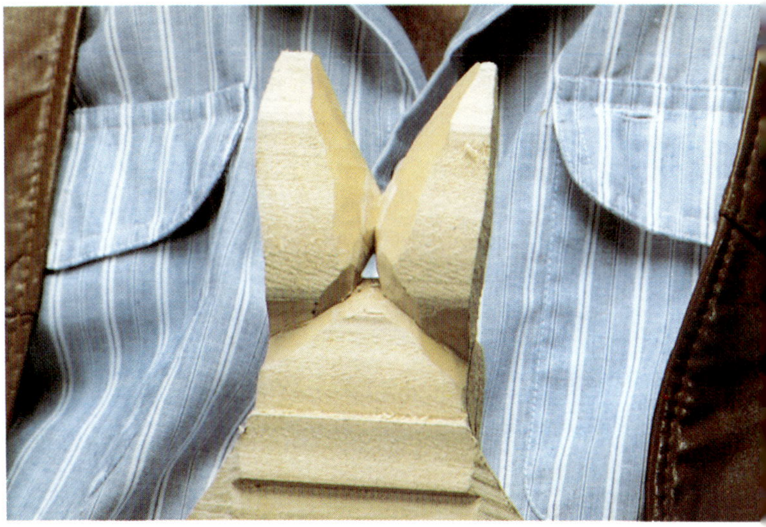

This cut-through gives the ears character and adds to the quality of the carving. It also forces the carver to keep proportions and planes regular and even.

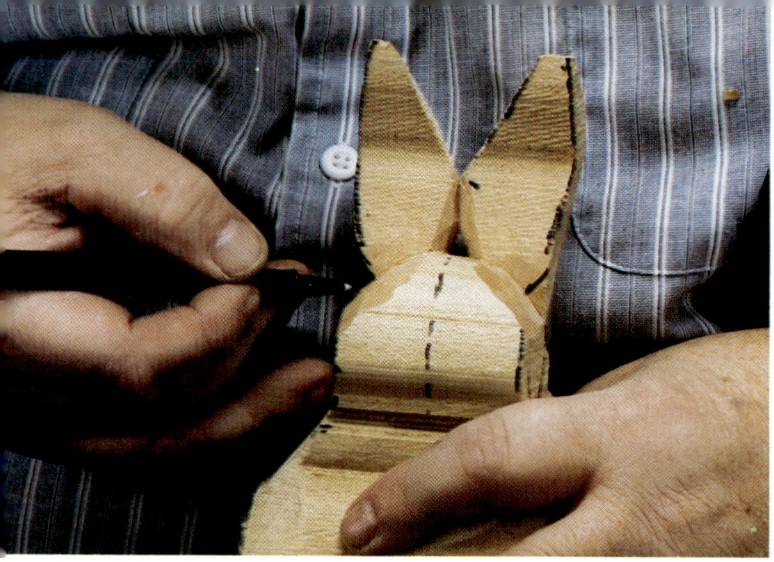

A nitch from the bottom of the ears will make them blouse out the way we want. Here they are marked.

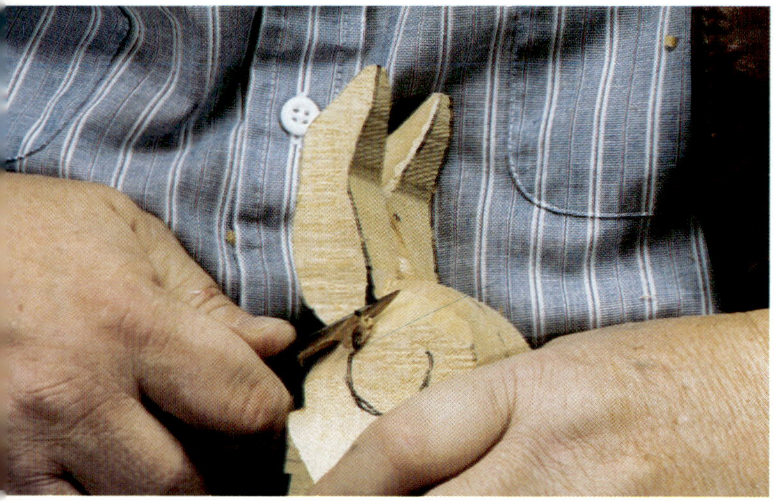

Cut a notch out at the base of the ears...

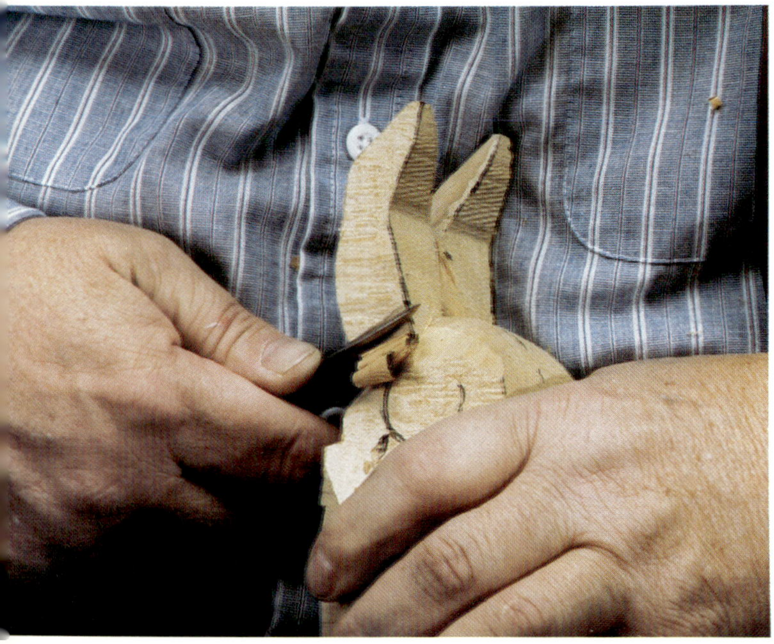

and trim the ear to the lines you have drawn.

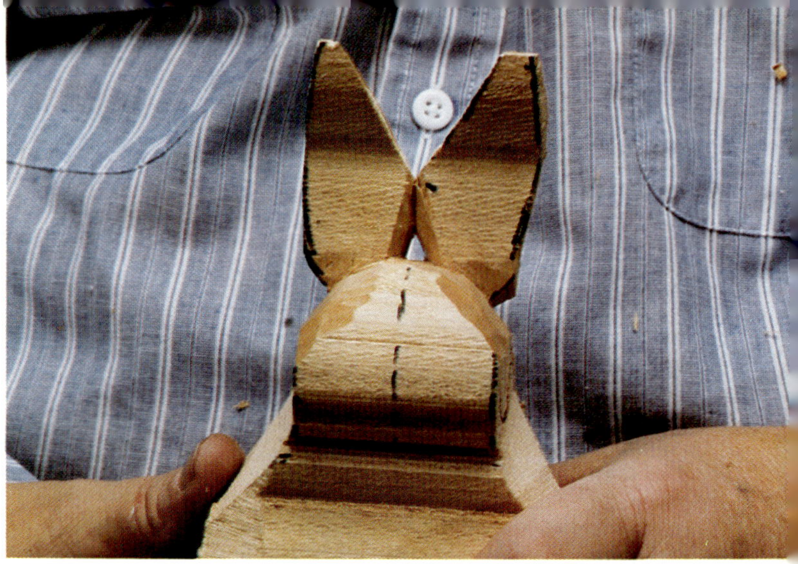

The ears are taking shape.

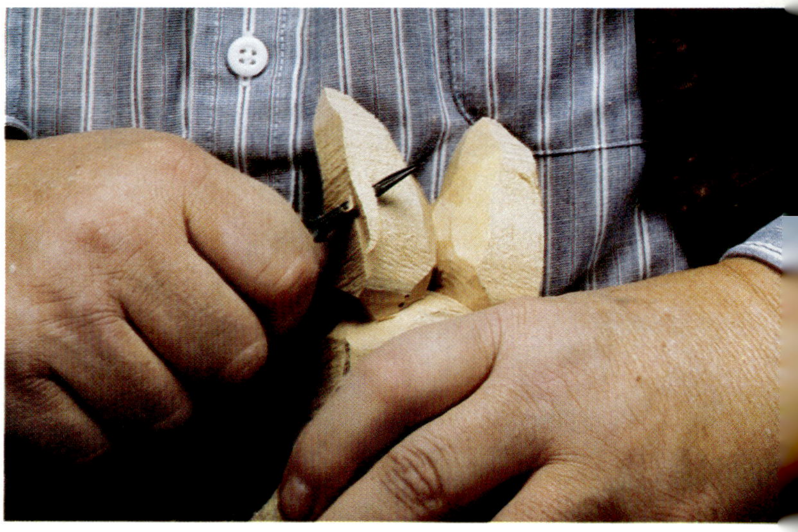

Continue to shape the ears by trimming down the square corners in the back.

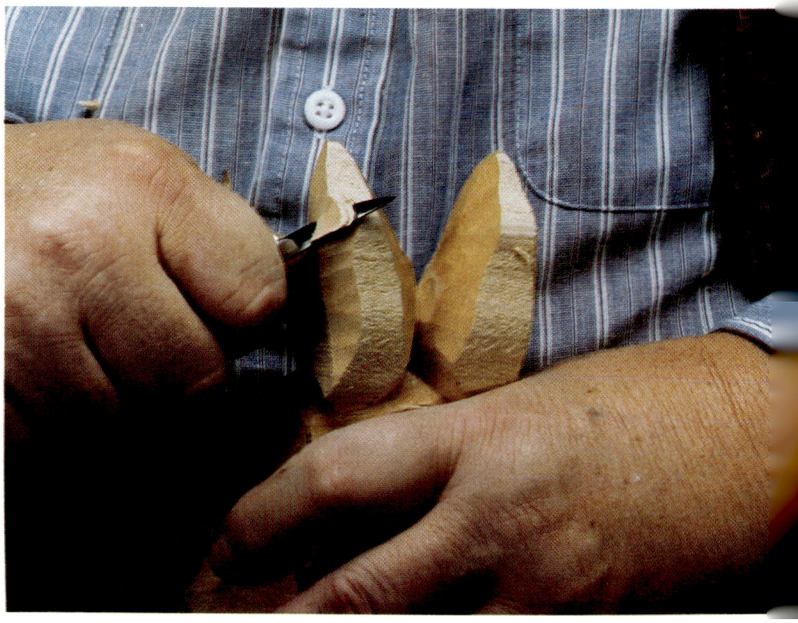

Continue up to the tip of the ears...

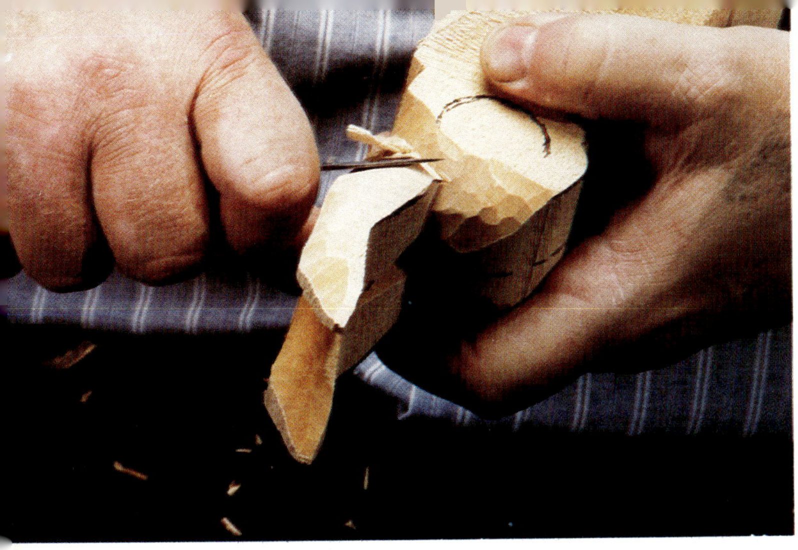

and down to the base.

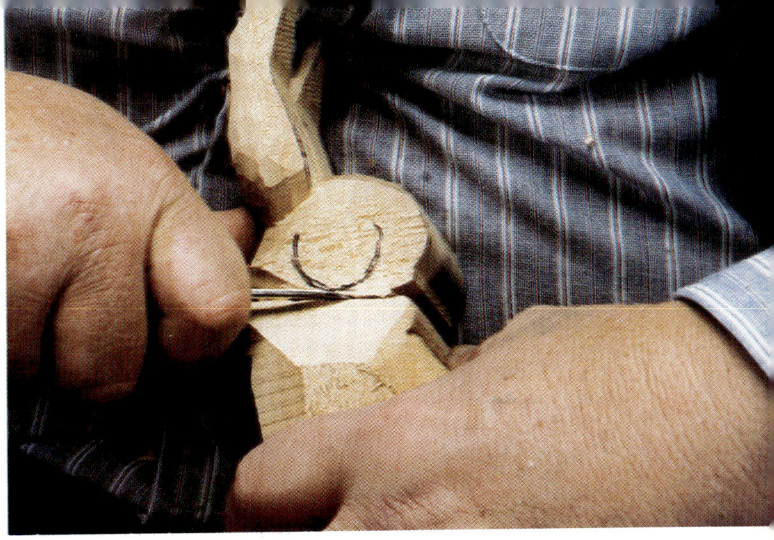

Cut a stop along the line...

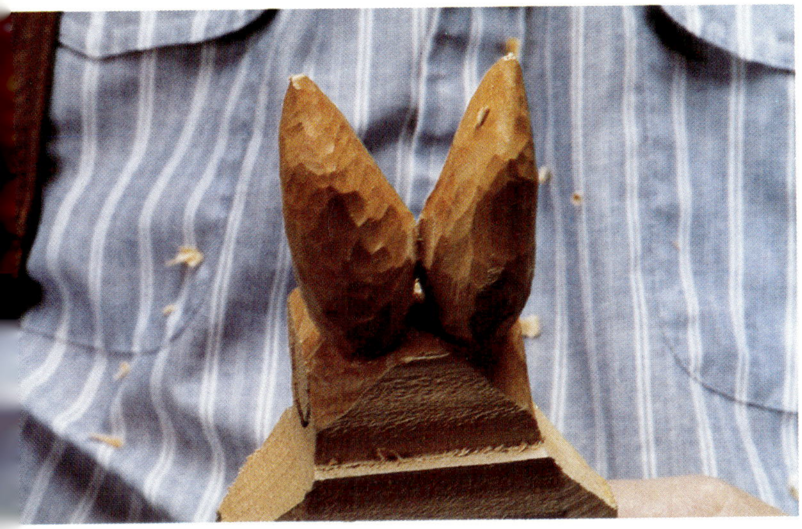

The back of the ears are rounded along each edge. The fronts will be hollowed, but that will wait until later.

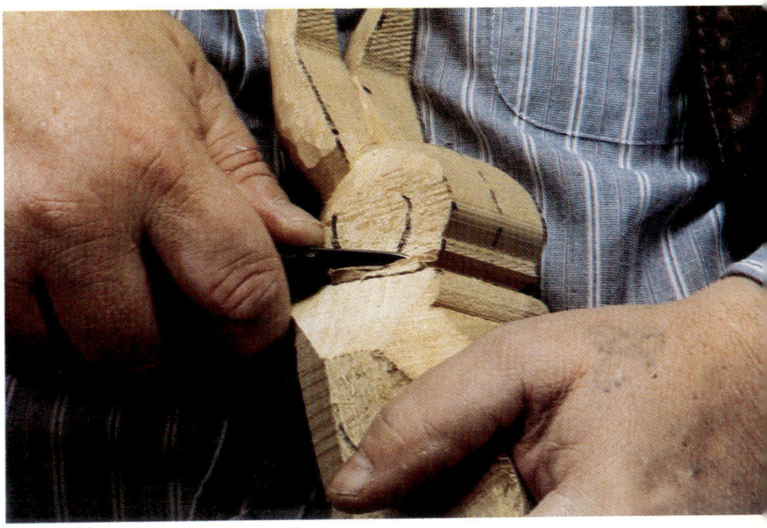

and cut into it from the head.

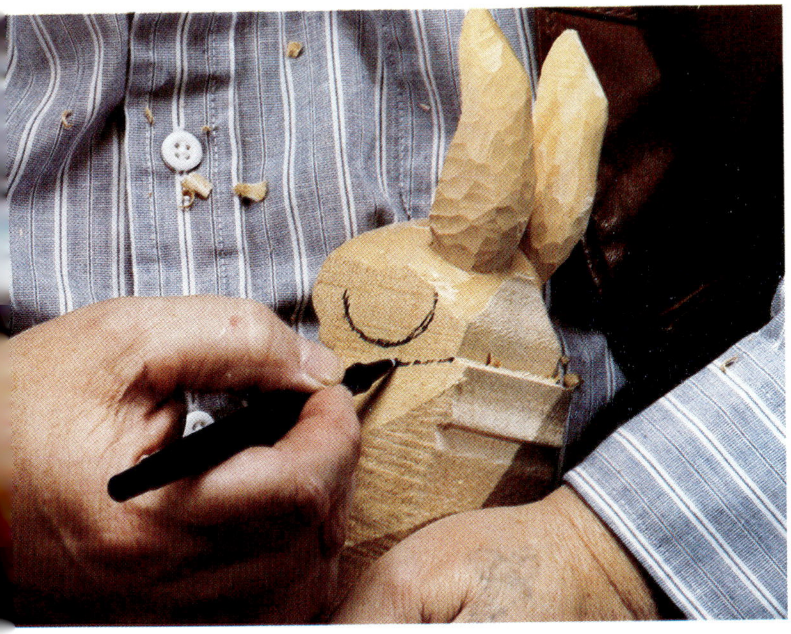

Draw in the top of the collar line.

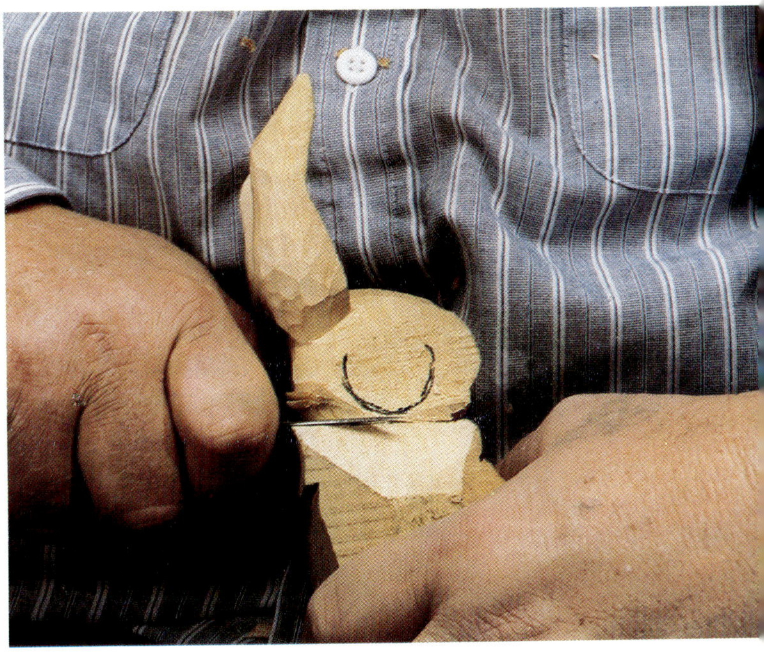

Cut a deeper notch at the back corners of the head.

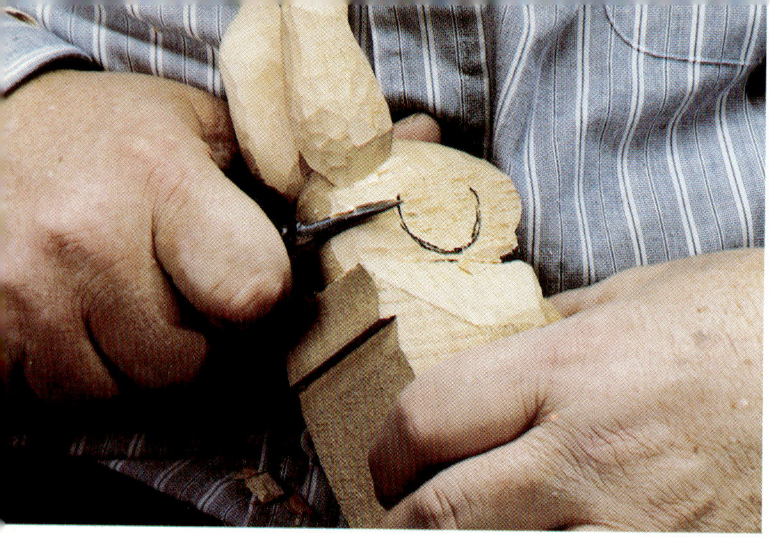

Continue to round the back of the head down to the neck and up to the ears.

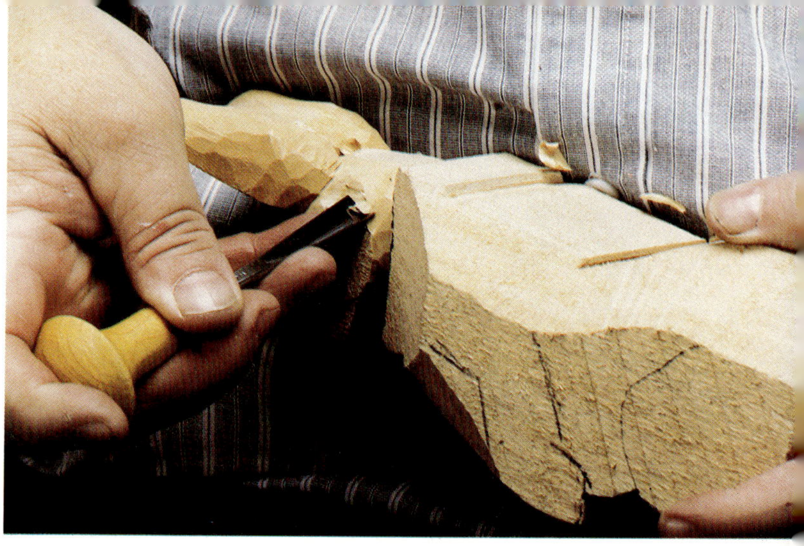

we will use a palm gouge and gouge around the cheek line. Stay aware of the back of the skull.

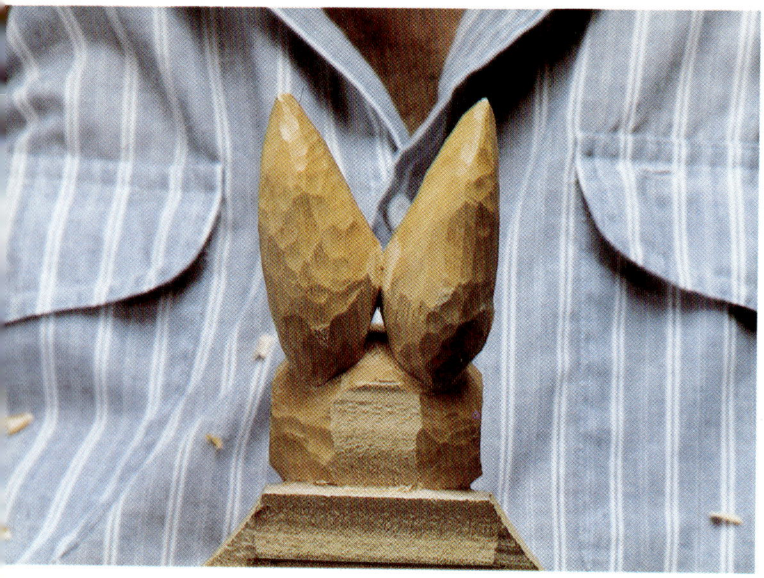

The back of the head so far.

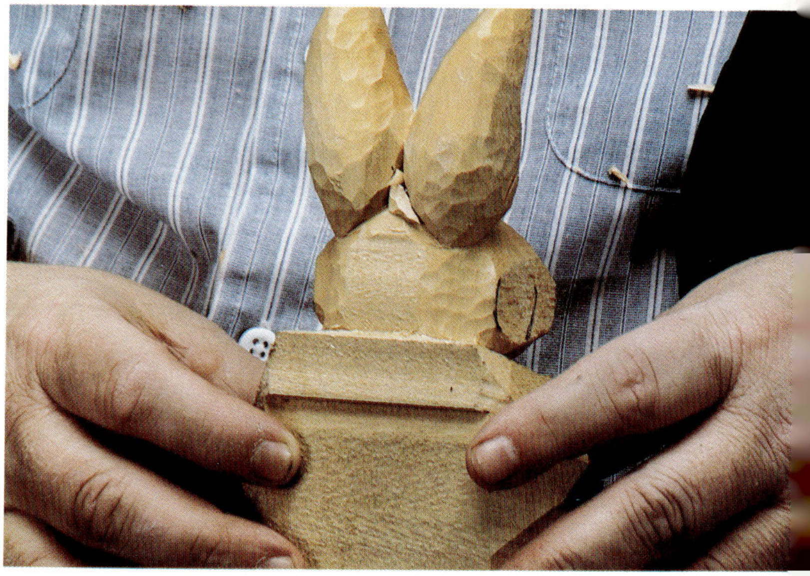

The rounded cheeks after gouging.

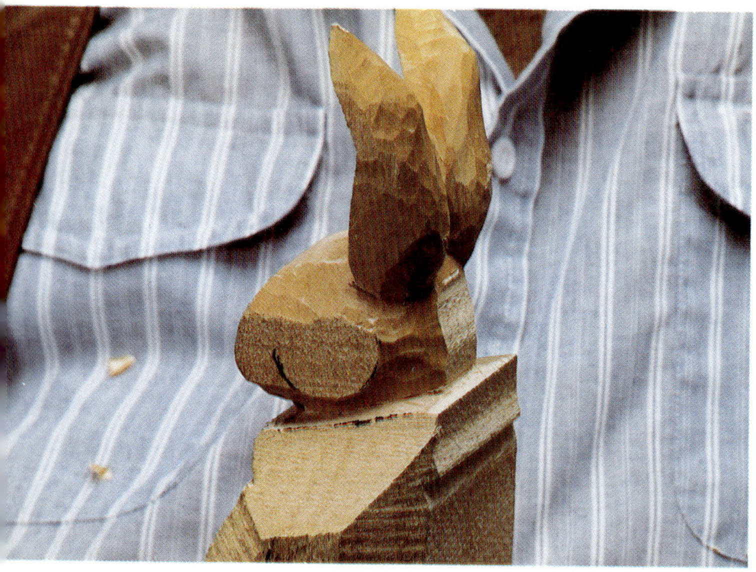

We want to be sure to keep the cheeks intact, so...

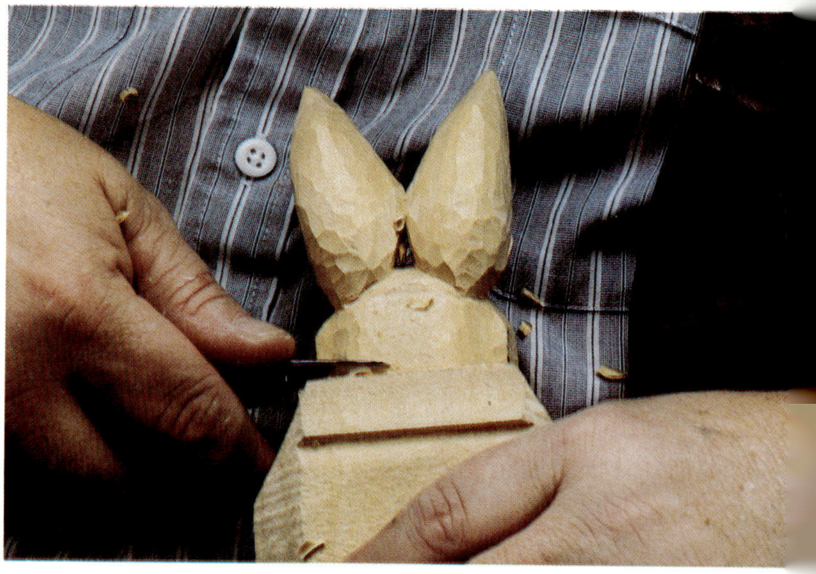

Smooth the gouge marks with a knife.

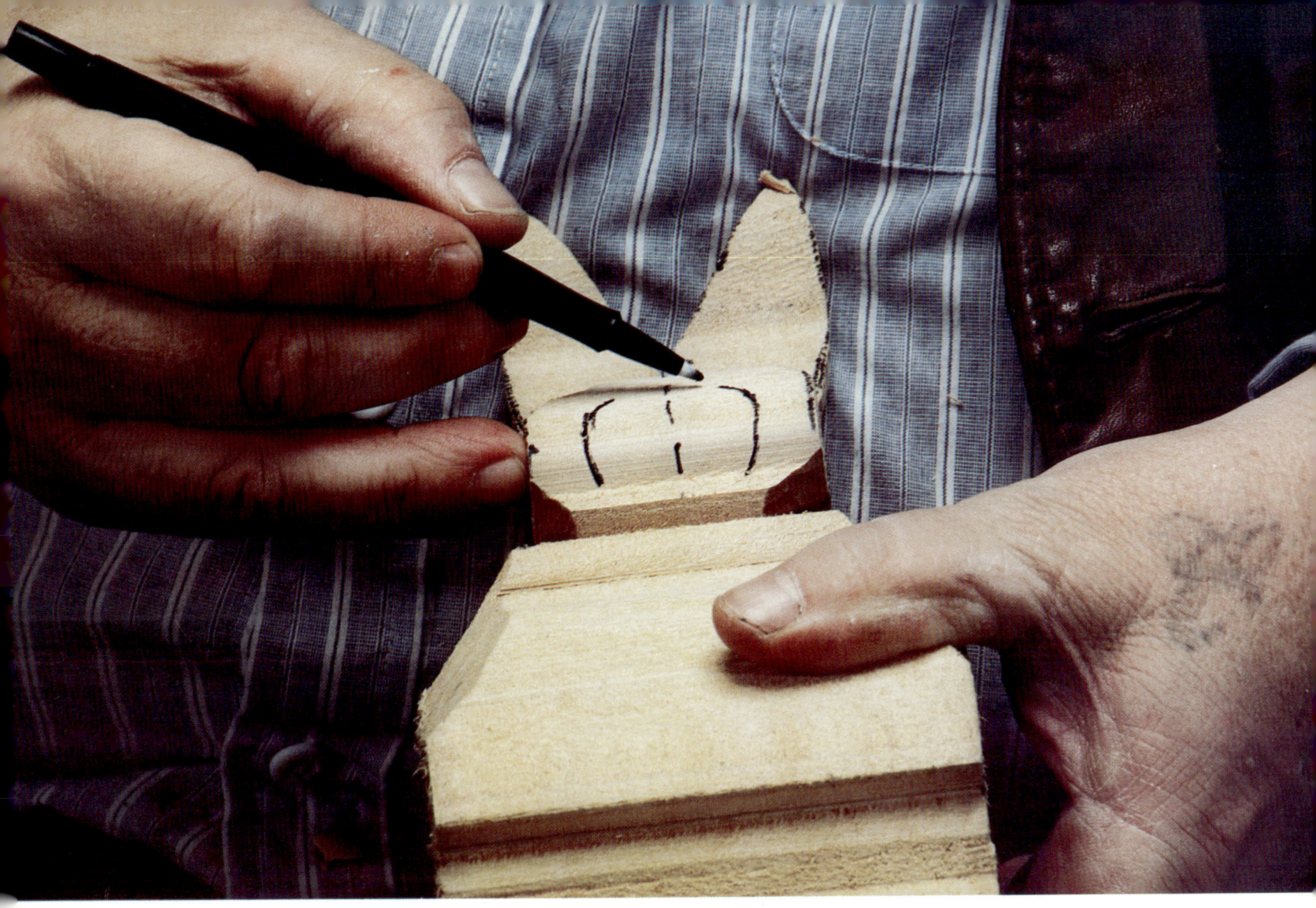

Draw in the face. The muzzle should be nice and wide, wider than you really want it at this point.

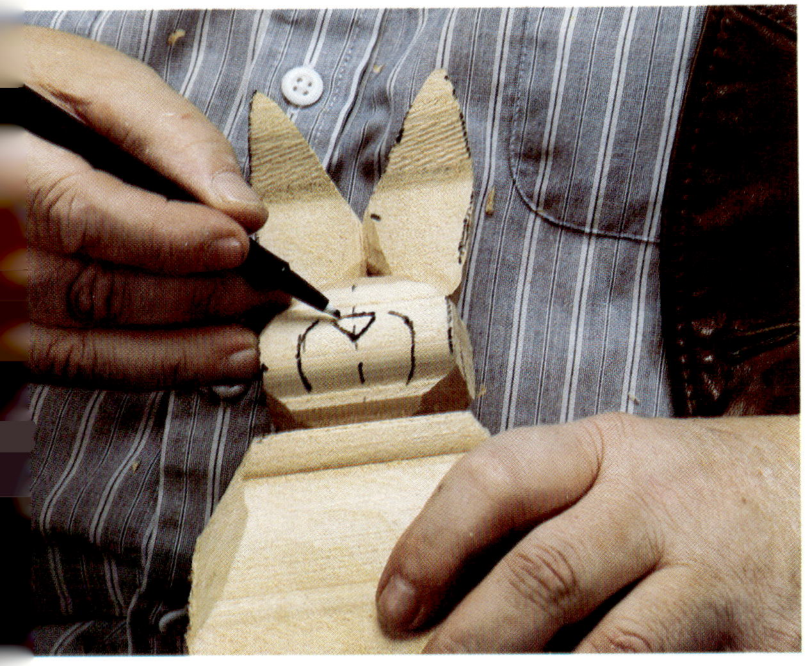

The nose is centered and in the shape of an inverted triangle.

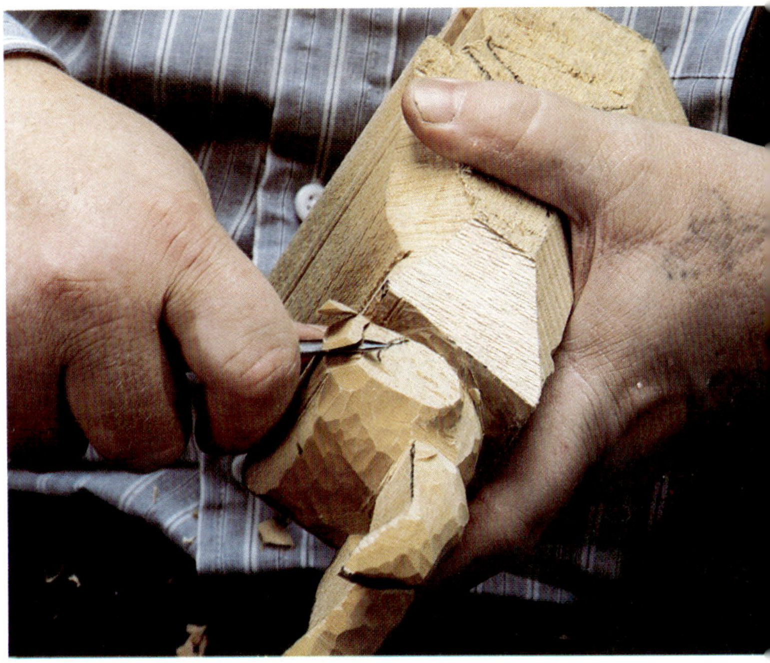

With the grain running with the cut, the excess beside the muzzle pops off fairly easily.

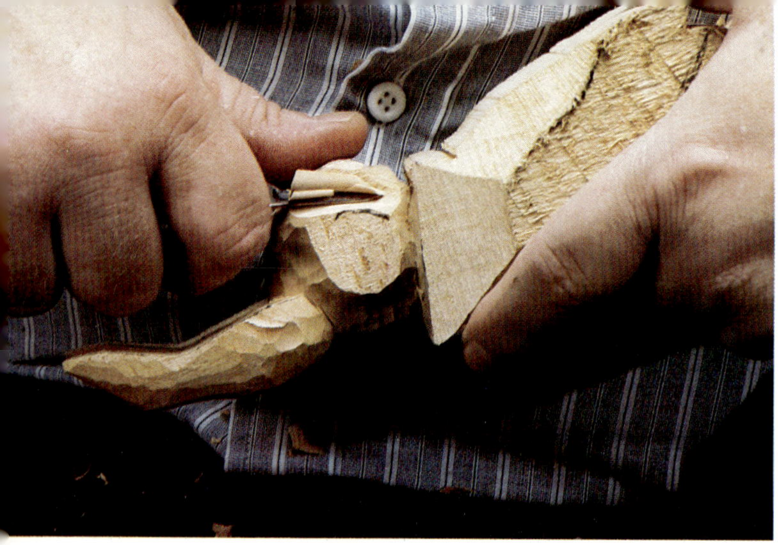

Be sure to keep the cheek intact.

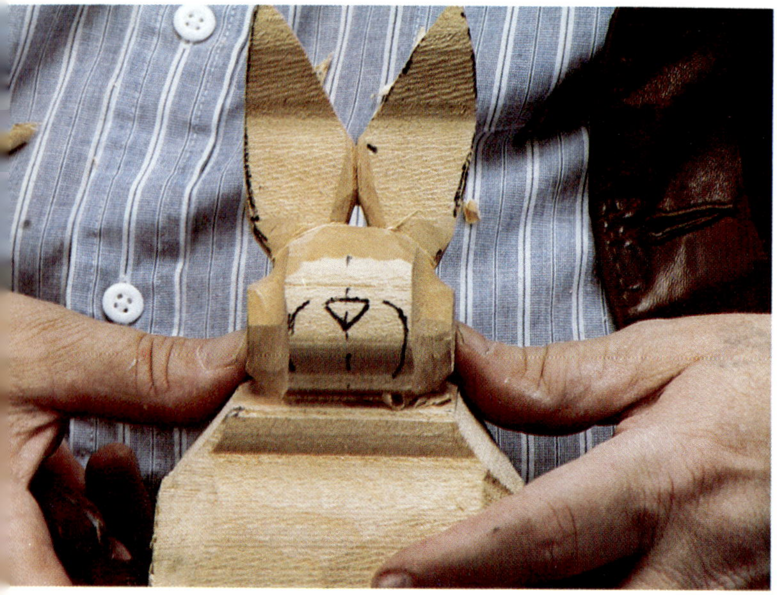

This shows how the cheek and muzzle are being defined.

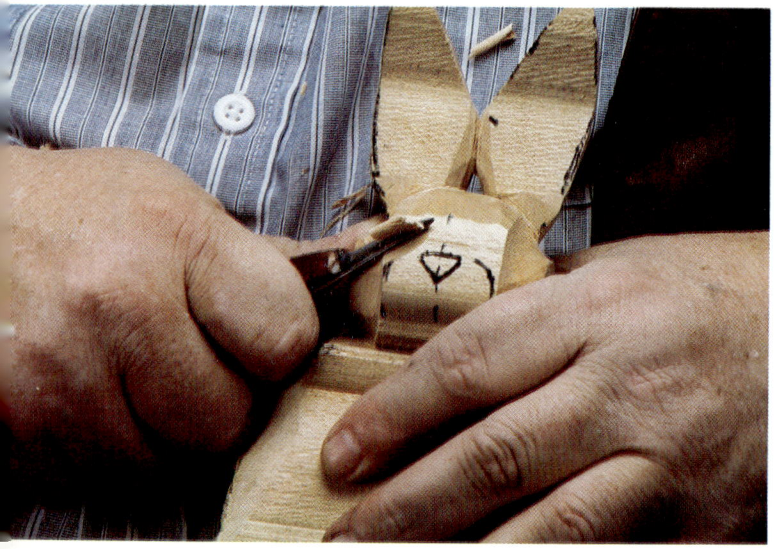

Hollow out the areas above the cheeks for the eye sockets.

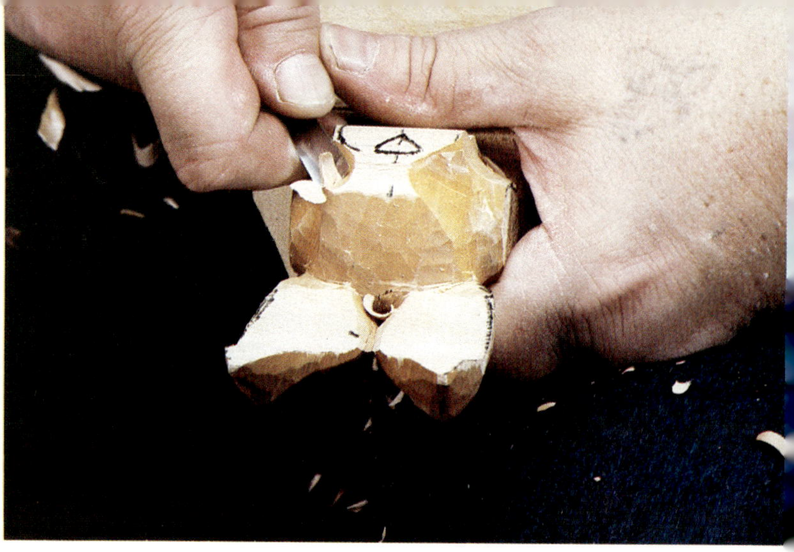

You can cut out the top of the muzzle with a knife or with a chisel.

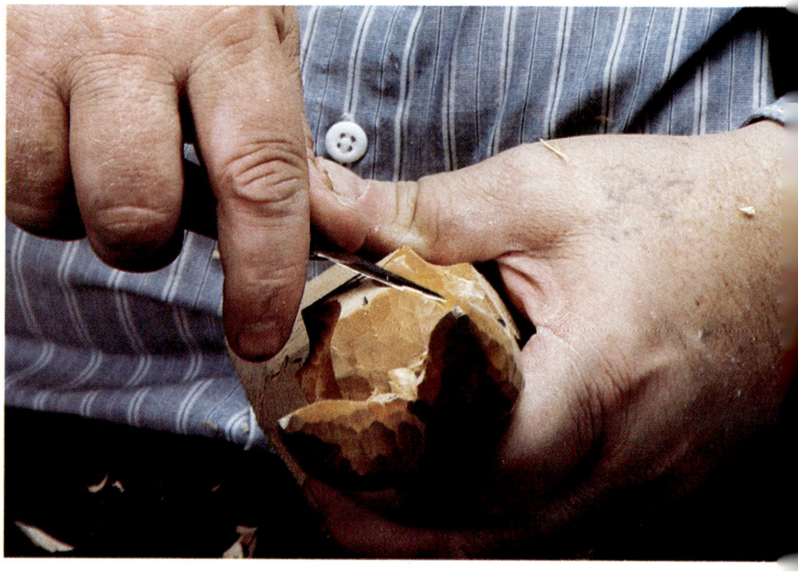

Go over the face with a knife, refining as you go.

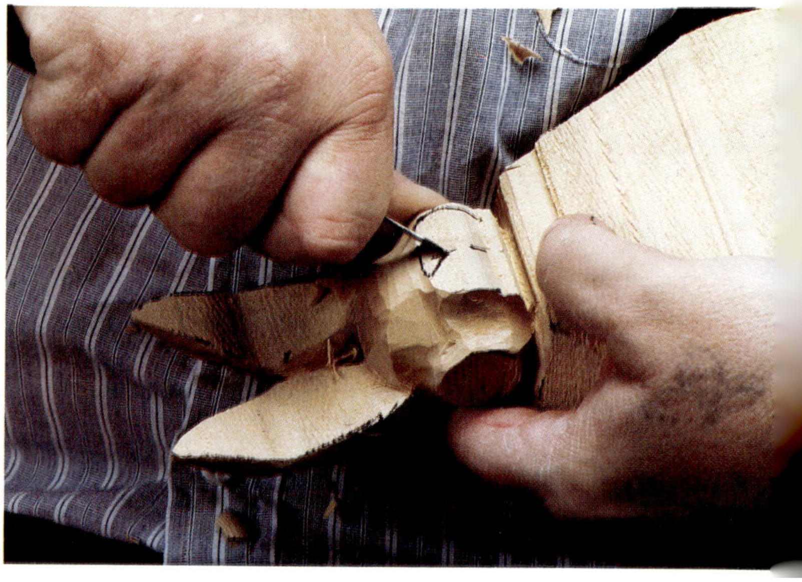

To carve the nose, cut a stop on both sides.

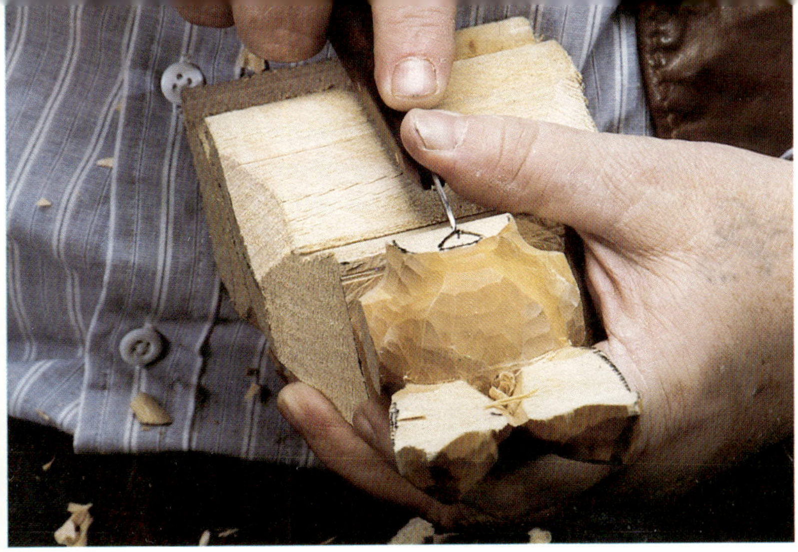

and a stop down the center below the nose.

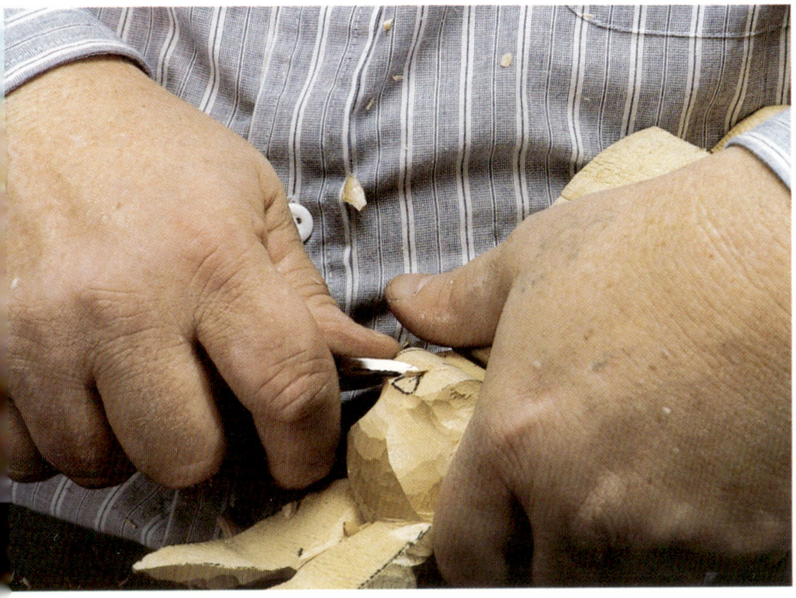

Carve back to the stops from both sides of the muzzle.

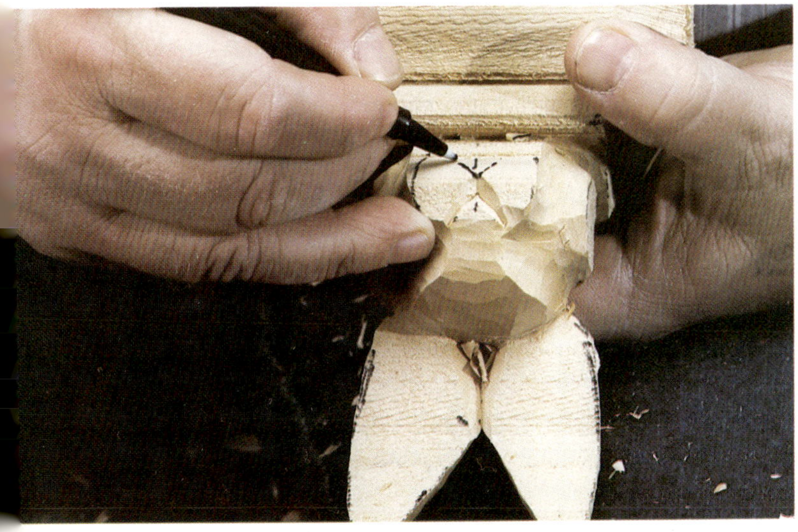

The distance between the nose and the upper lip is not very great in the rabbit. The mouth almost forms an X with the lines of the nose.

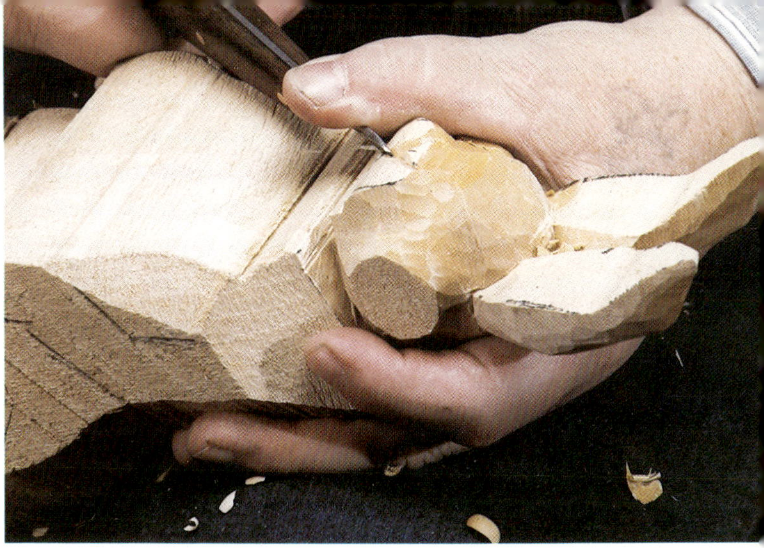

Cut a stop straight in on the mouth lines, but not too deep. You need to leave room for the buck teeth.

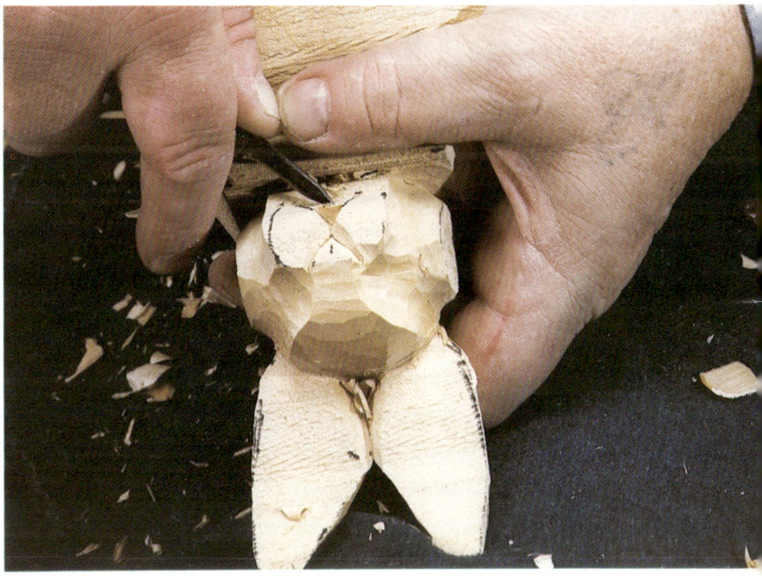

Trim back to the stop with a shallow cut so there is wood left for the teeth.

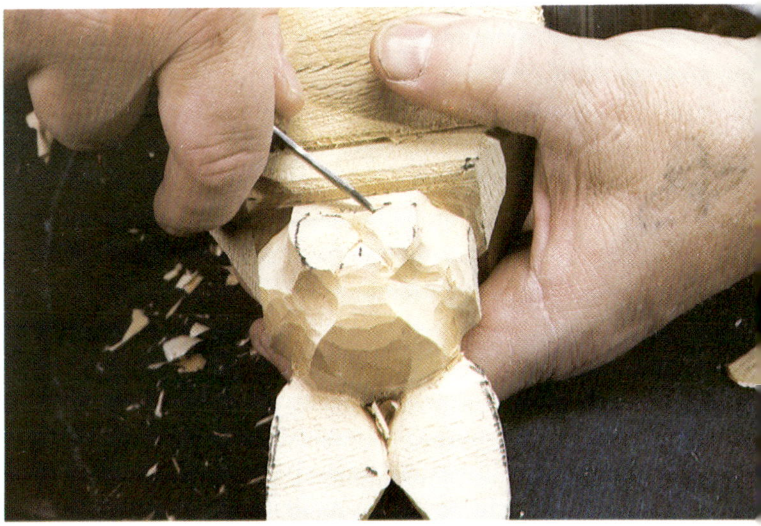

A v-shaped notch at each corner of the mouth will create the teeth. Cut this way...

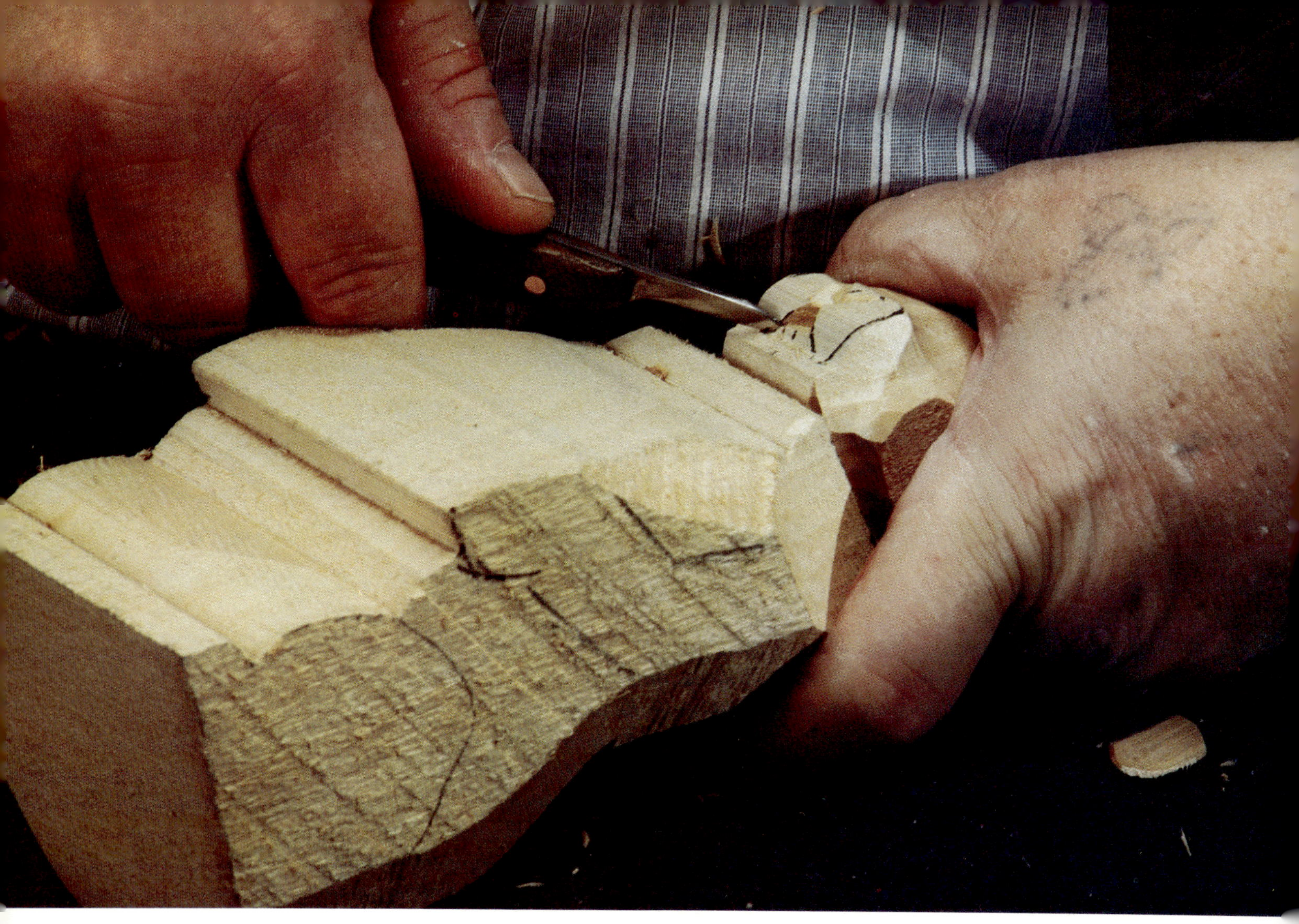

then along the mouth line...

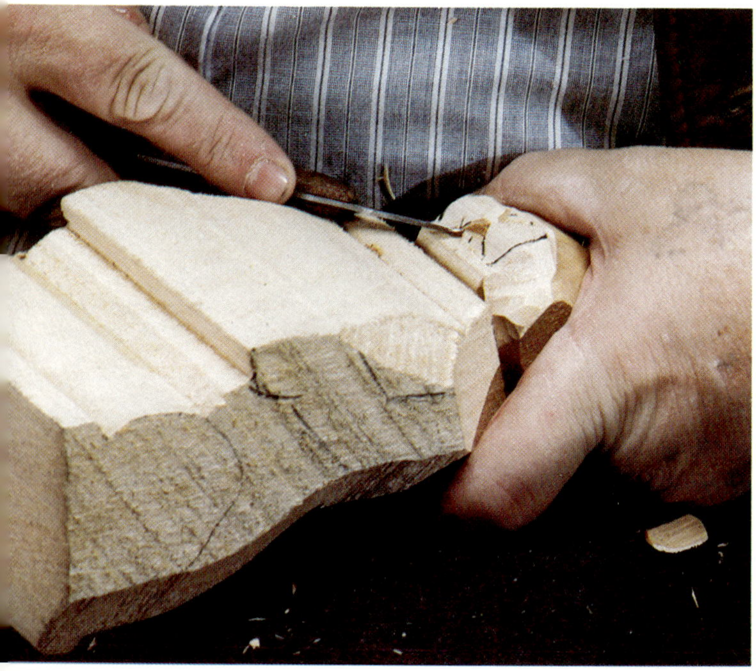

and then across the bottom to pop out the little triangle.

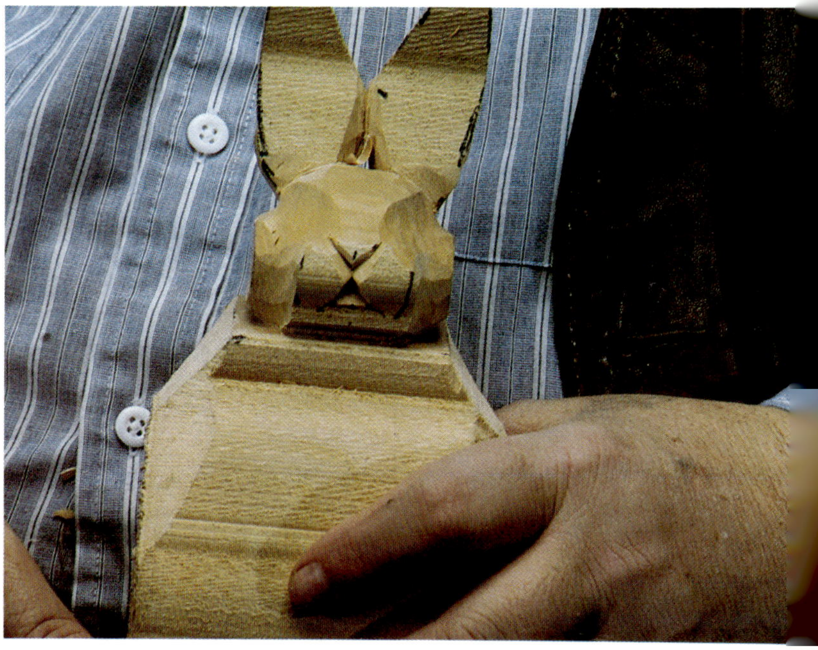

Removing the triangles at the corners of the teeth creates this appearance.

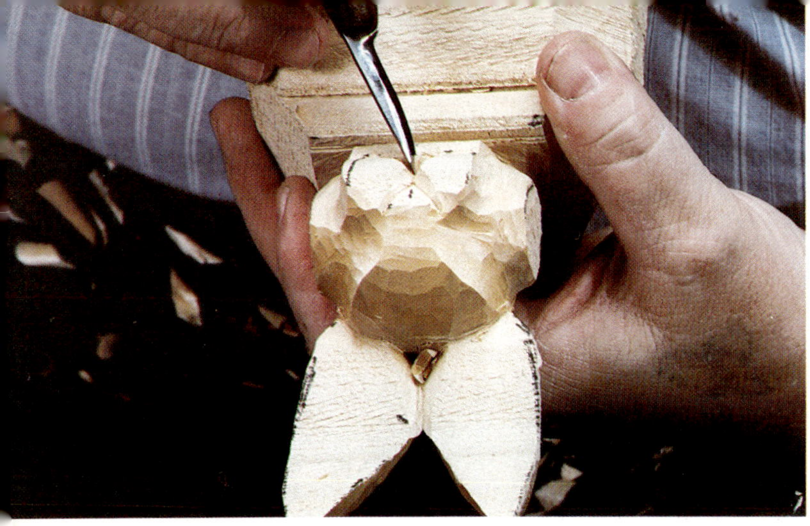

The teeth are defined and separated with two cuts creating a v-line between them.

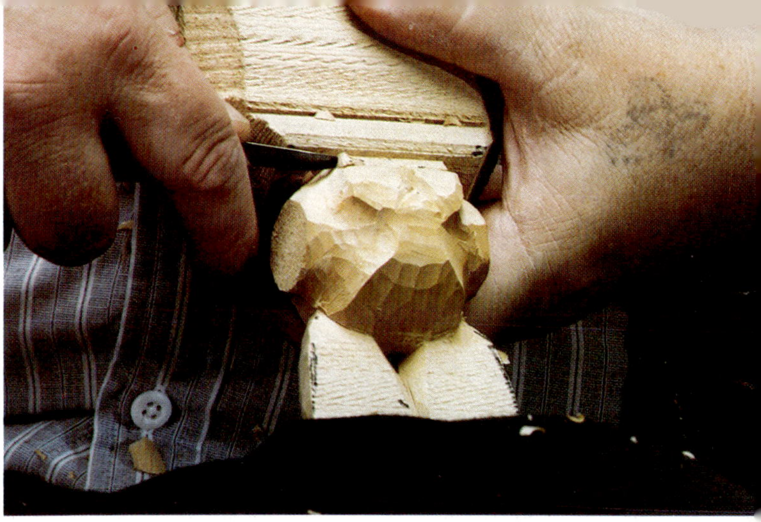

Carry the line of the mouth around the jaw by notching a v-line.

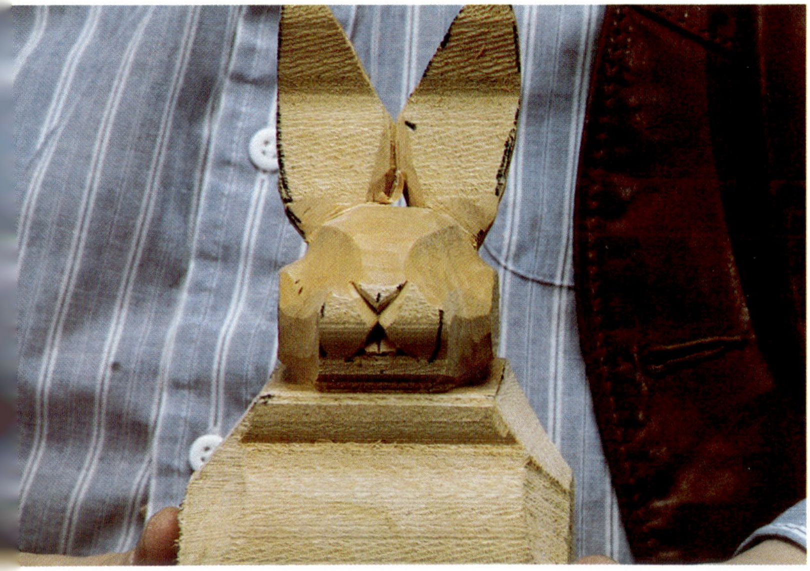

This is the result.

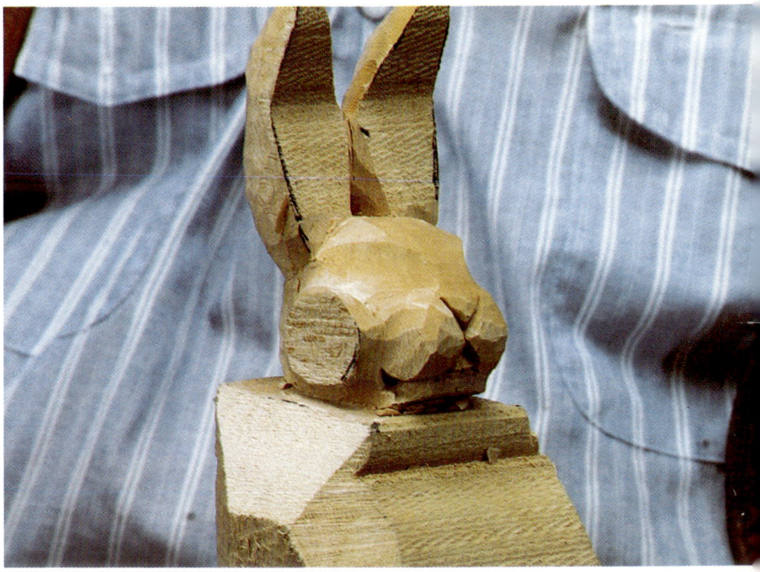

Bring the mouth line up at the back, giving the bunny a smiling look.

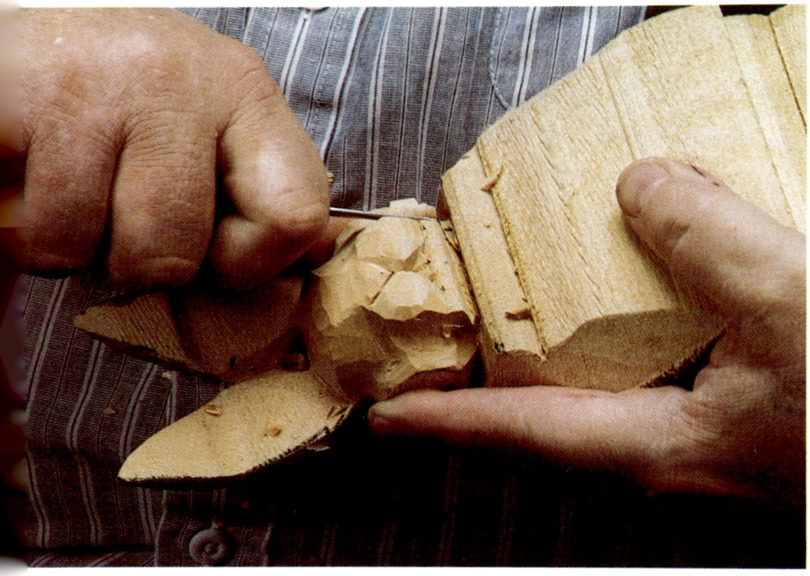

Clean up the face a little, removing unnecessary pencil marks which may confuse the eye.

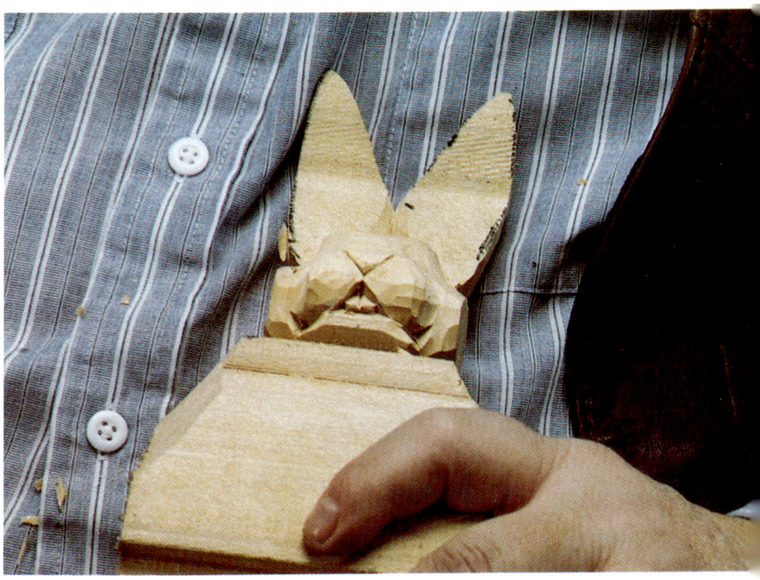

The lower jaw is a bit too strong...

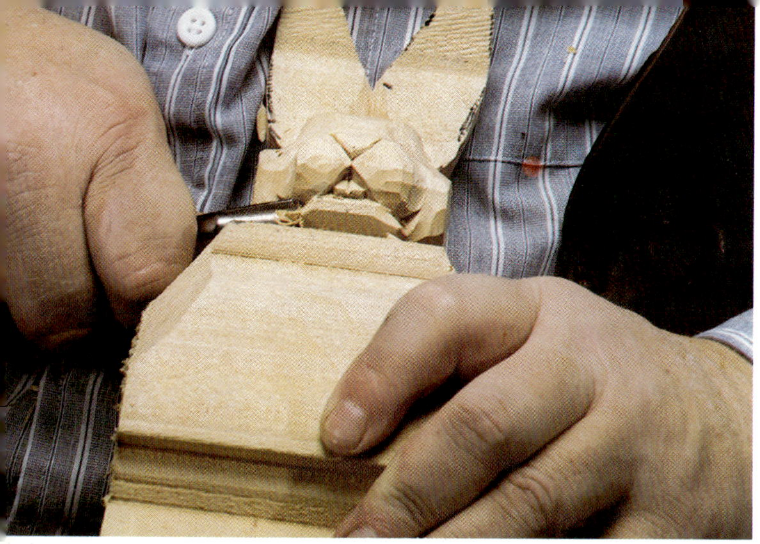

so I'll take the gouge and trim it up. When using the gouge it is best, and safest to keep the piece in a vise. Having said that, you will see that I don't follow my own advice. After years of experience I have learned to use finger position to keep control over the tool. Still, sometimes I slip, and when I do it hurts.

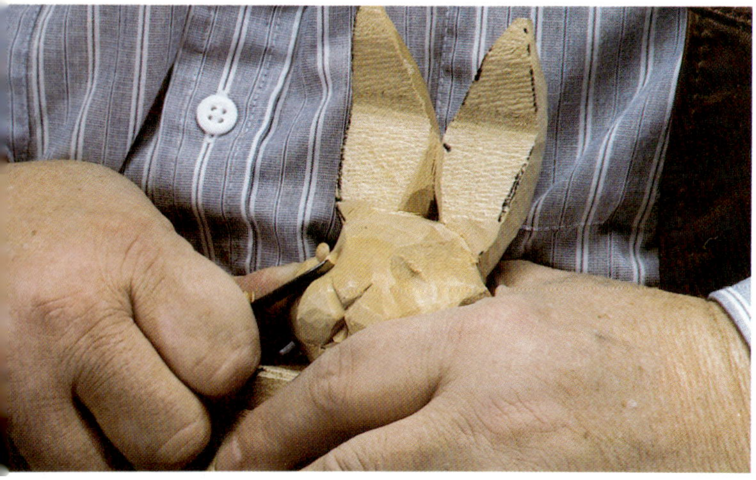

Use the gouge to bring out the muzzle and create a space for the eyes. A rabbit has a pretty wide bridge between the eyes, so don't narrow it too much.

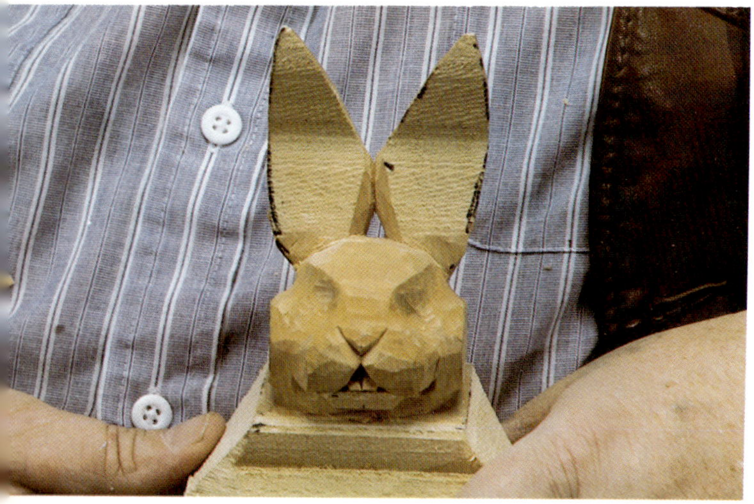

The face is taking shape.

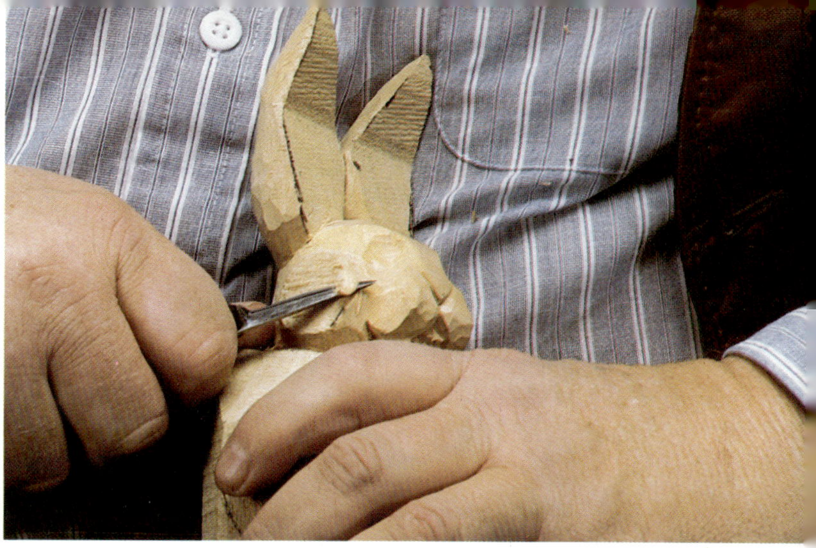

Next we go around the cheek. It should be fuller at the bottom. I use a knife to shape it. Start at the top front section...

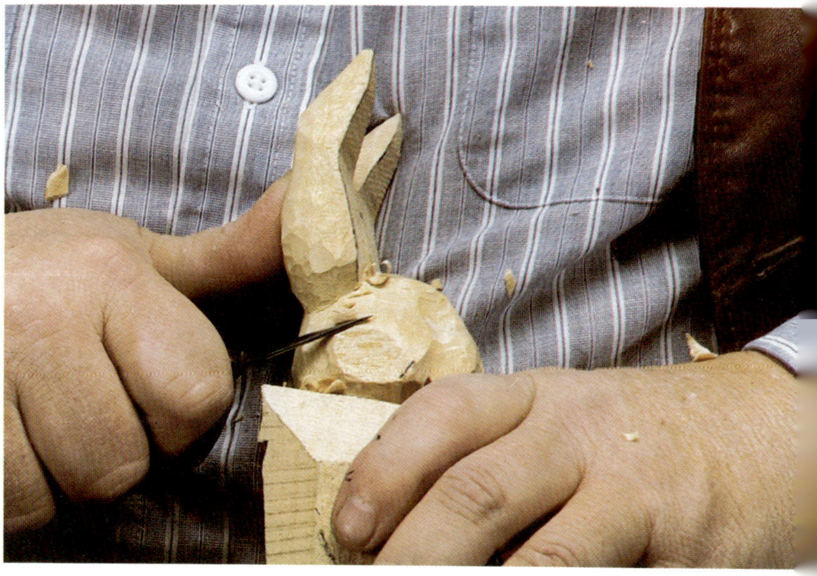

and work your way around the back...

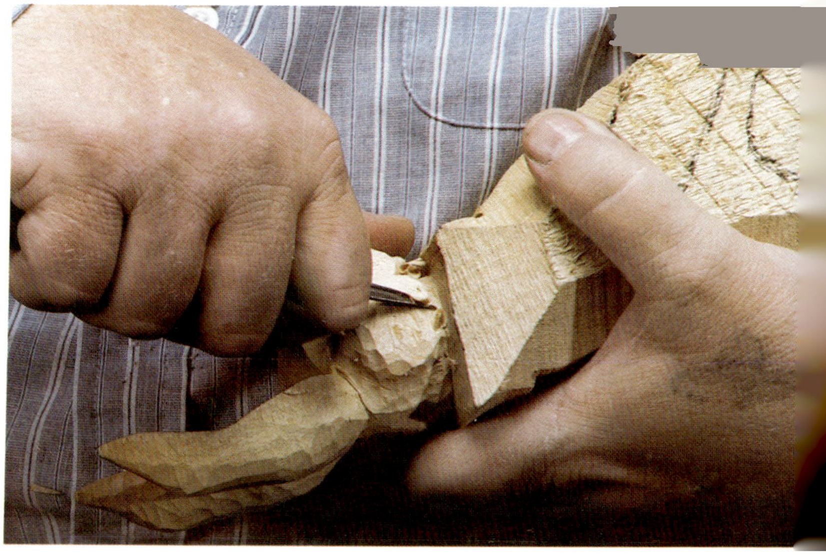

and the bottom.

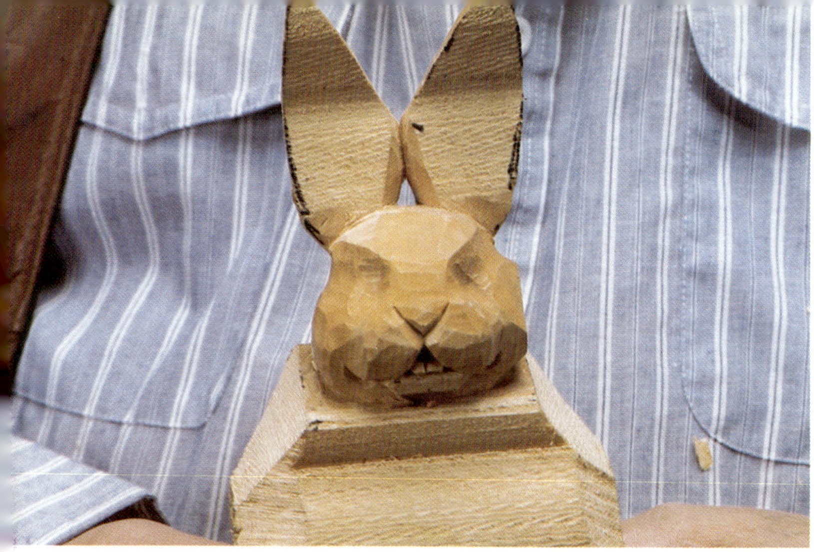

One side done, from the front...

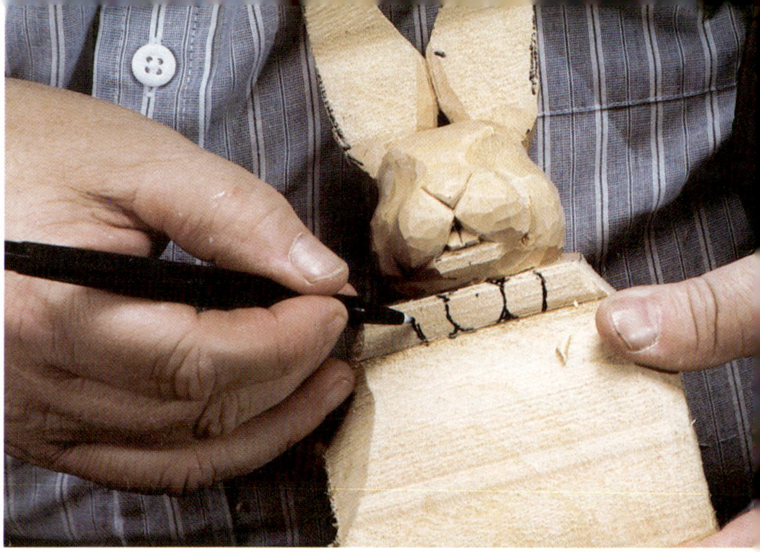

Draw in the bow tie...

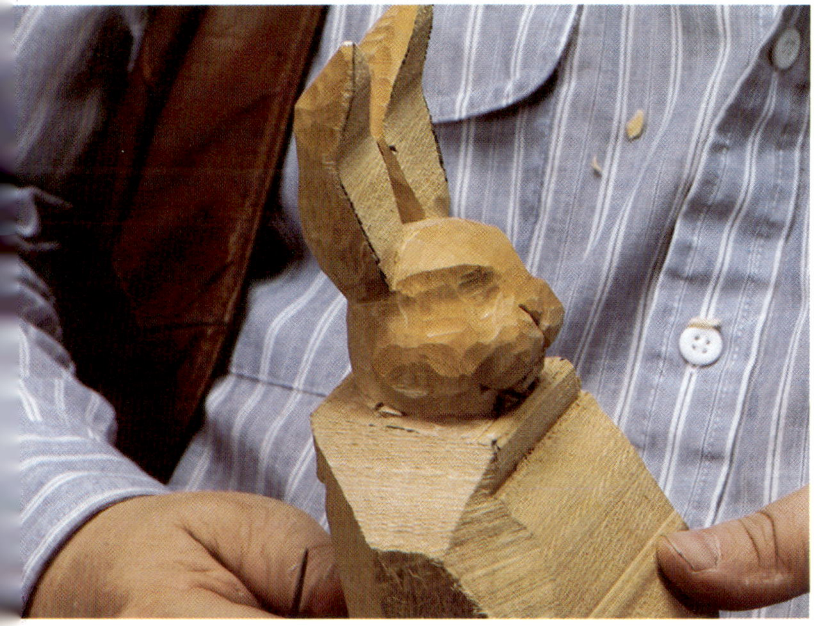

and the side.

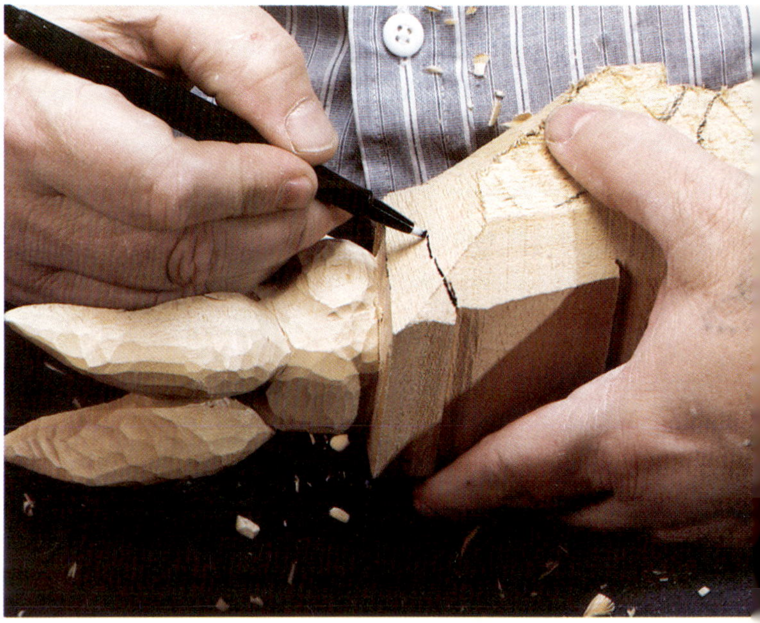

and the bottom line of the collar.

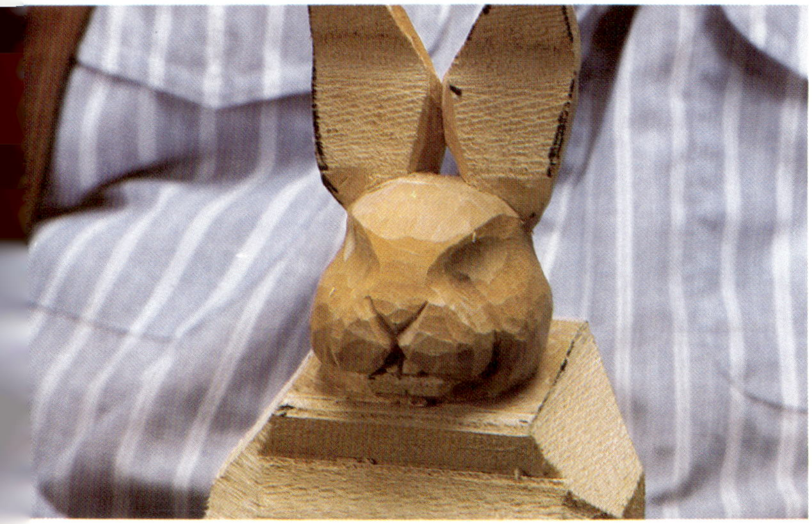

After the other cheek is rounded we have the face in the early stages of refinement.

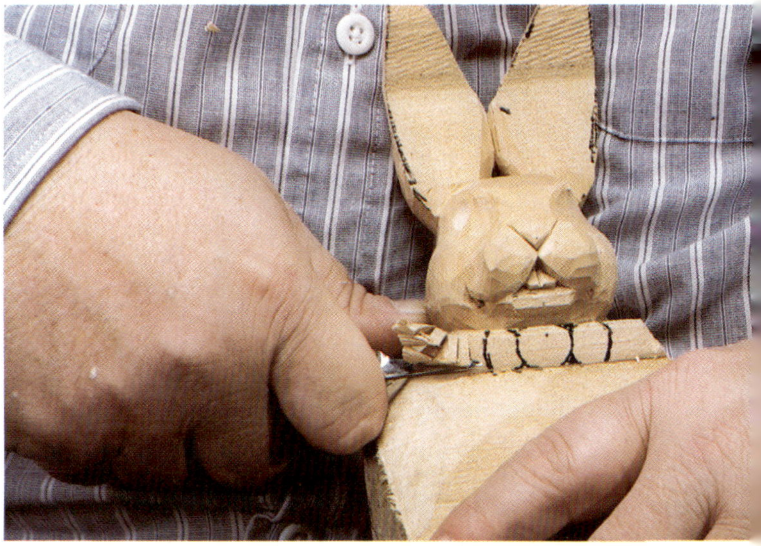

Chip off the front corners of the collar to the bow tie.

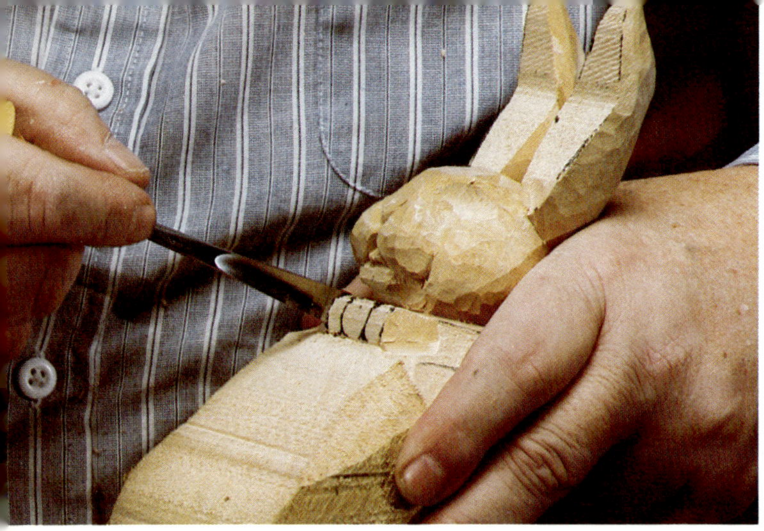

Use a fairly flat gouge to cut a stop on either side of the bow tie, holding the cupped side of the gouge against the line of the tie.

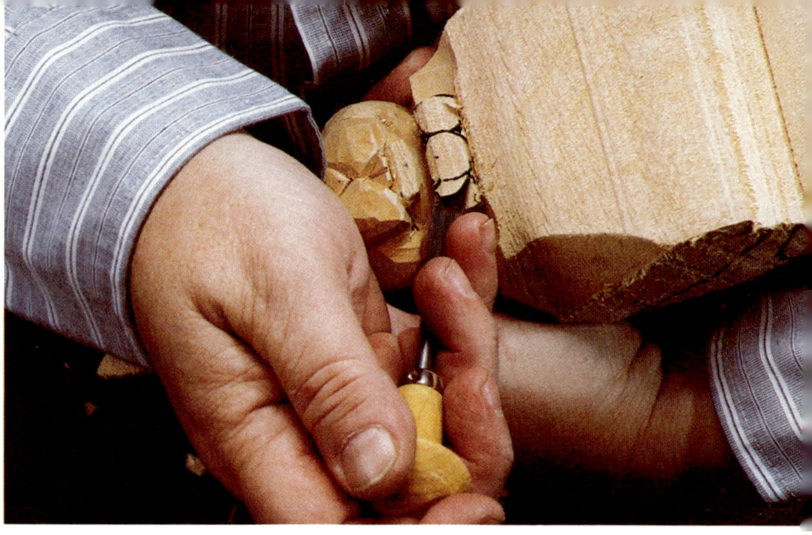

Cut back to it with the cupped side out. Using the gouge for this produces a rounded knot and gives a convex shape to the sides of the tie.

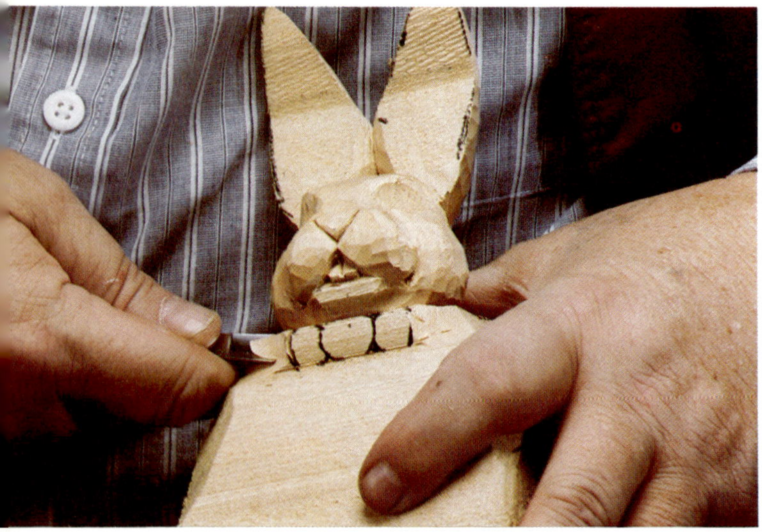

Trim back to it from the outside. Note how the forefinger is used as depth gauge when using the gouge.

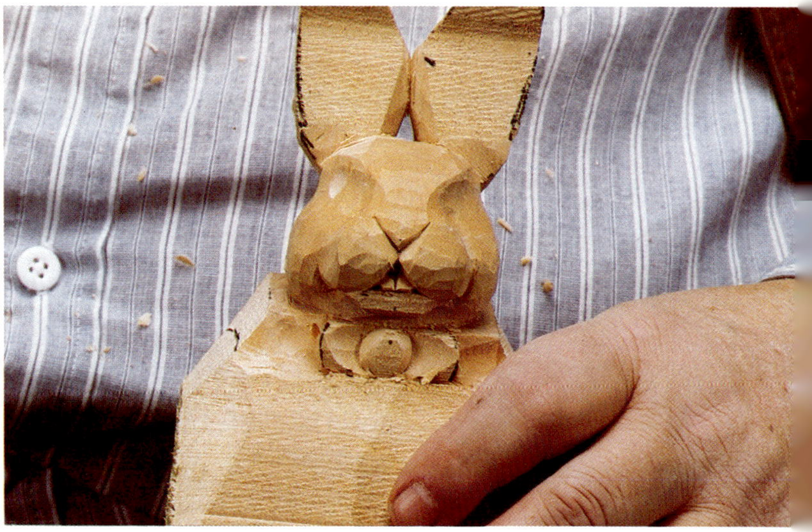

The tie so far.

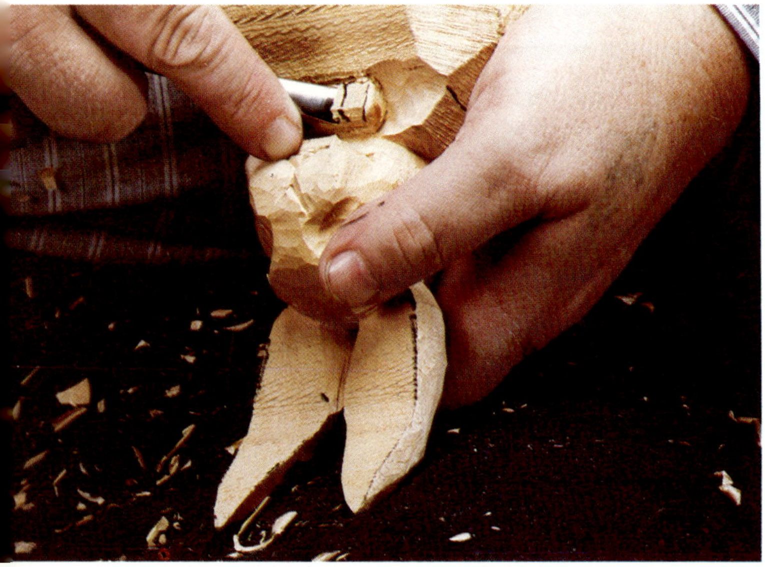

Cut an angled stop with the gouge over the knot, again with the cupped side toward the knot.

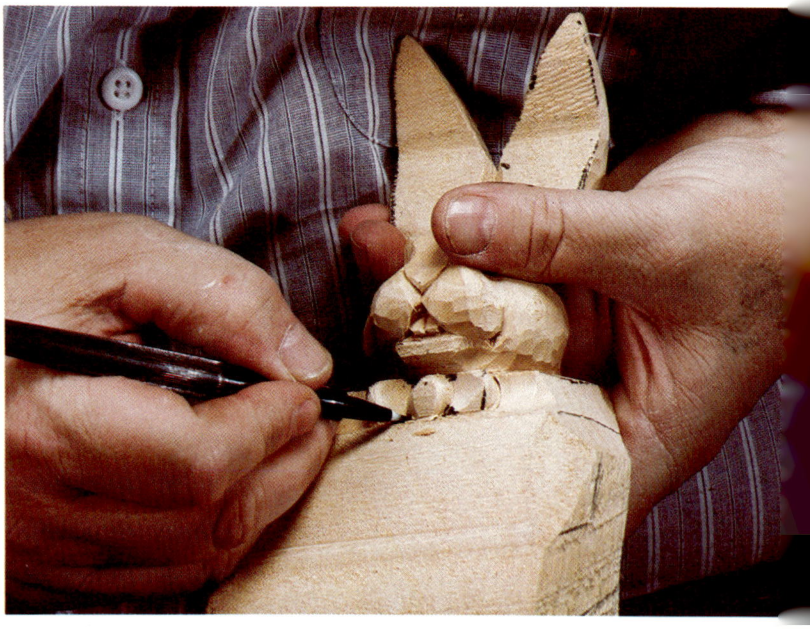

Mark the corners and edges of the tie.

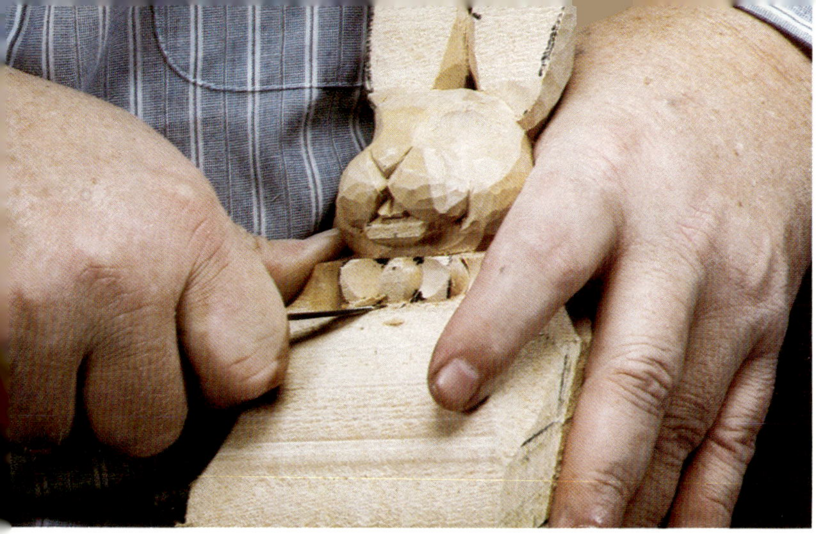

These areas will be removed with a knife to give the tie more definition, and a more three-dimensional look.

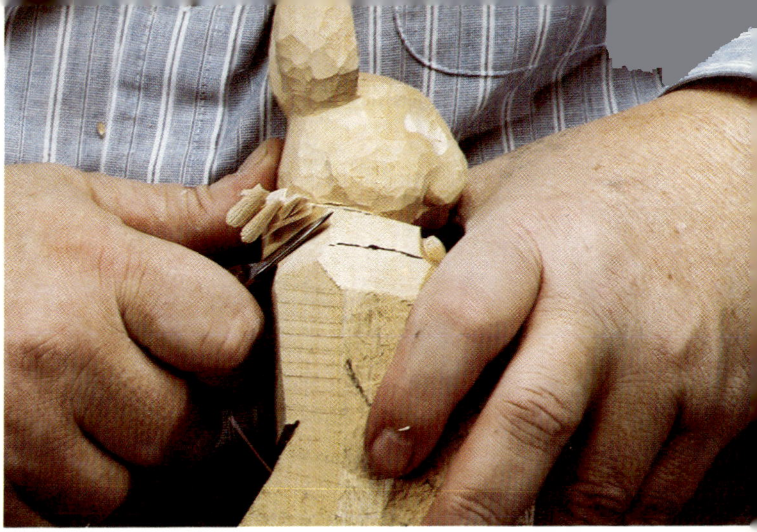

Round the back of the collar, sloping it up toward the neck.

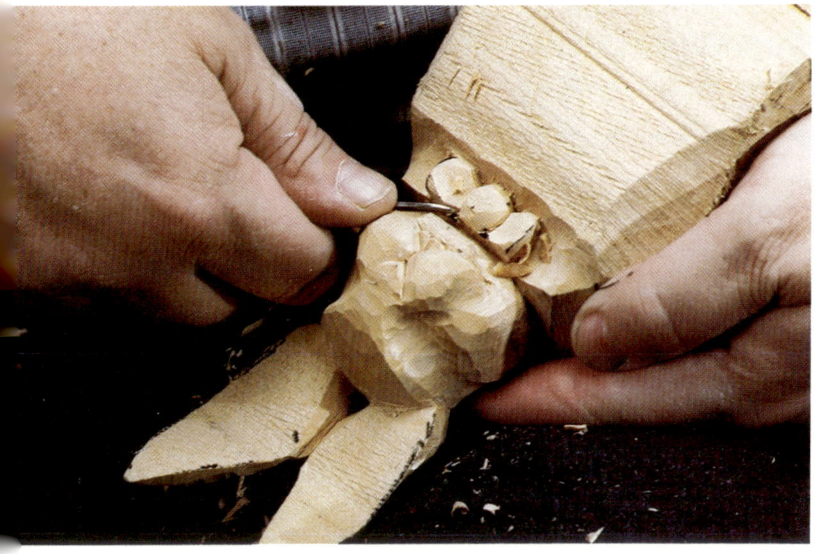

Do the same thing at the top of the tie.

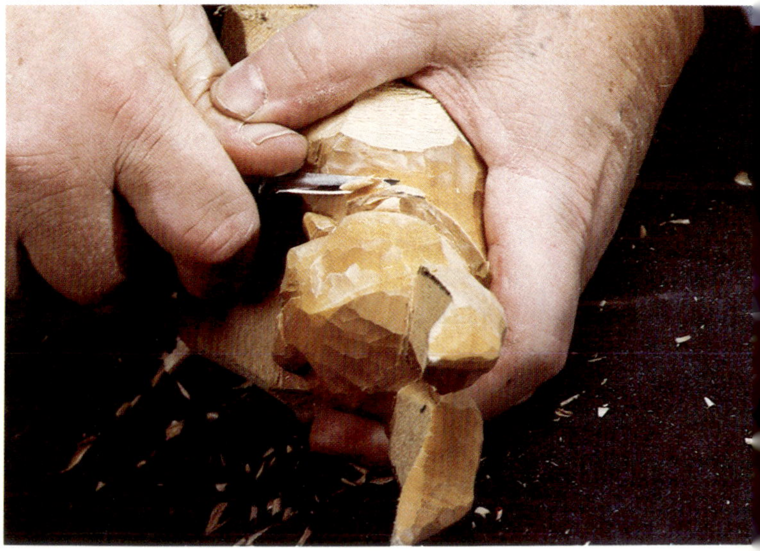

Go all around the collar to give the starched, stand-up effect.

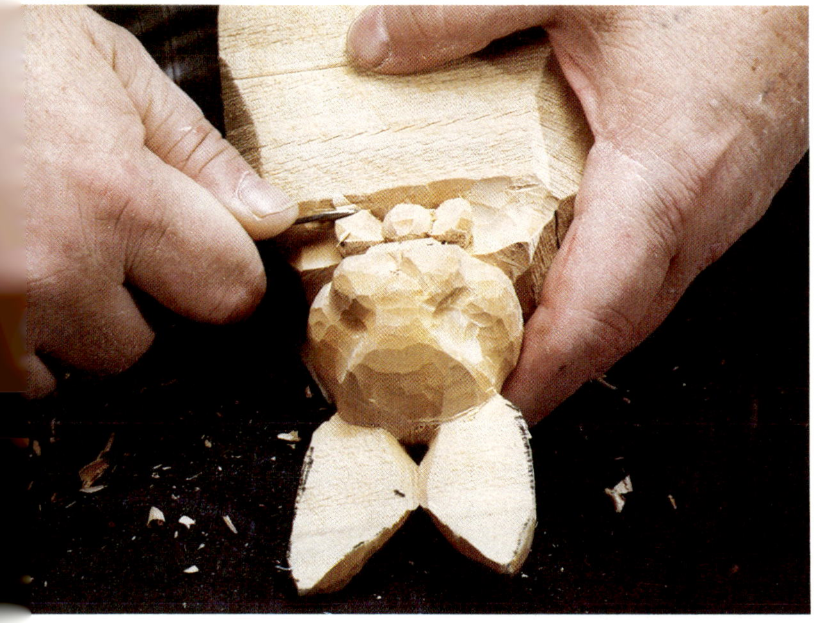

Clean up the tie and round the surfaces.

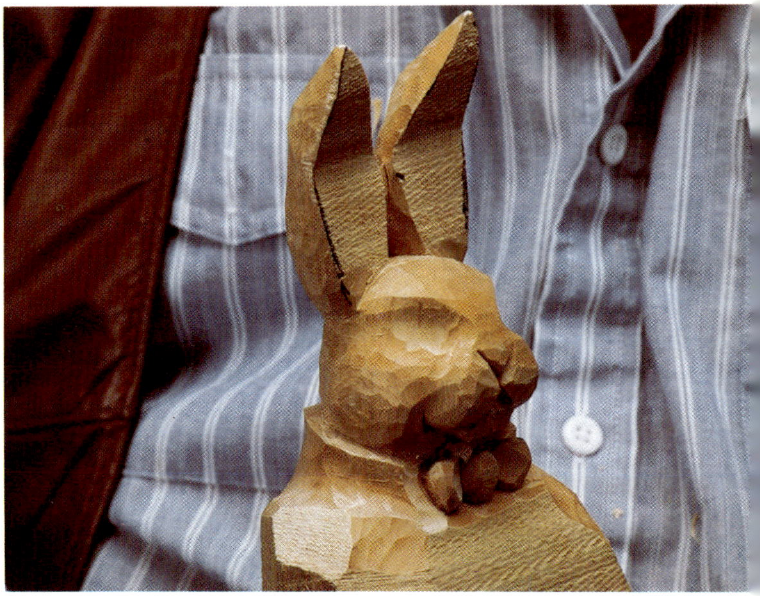

The collar for now.

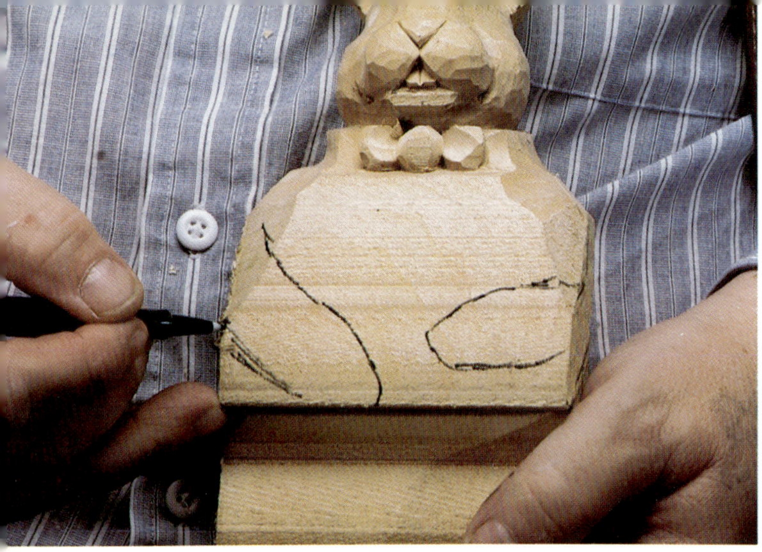

Begin shaping the body and the arms. A sitting bunny will normally have one arm above the other, so we'll draw it like this.

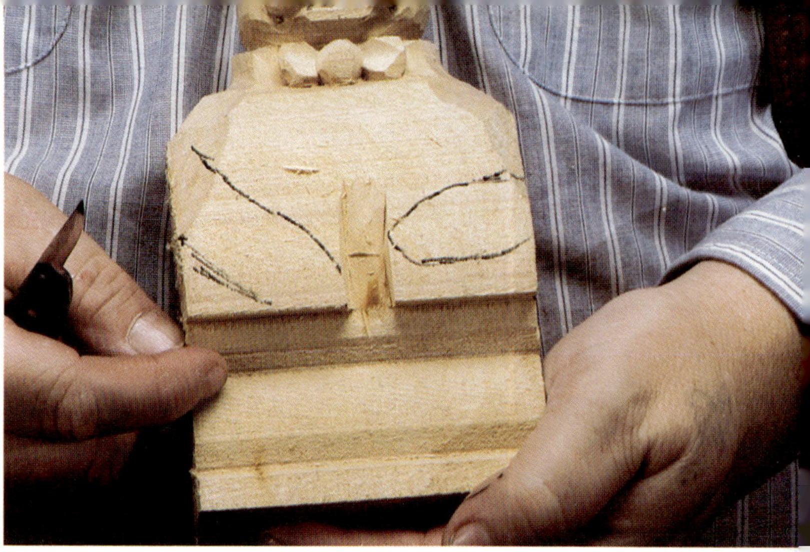

Use the knife to get to this point.

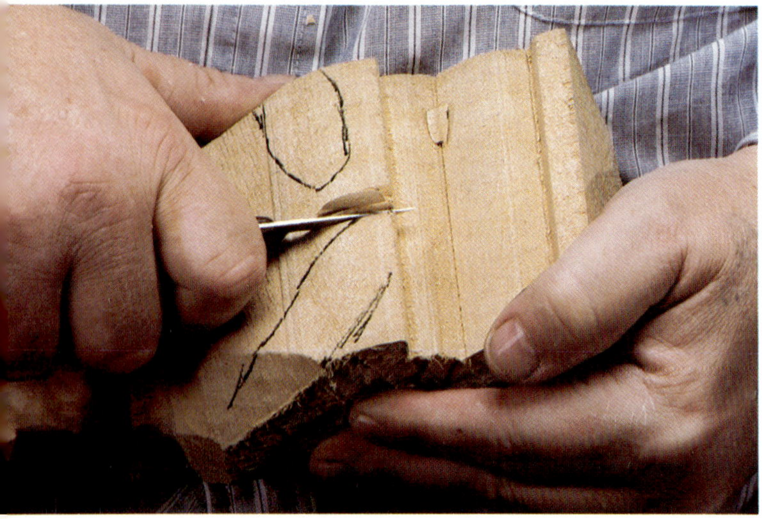

Separate the hands by cutting a good, deep stop...

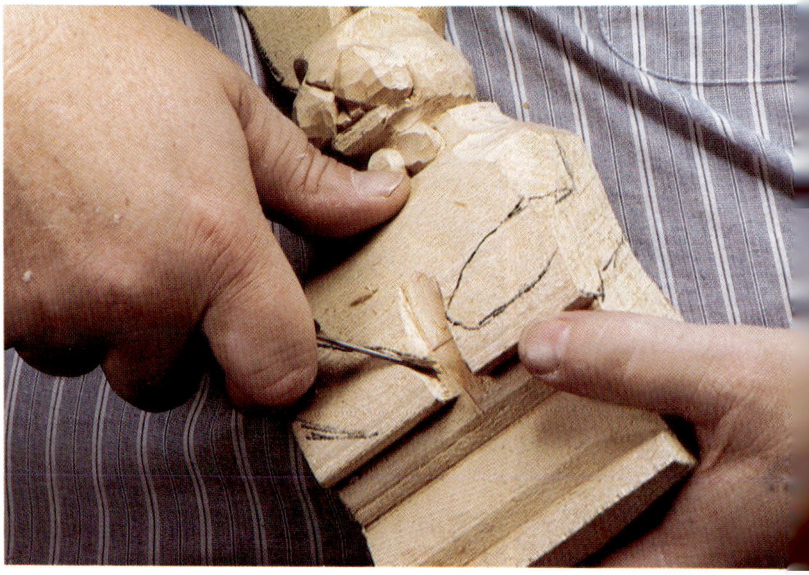

Cut a stop along the upper edge of the arm...

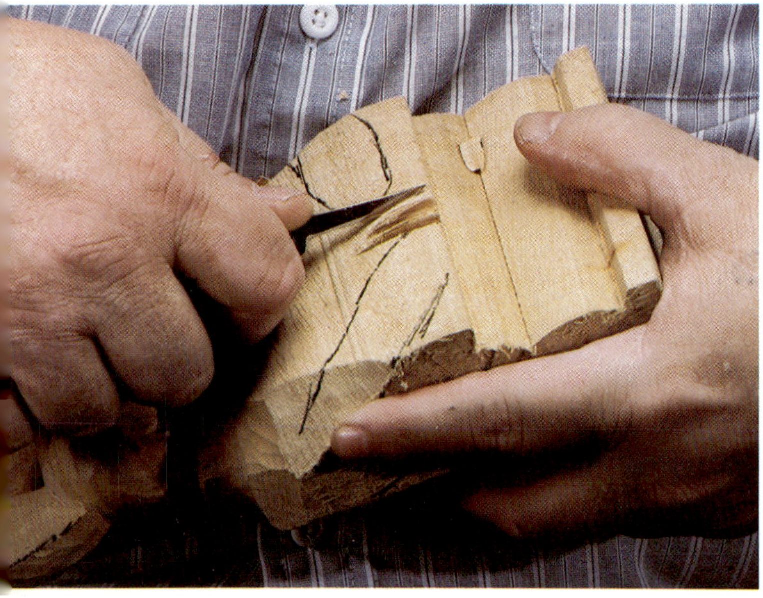

and carving back to it.

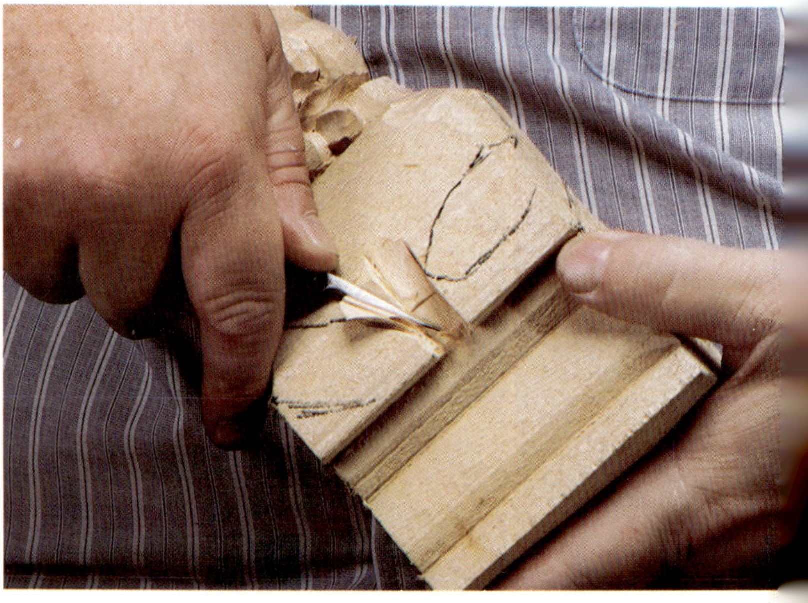

and come back to it from the body.

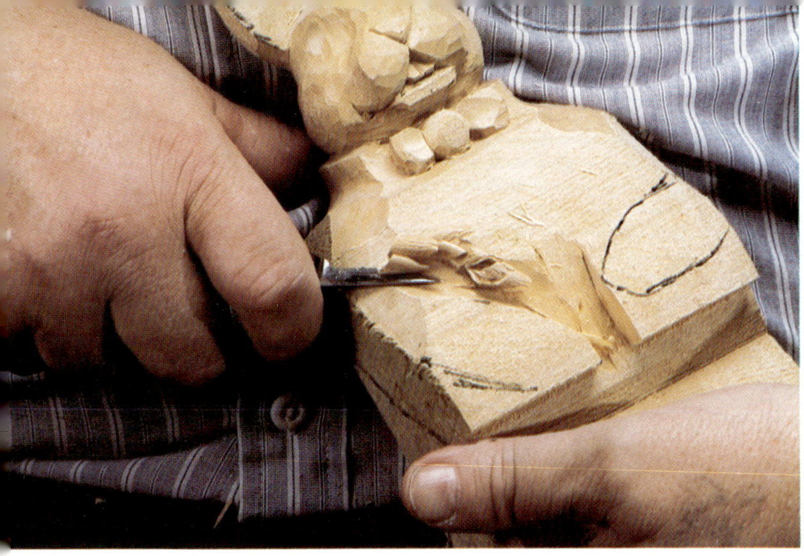

Use the knife to bring out the arm, carving up into the body.

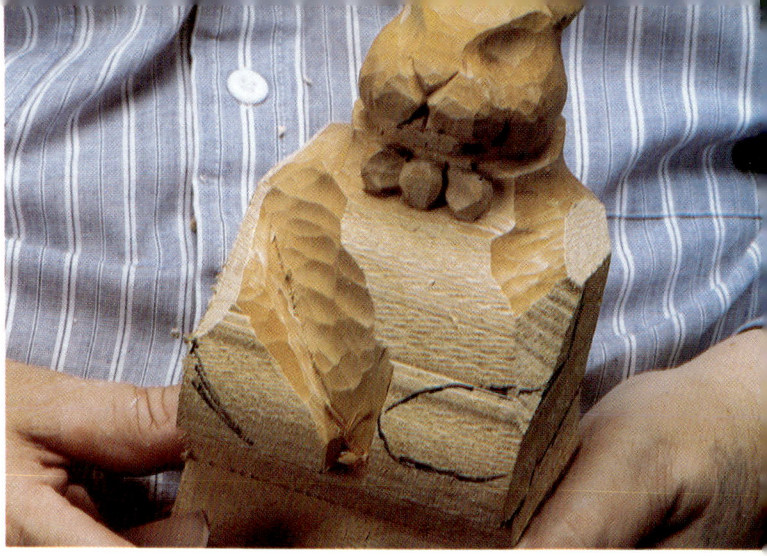

The right arm is gradually emerging from the body.

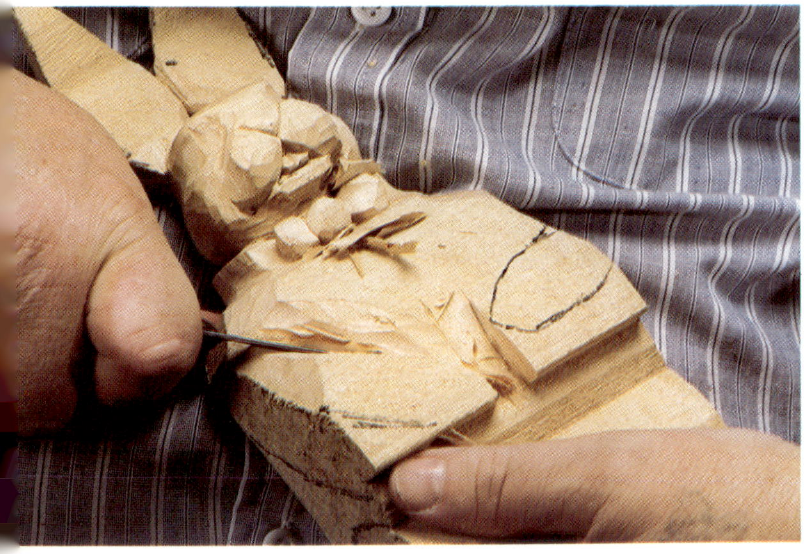

Continue to deepen the space between the arm and the body.

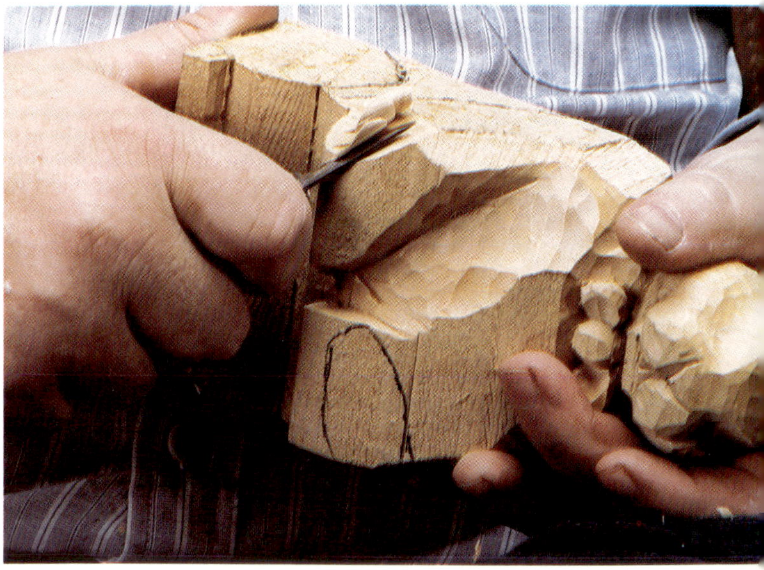

Use the knife to remove the excess wood beneath the right arm.

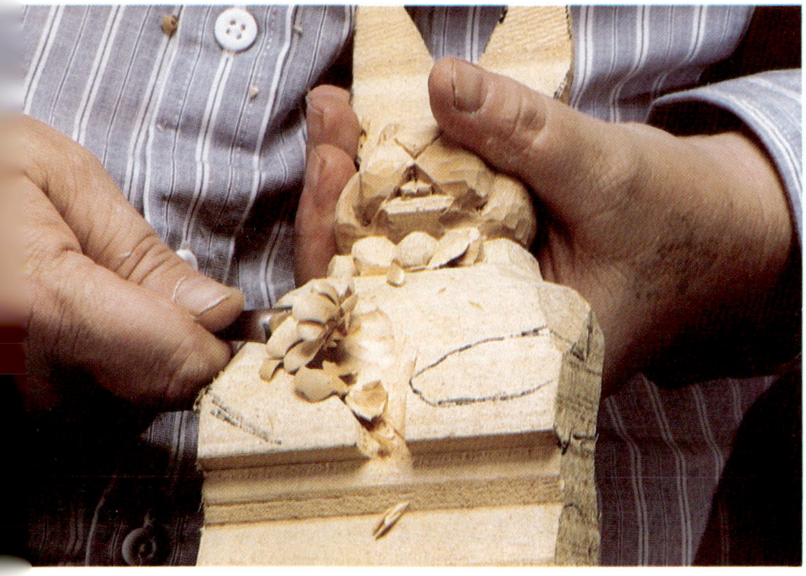

Remove excess wood with the palm chisel.

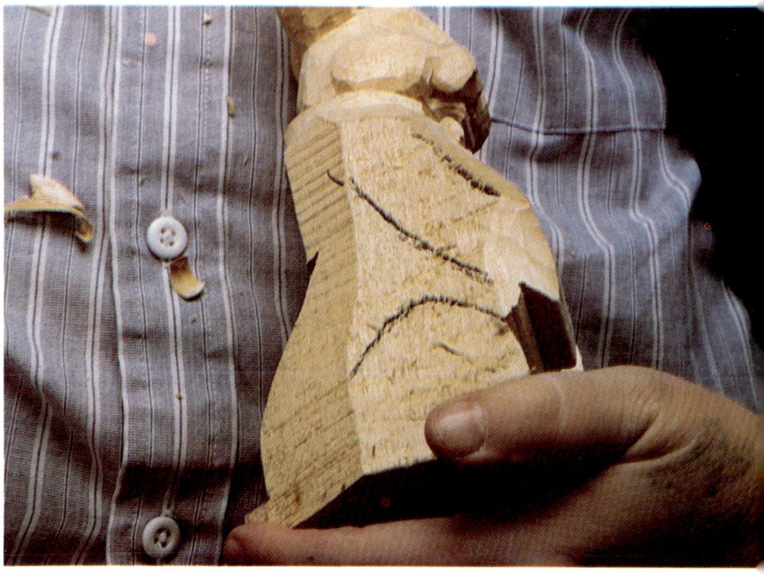

It may be helpful to re-mark the lines.

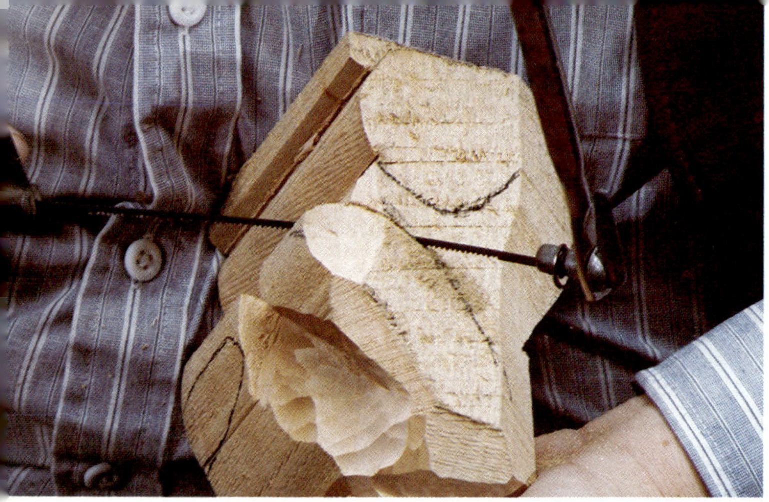

A coping saw at this point will save some work. Cut along the lower line of the arm until it looks as though you've gone deep enough. I put my coping saw blade in backwards so that the cutting stroke comes when I pull. This gives me more control.

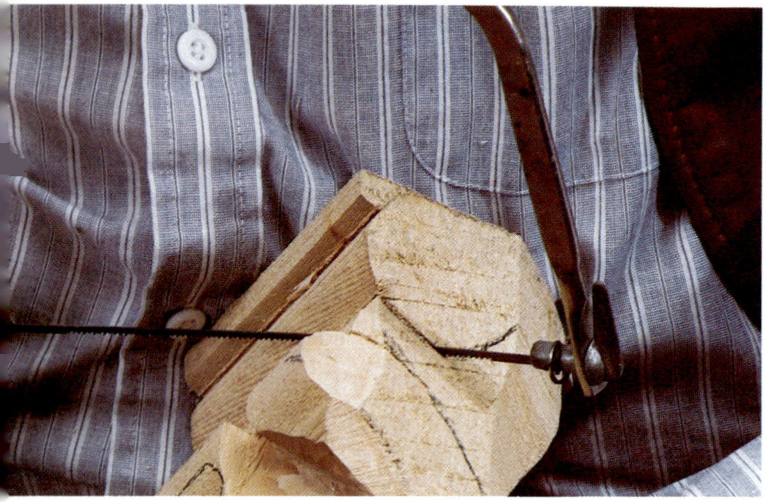

Do the same on the top of the hind leg.

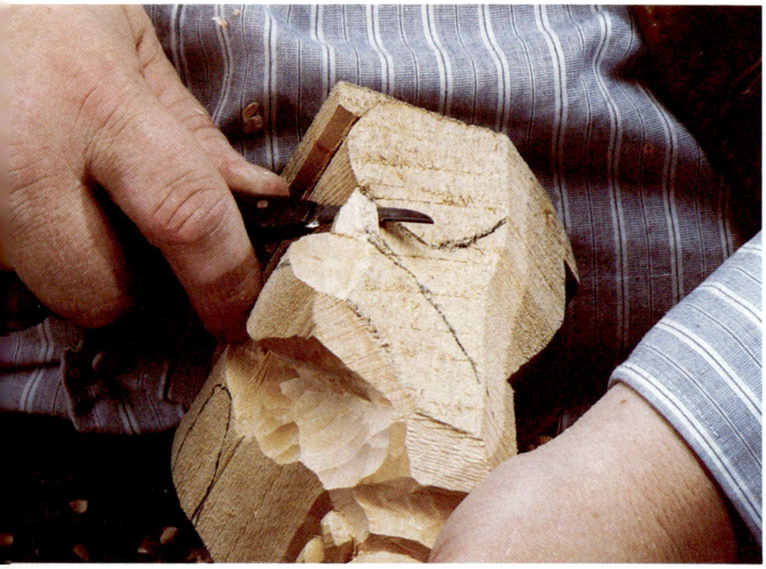

Use a knife to pop out the wood between the fore leg and the hind leg.

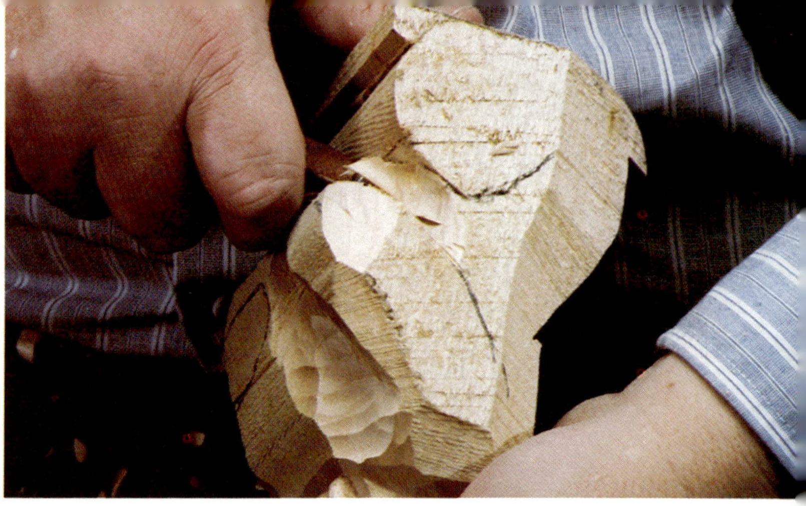

A turned up knife will do nicely to further clean out this space.

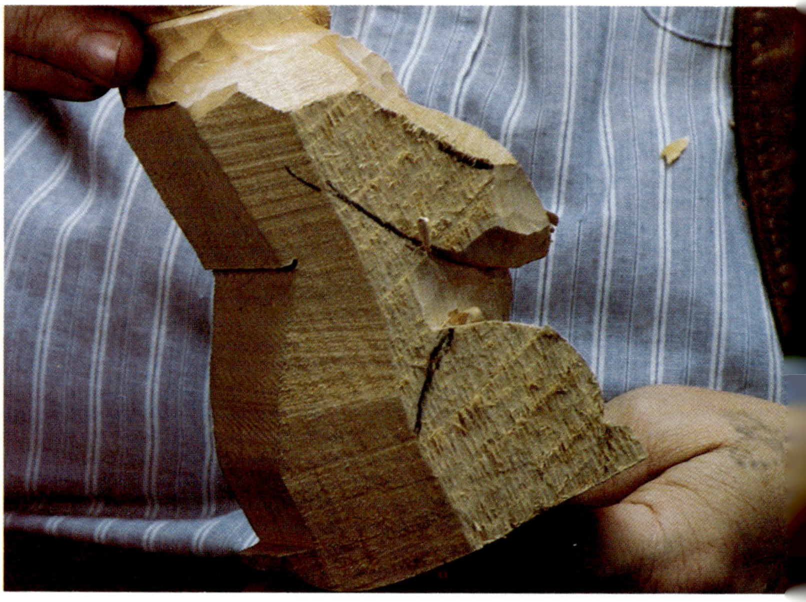

This gives an idea of how much wood to remove.

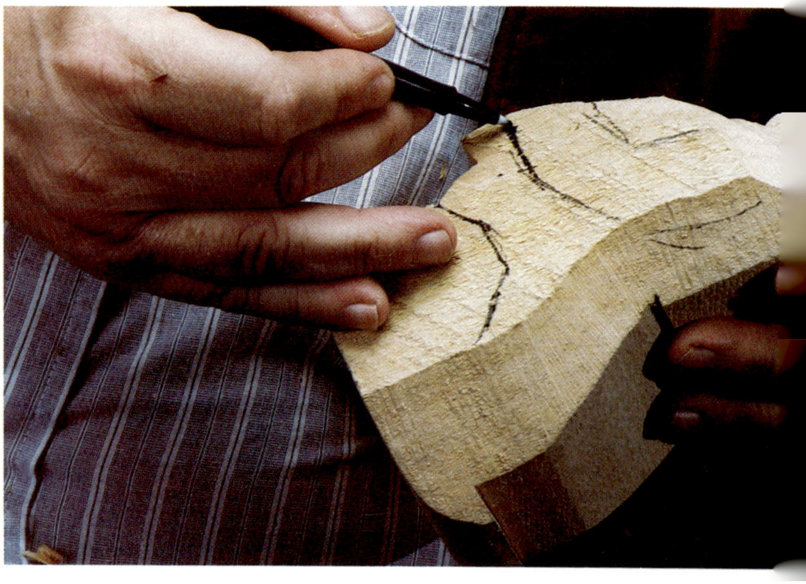

Re-mark the left side to raise the left front paw higher than the right. Then proceed as on the right side.

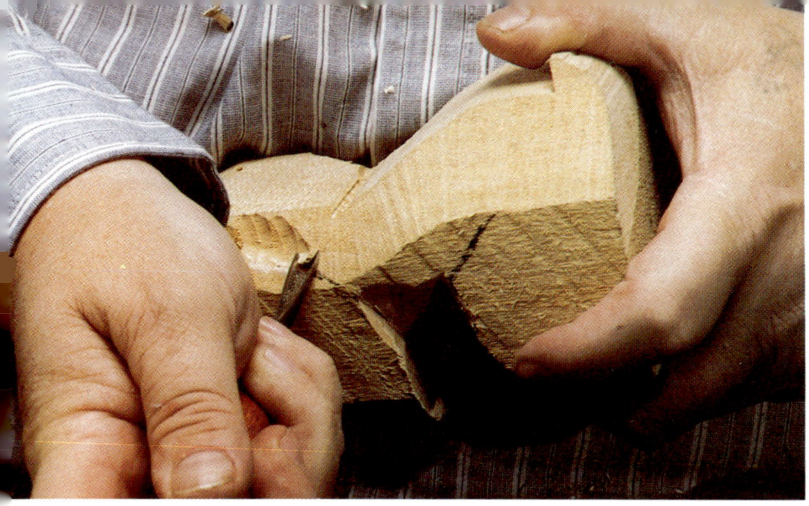

Remove the material behind the arms using a gouge and cutting away from the arm line.

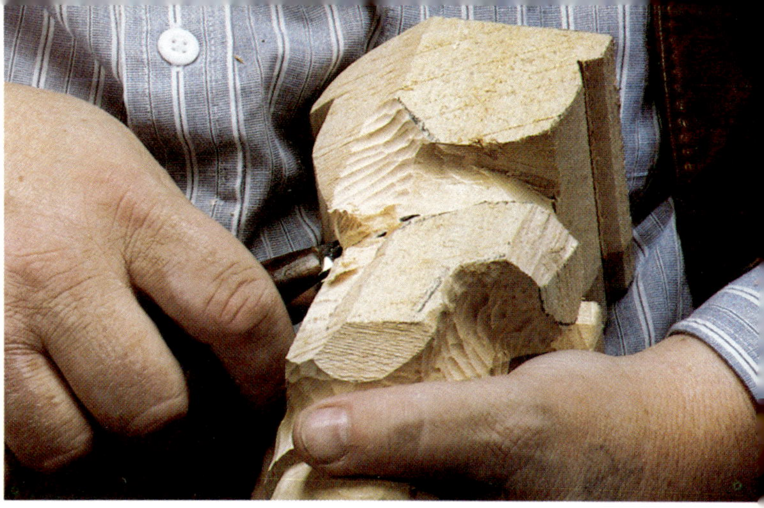

Clean up the gouge marks and round things off with the knife.

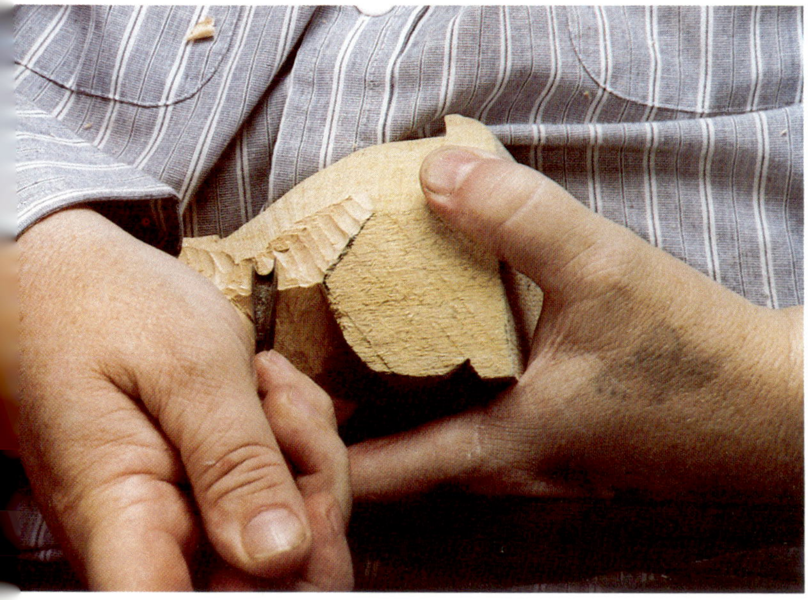

Continue with the gouge behind the hind legs and through the mid-section.

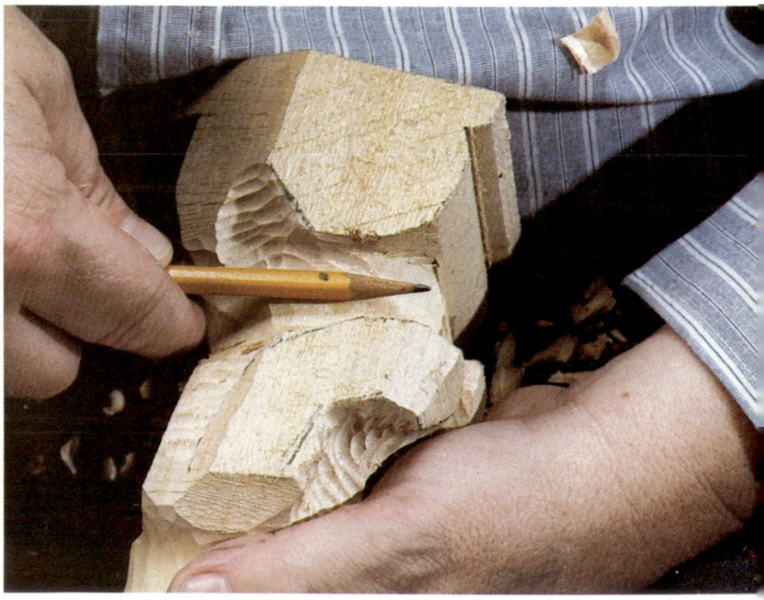

The bunny is a bit broad in the middle. You can see this by using a pencil as a gauge. The mid-section should be more or less round. Here is the depth measurement....

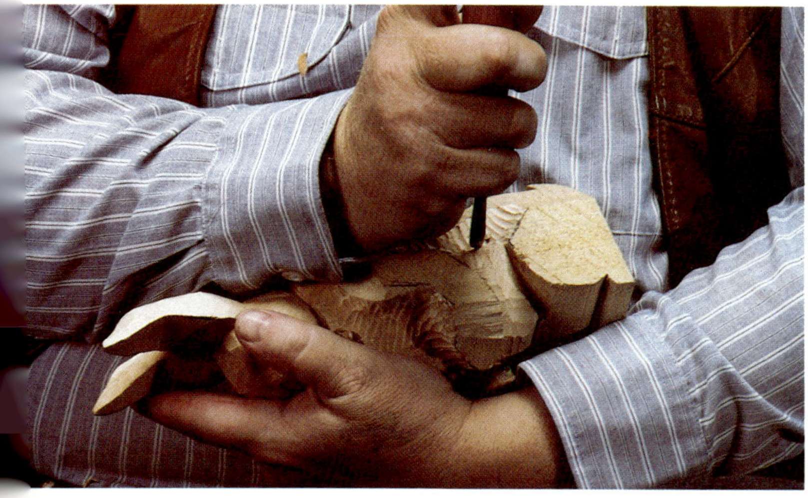

This is a relatively safe position for doing this kind of gouge work. Hands are out of the way and the gouge is used with short arching movements of the wrist and no heavy pushing.

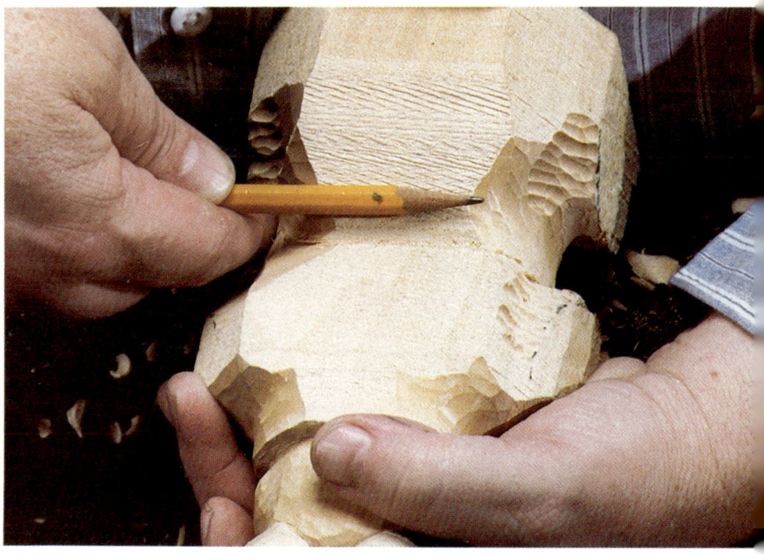

and here is the width. Time for a diet.

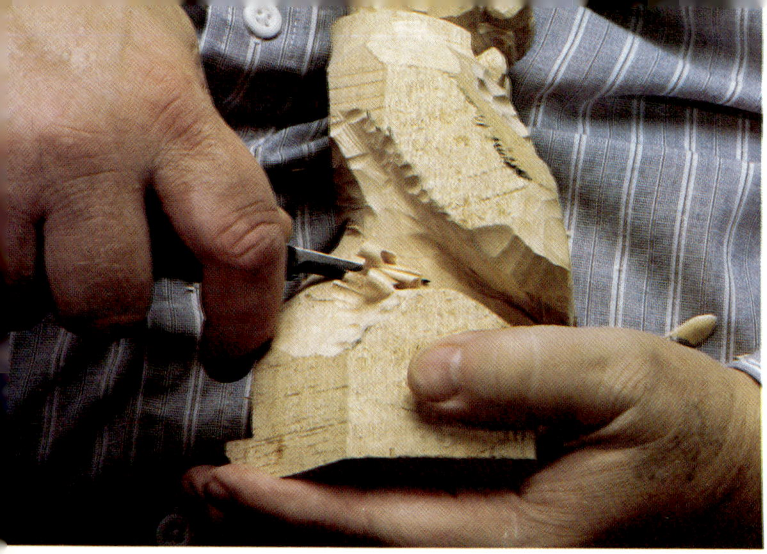

Trim down each side with the knife.

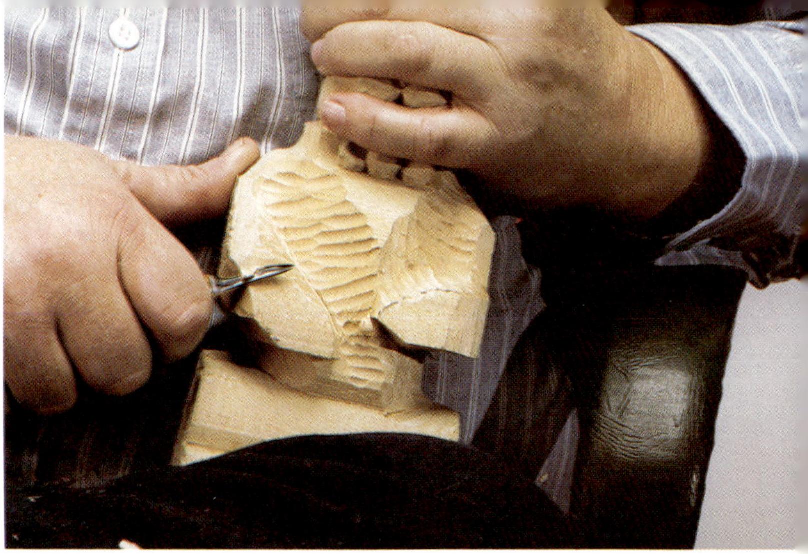

Round and shape the arms to remove thick places and clunky edges.

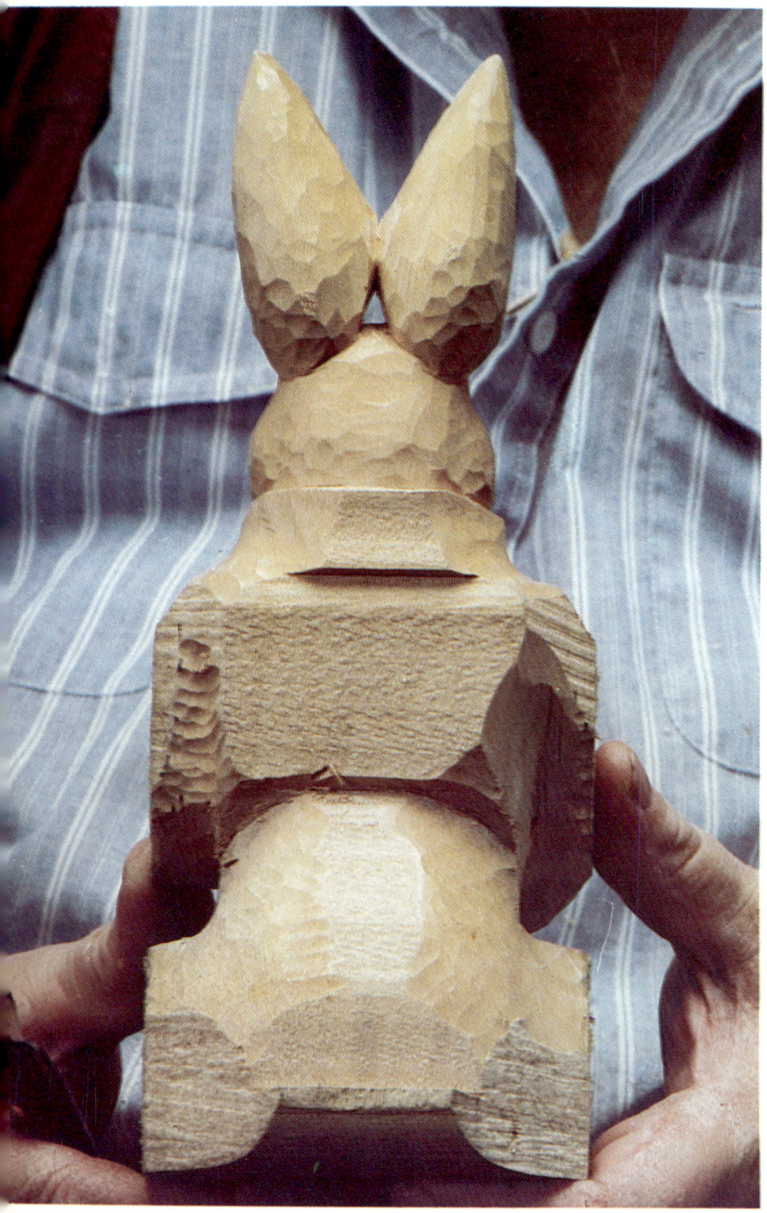

The diet works!

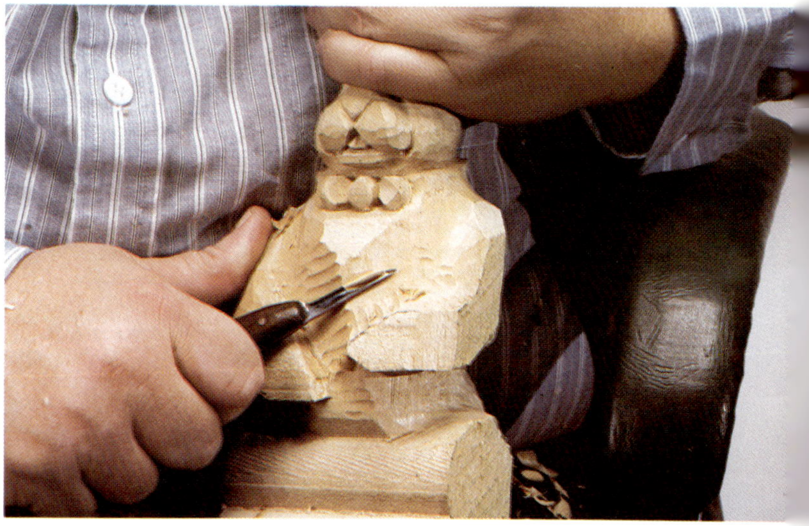

Continue to shape and clean-up the chest area.

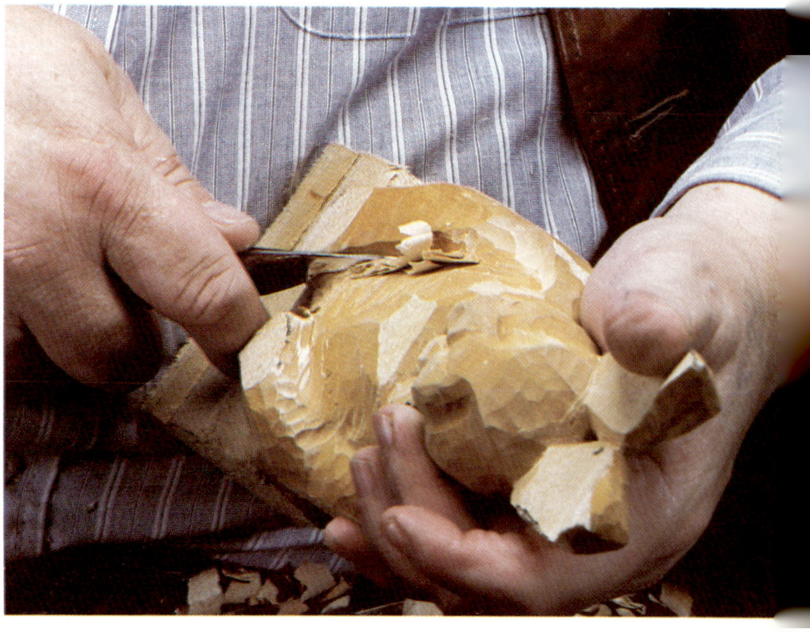

Define the space between the arm and the stomach.

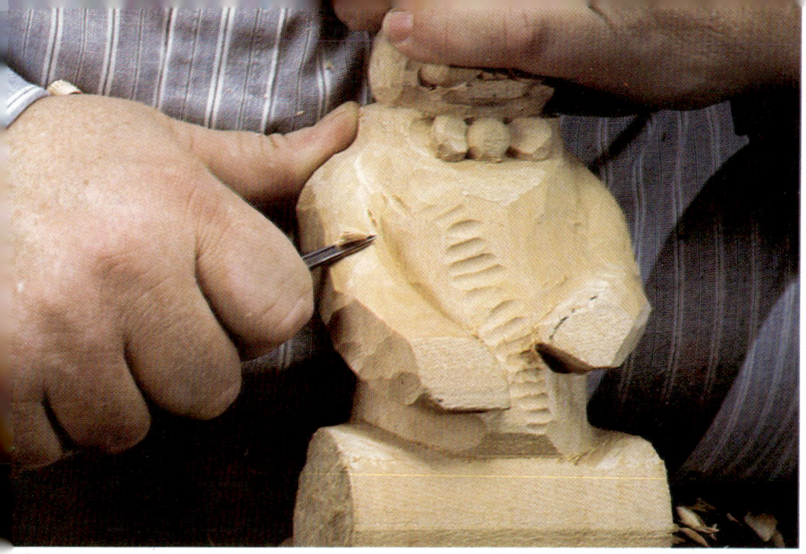

Keep going over the arms until they look balanced and correct.

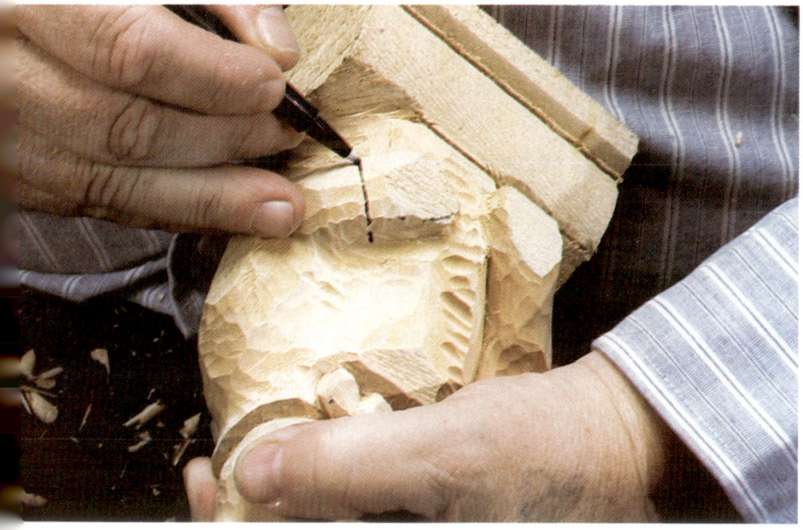

Decide on the length of the left sleeve...

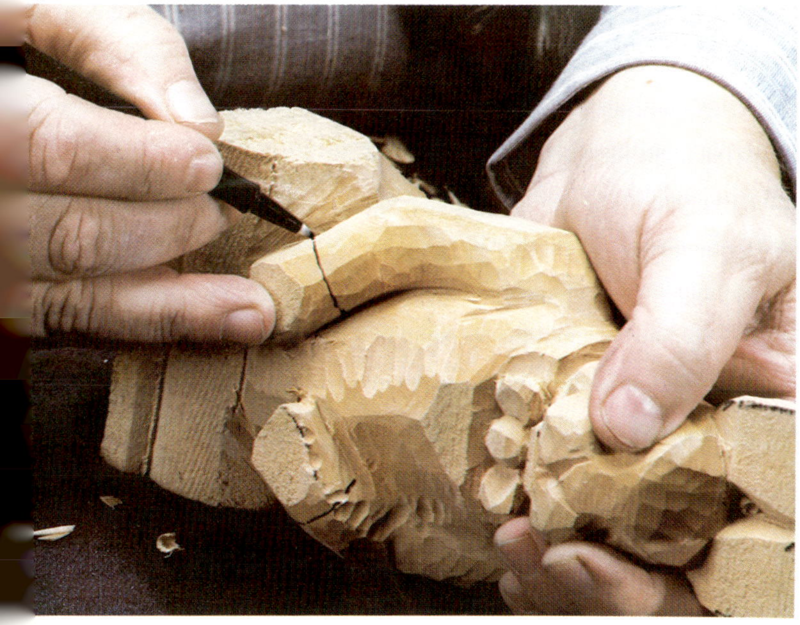

and the right, and mark them both.

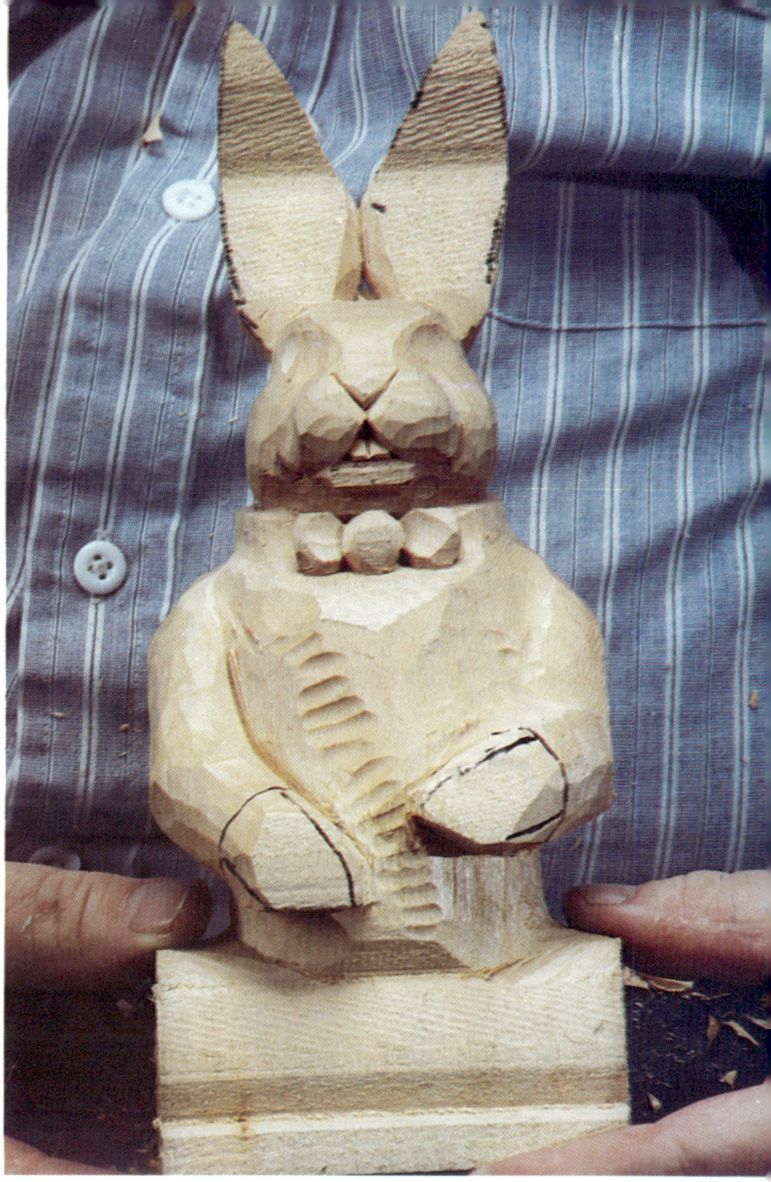

Mark the outline of the paws.

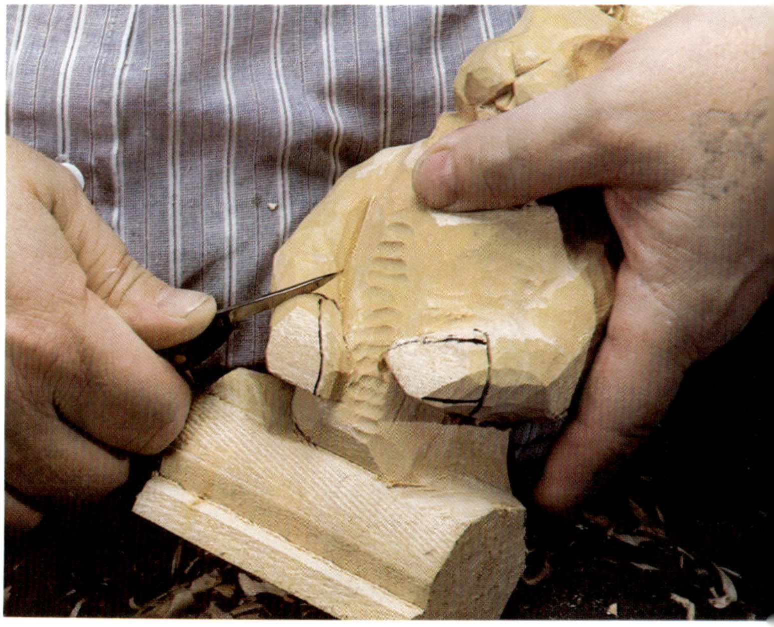

Cut a stop on the end of the sleeve...

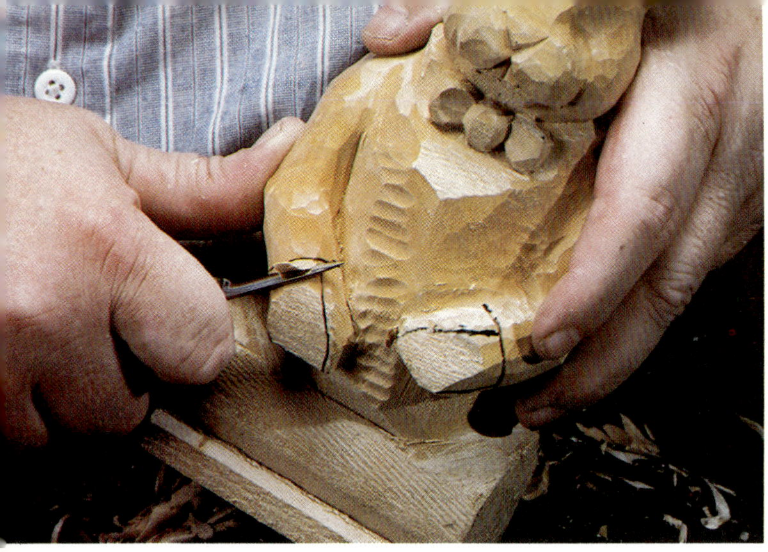

and cut back to it from the paw.

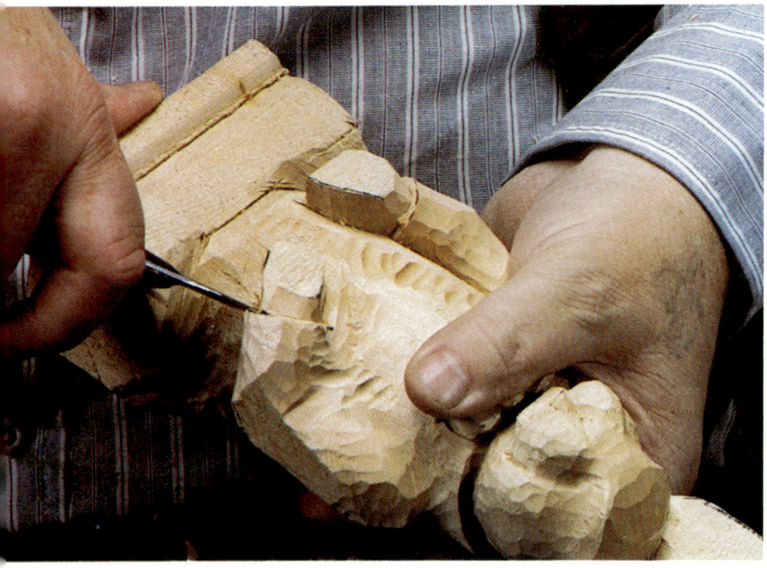

Trim the paws to the outline.

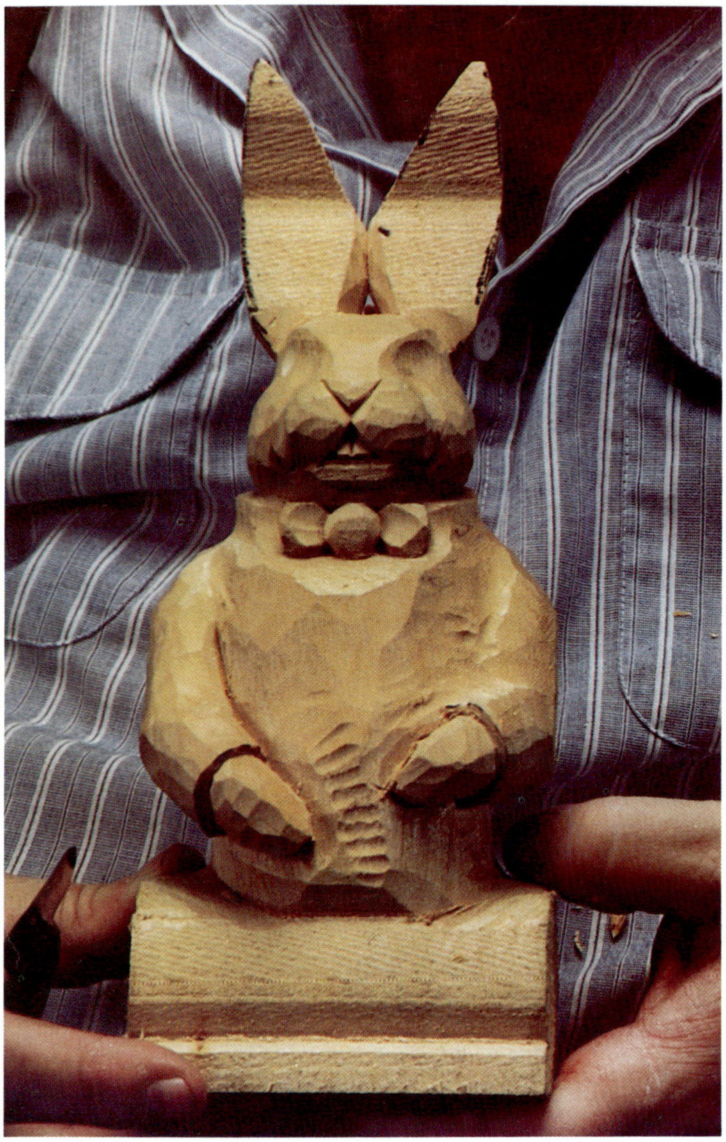

The shaped paws.

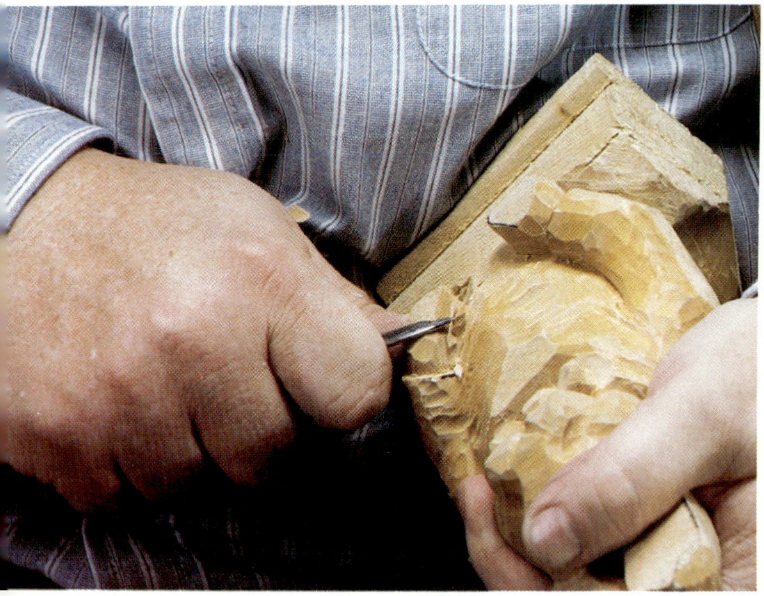

Round them off.

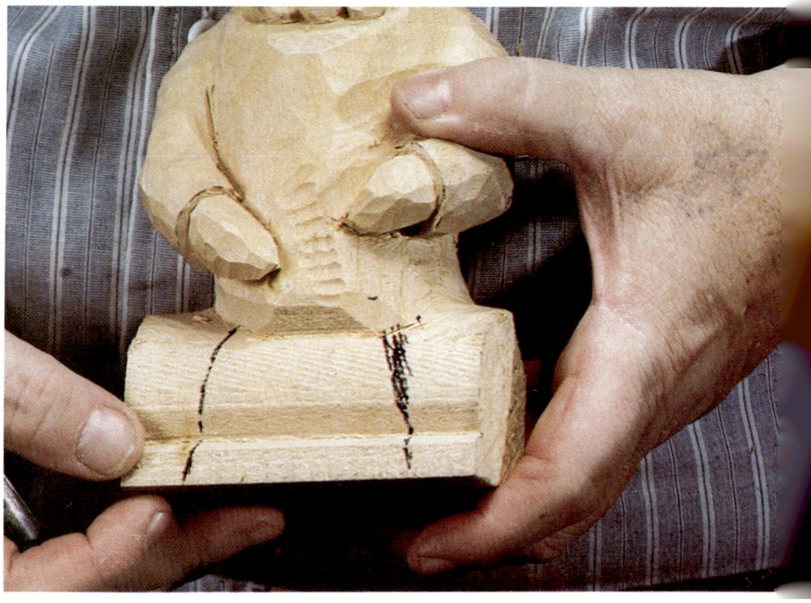

Mark out the space between the legs.

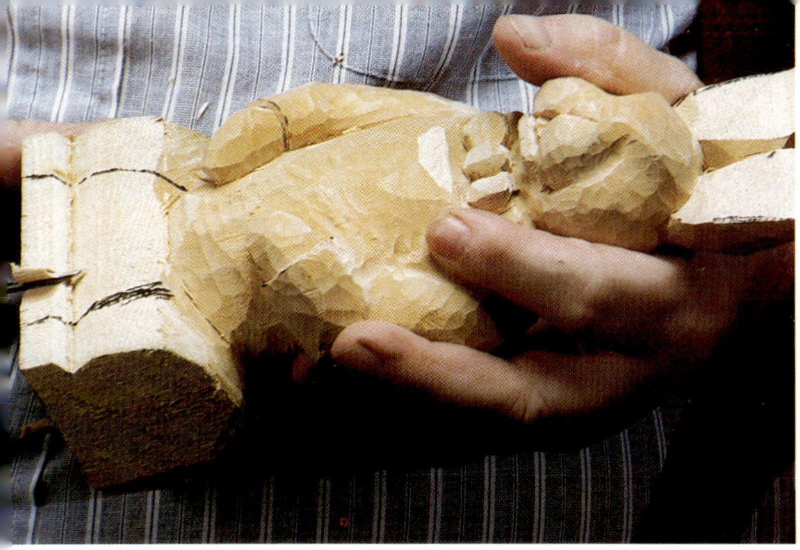

Use a knife to pop out as much of this excess wood as possible.

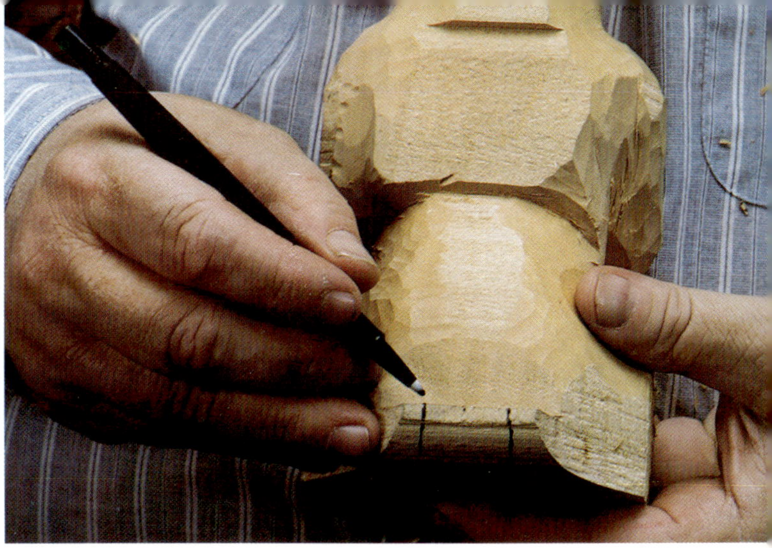

Draw in the cottontail.

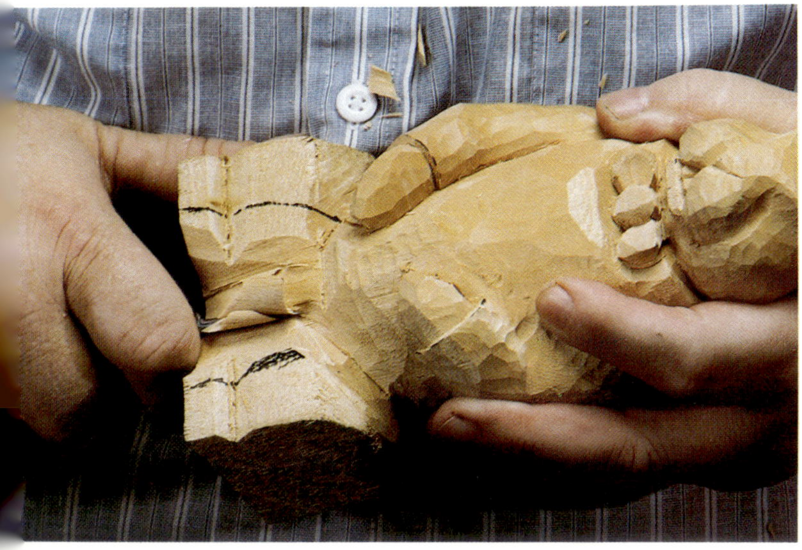

You want to maintain the line of the stomach...

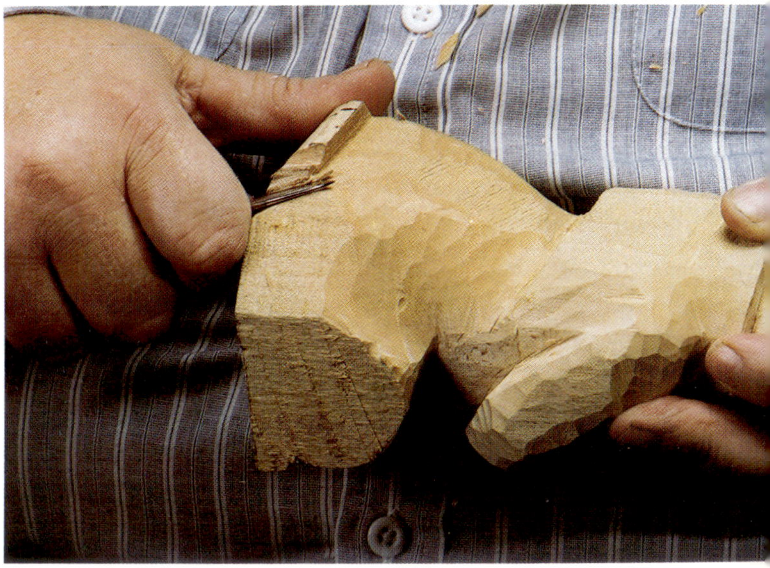

Trim the sides of the tail to bring it to proper width.

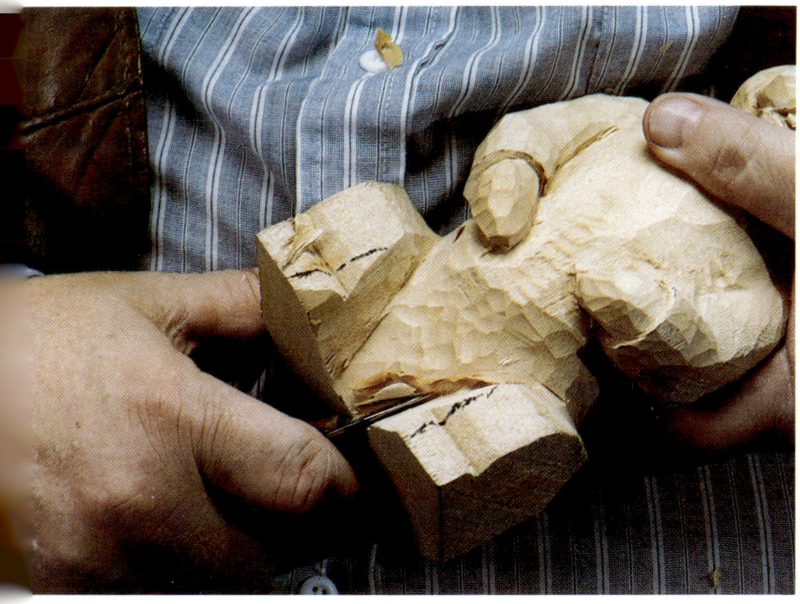

going down between the legs.

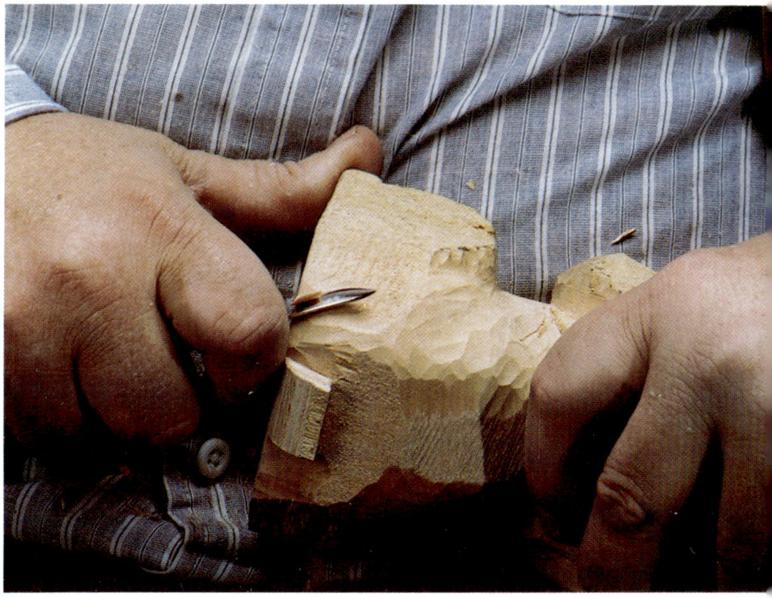

Round the back of the haunches.

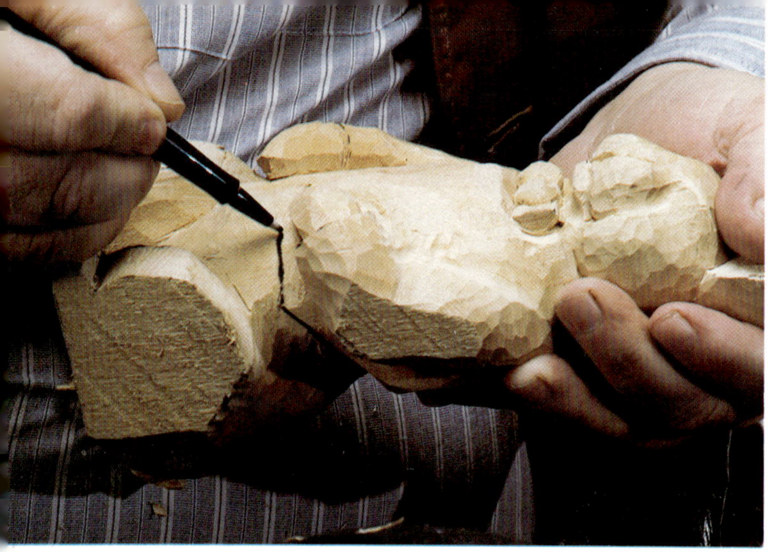

Mark the bottom edge of the coat.

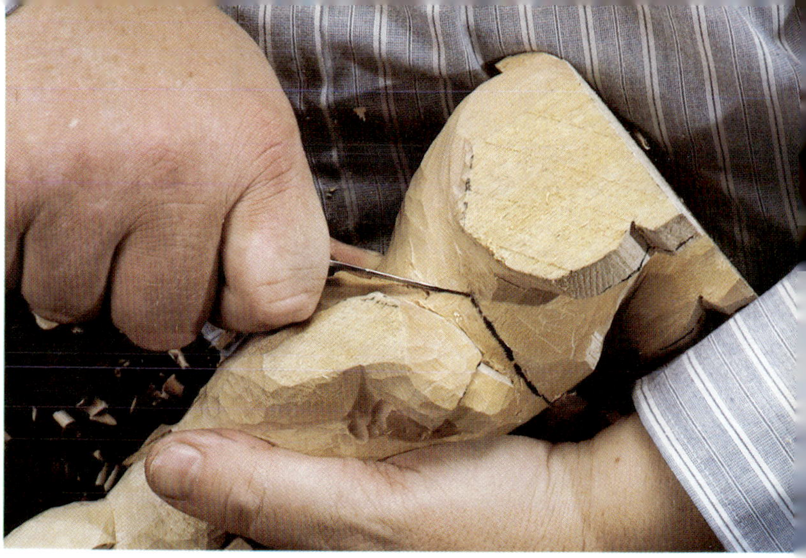

Cut a stop along the bottom of the coat...

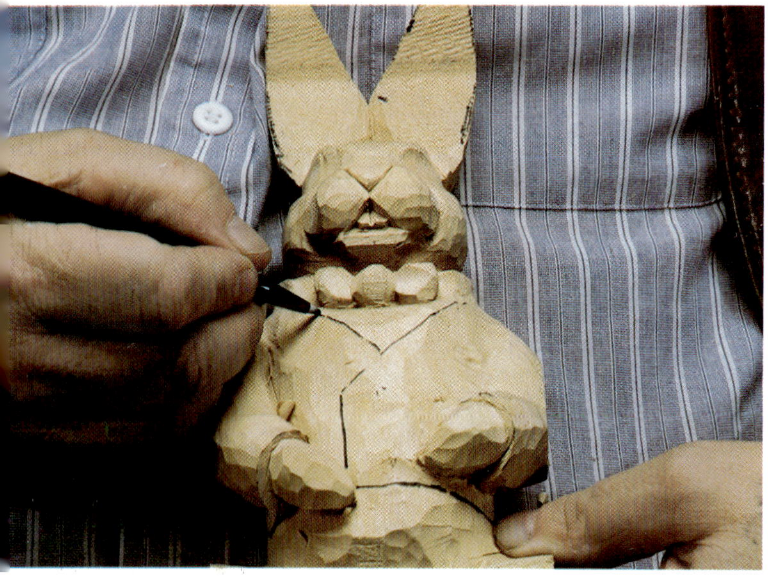

Continue to mark the details of the coat.

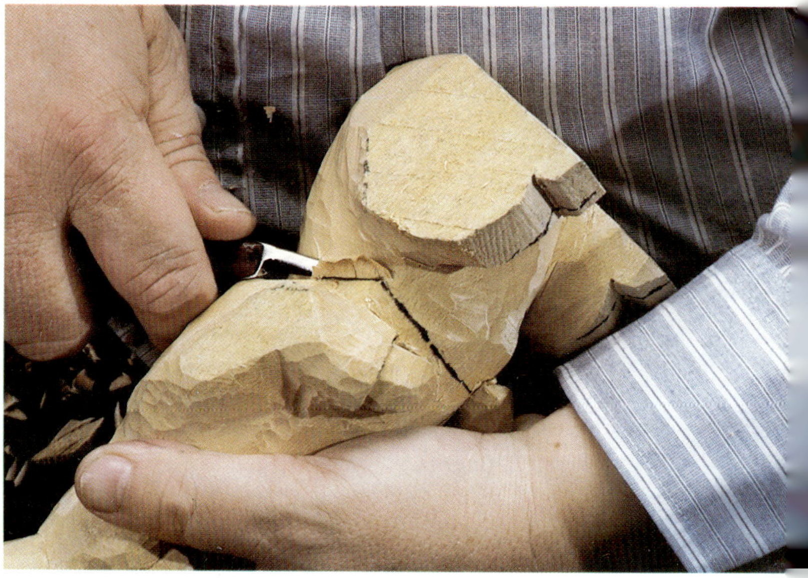

and cut back to it from the leg.

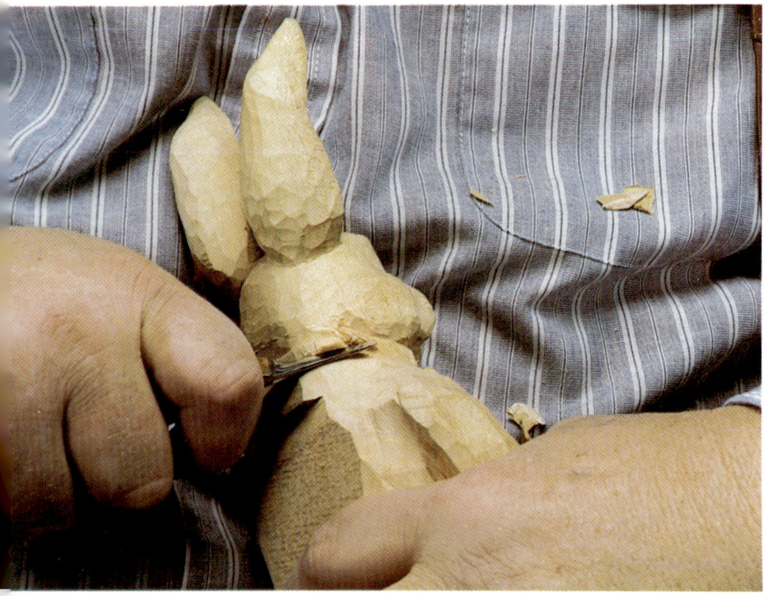

Thin the collar.

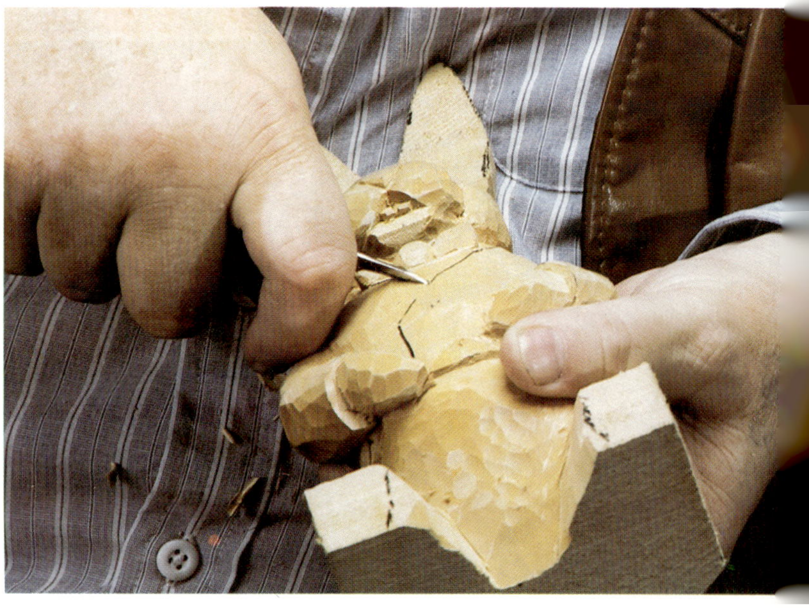

Cut stops in the "V" of the jacket...

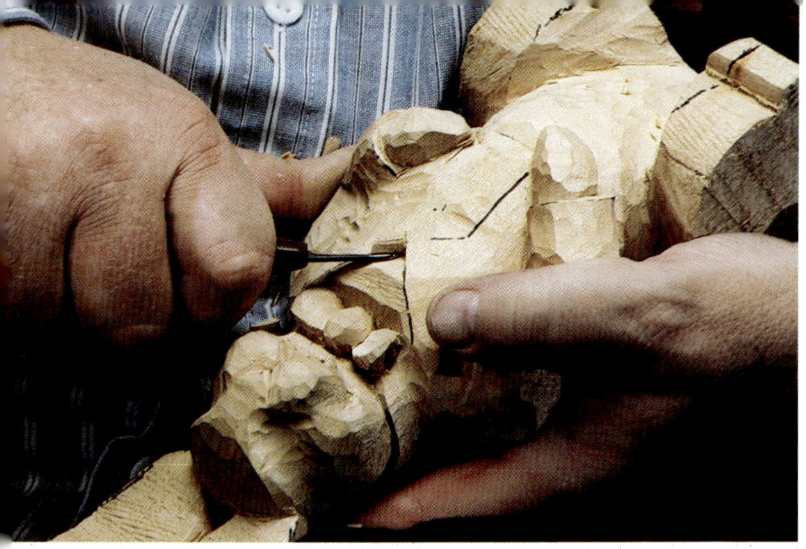

and trim back to them from the shirt front.

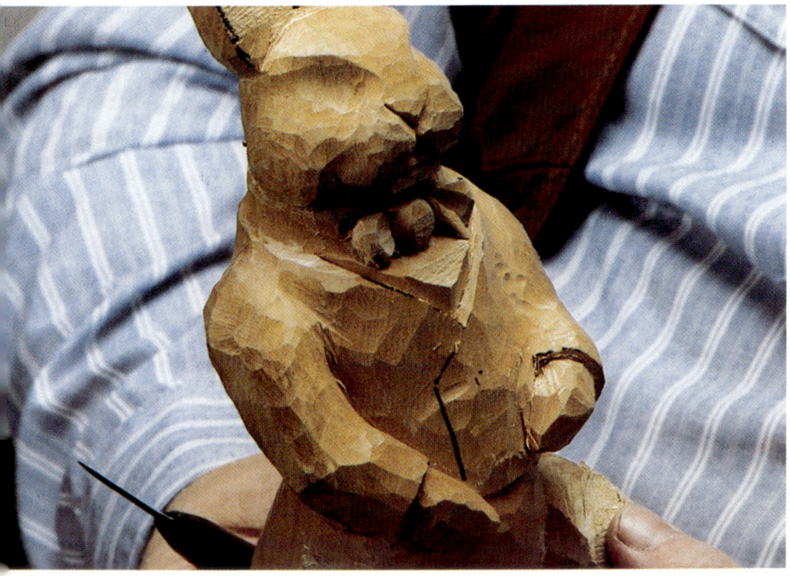

At this point we need to decide the shirt style, particularly whether or not the bunny needs ruffles. They seem appropriate for his Easter best, so we leave the wood to make them.

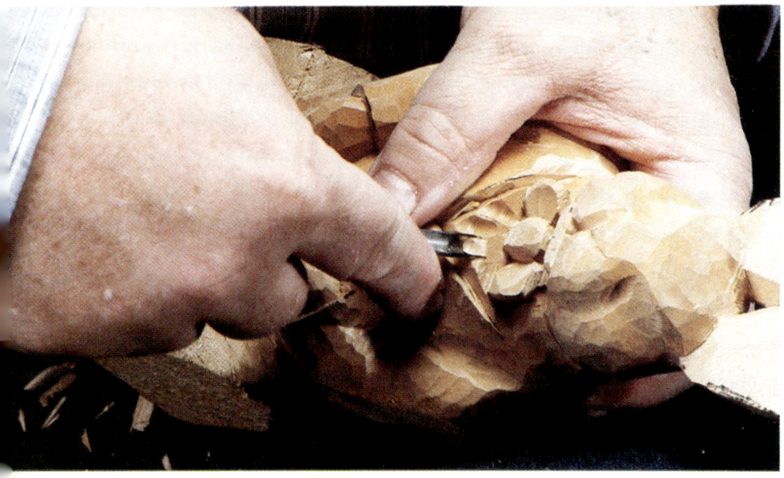

Ruffles are made with a half round gouge, pushed up toward the neck of the shirt. Do this around the shirt front, making the ridges and valleys of the ruffle.

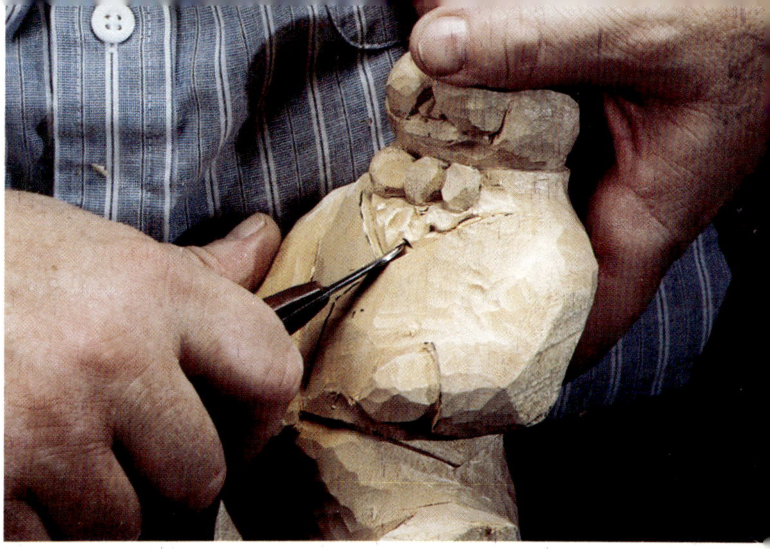

The ruffle is accentuated by taking a little nitch out of the edge of fabric under each ridge of the ruffle.

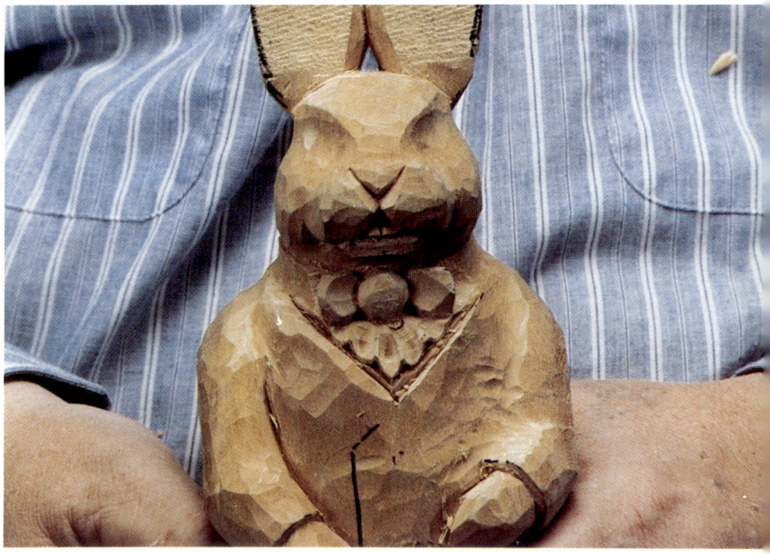

The effect is very nice.

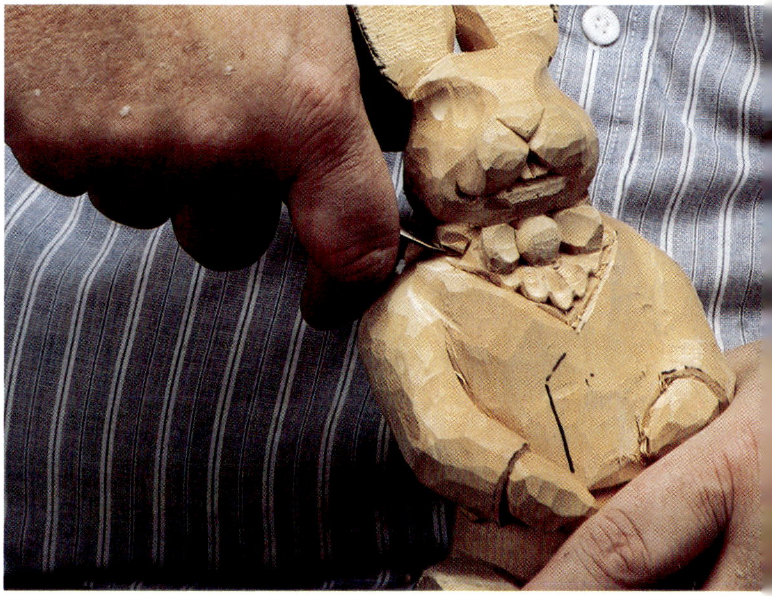

Taking a little nitch at the top corner...

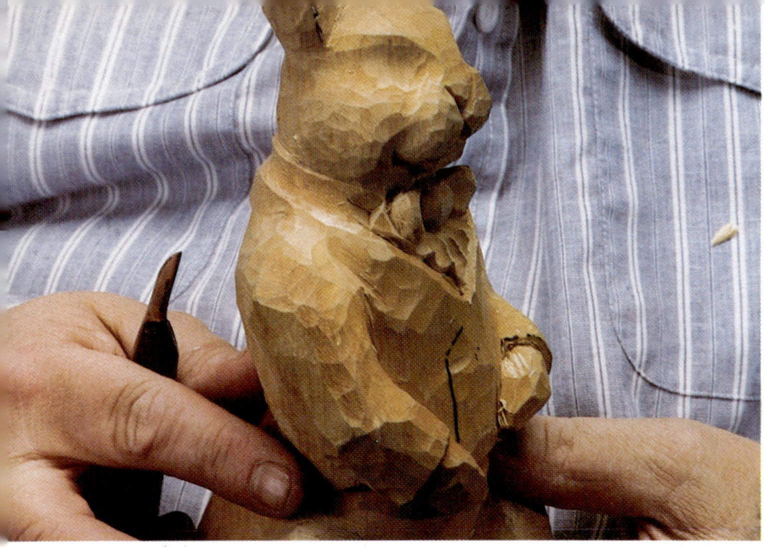

helps define it more.

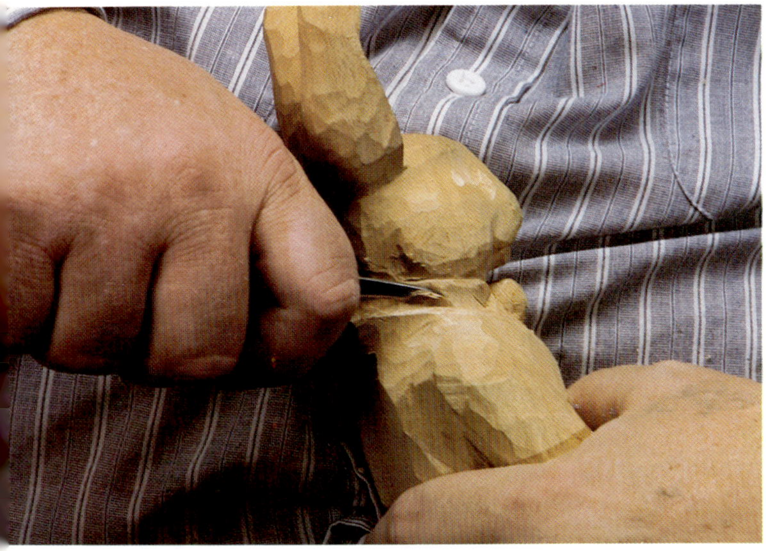

Make the shirt appear to go under the jacket by cutting down the collar of the shirt...

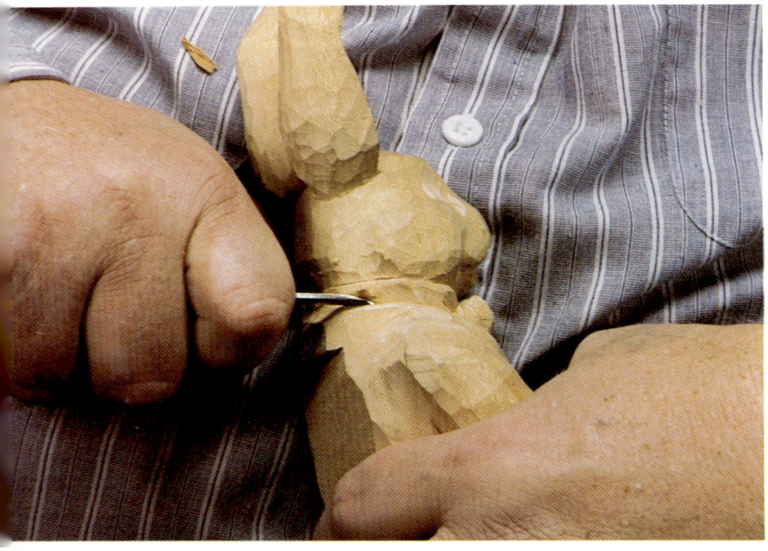

then cut down into it from the edge of the jacket collar, making it appear rolled over. Carry this all around the back of the jacket.

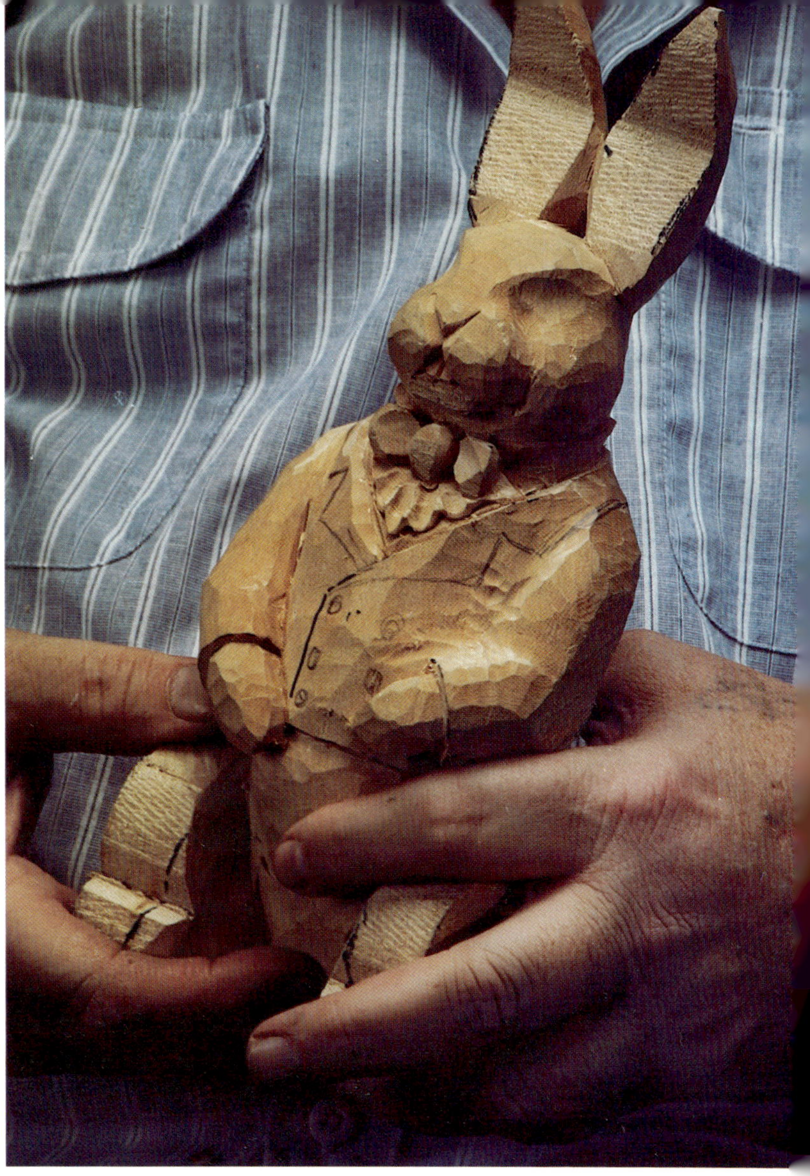

Draw in the design of the coat.

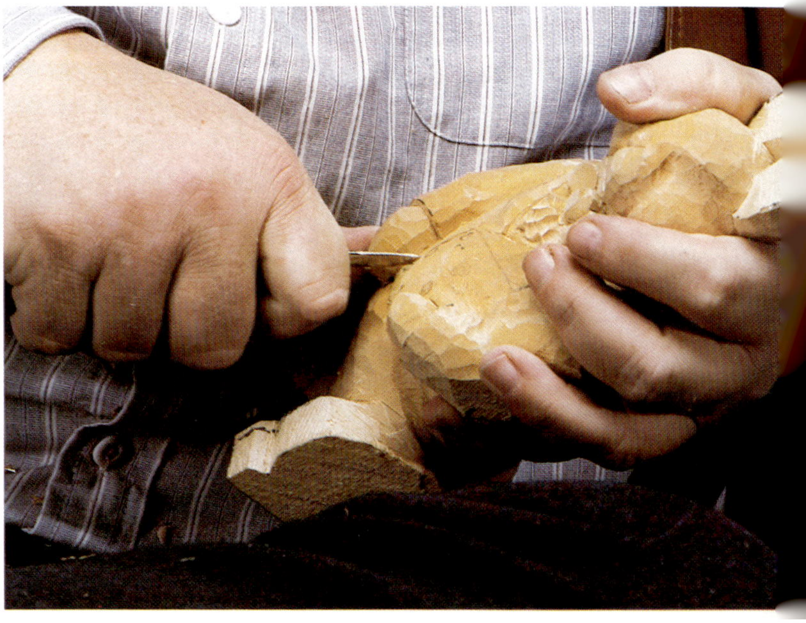

Cut a stop along the opening of the coat...

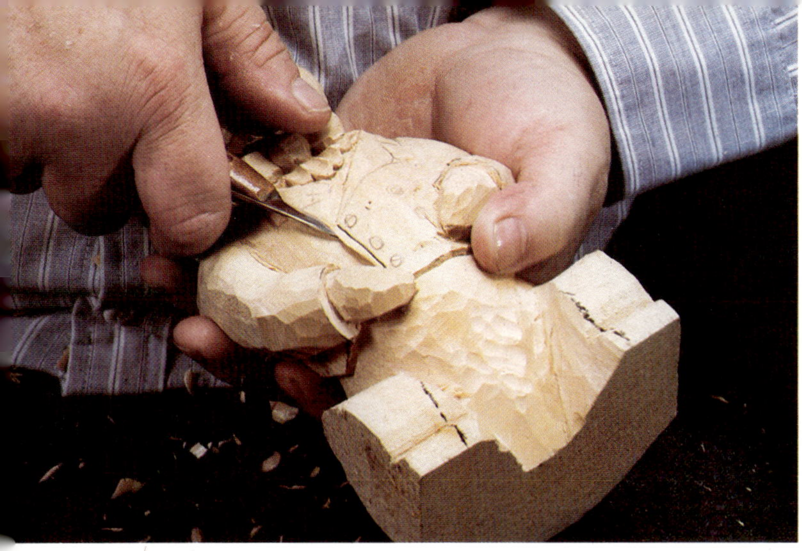

and trim back to it.

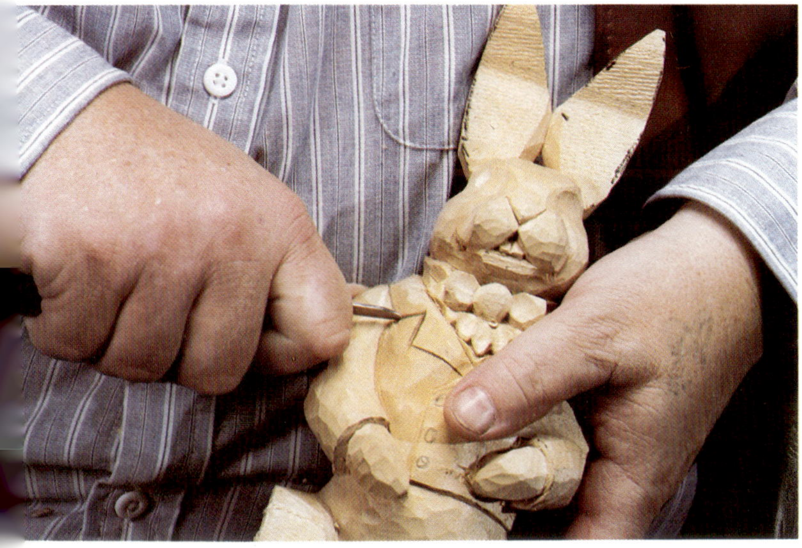

Go around the collar and lapel with stops...

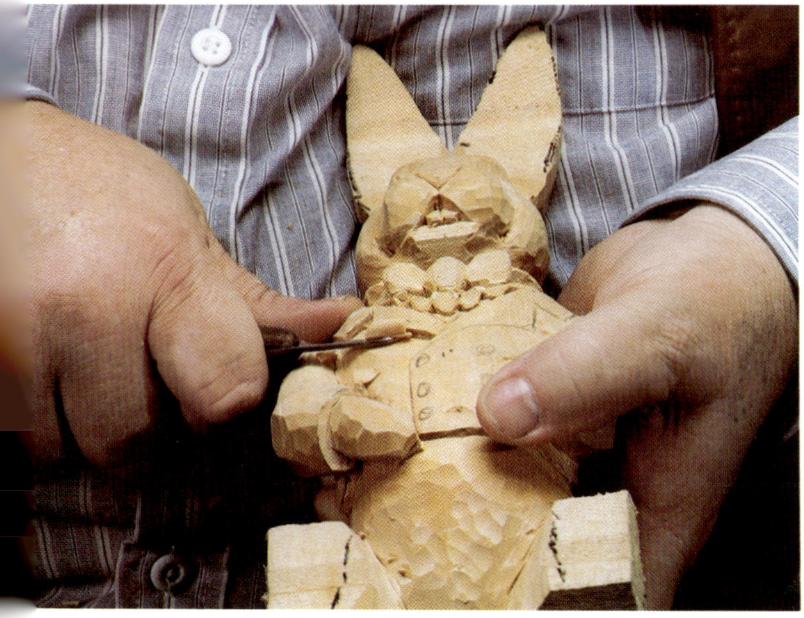

and trim back to them from the jacket.

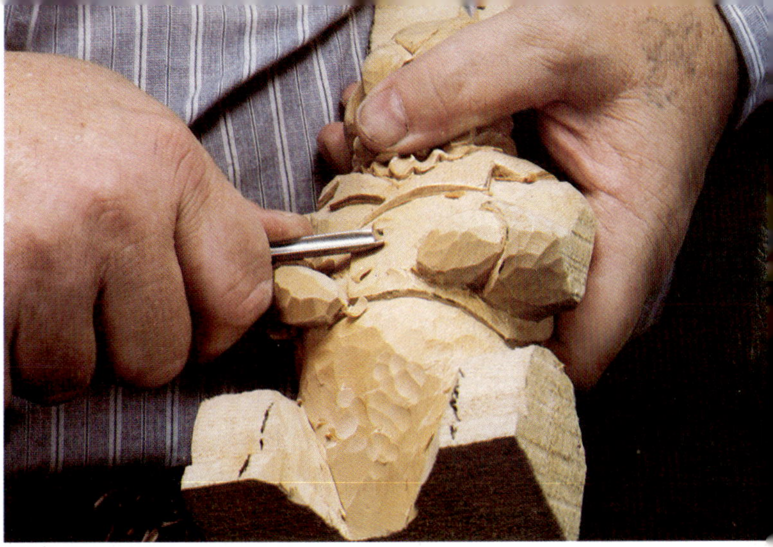

I want the jacket to appear tight, so, where the buttons are going to be, I use a gouge to cut some "strain" lines.

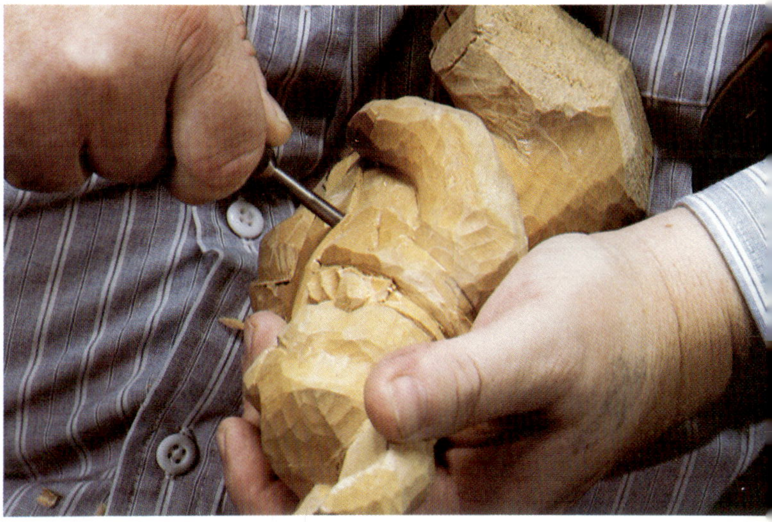

Use a eyepunch to form the buttons. Simply push and twist.

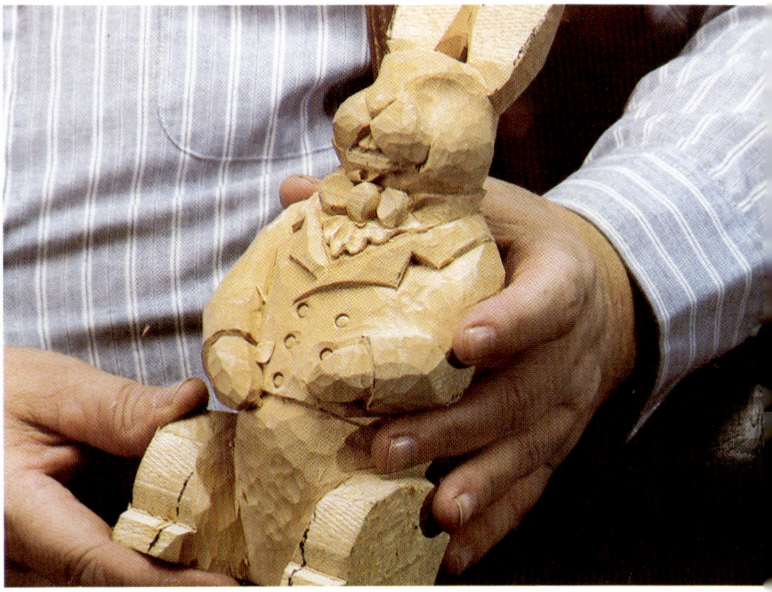

The result.

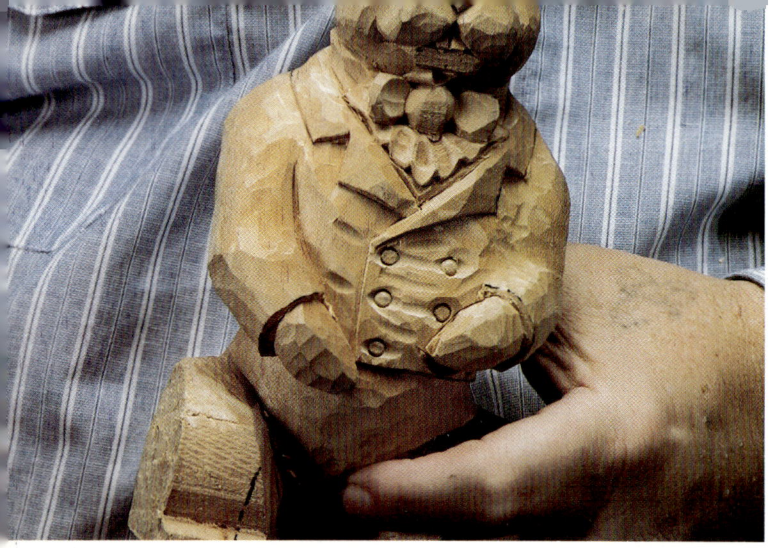

Deepening the "strain" lines makes the jacket appear tighter.

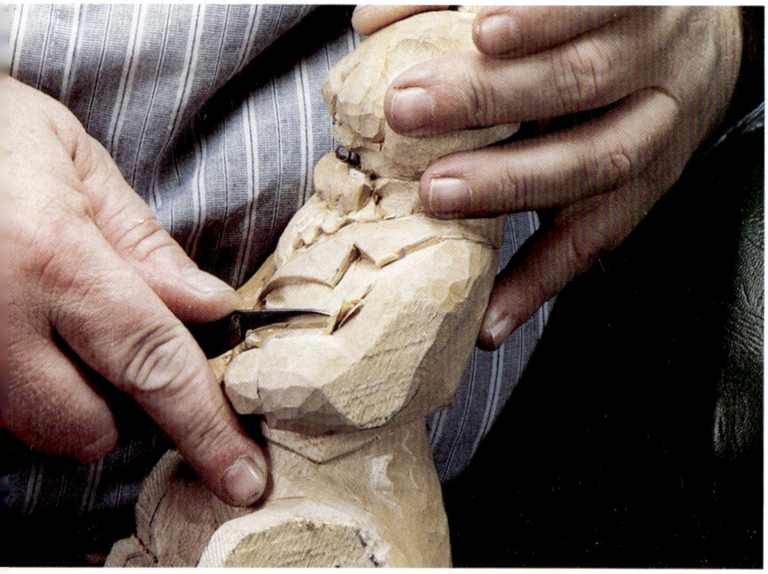

The arms need a little more defining so they won't seem attached to the body.

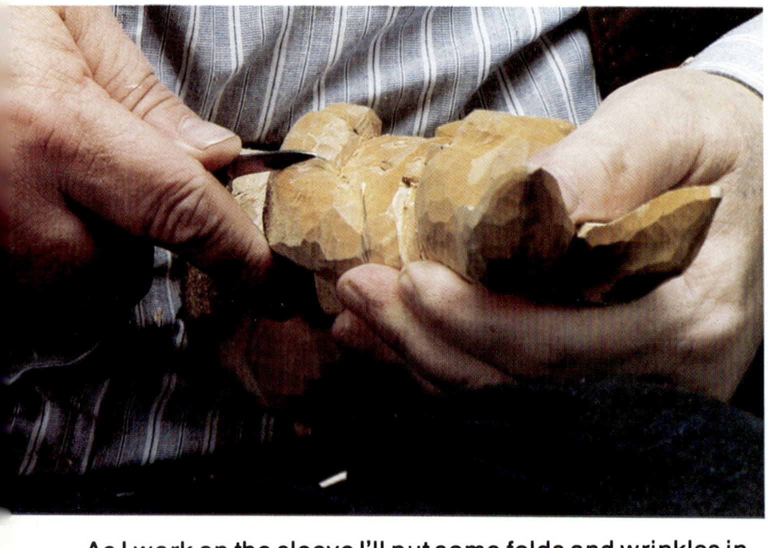

As I work on the sleeve I'll put some folds and wrinkles in it to give it more character.

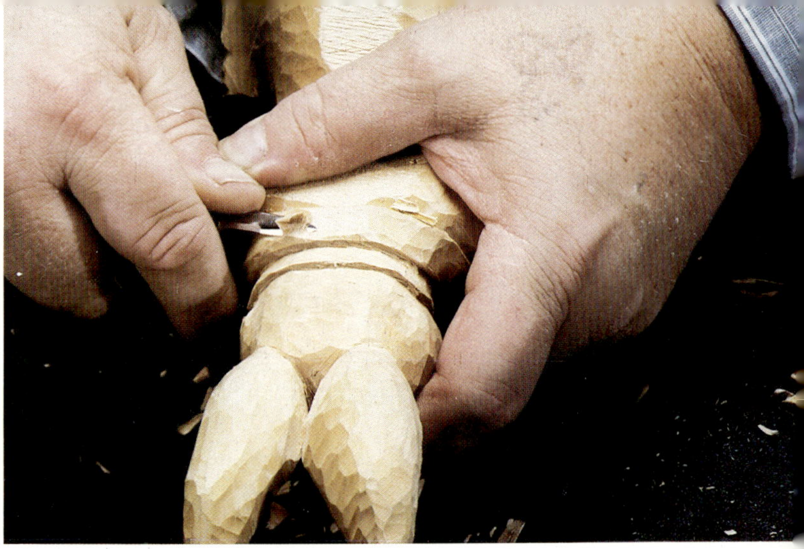

The coat collar and back need some dressing up.

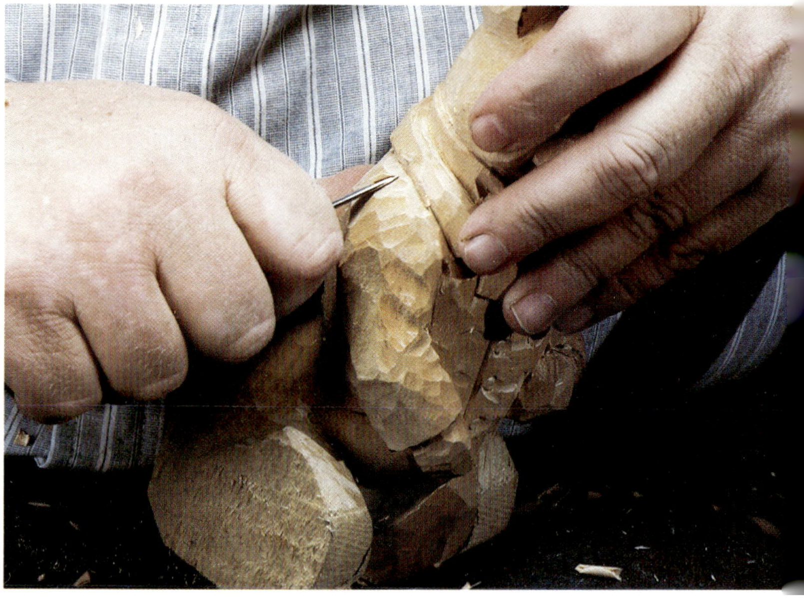

Round the shoulders...

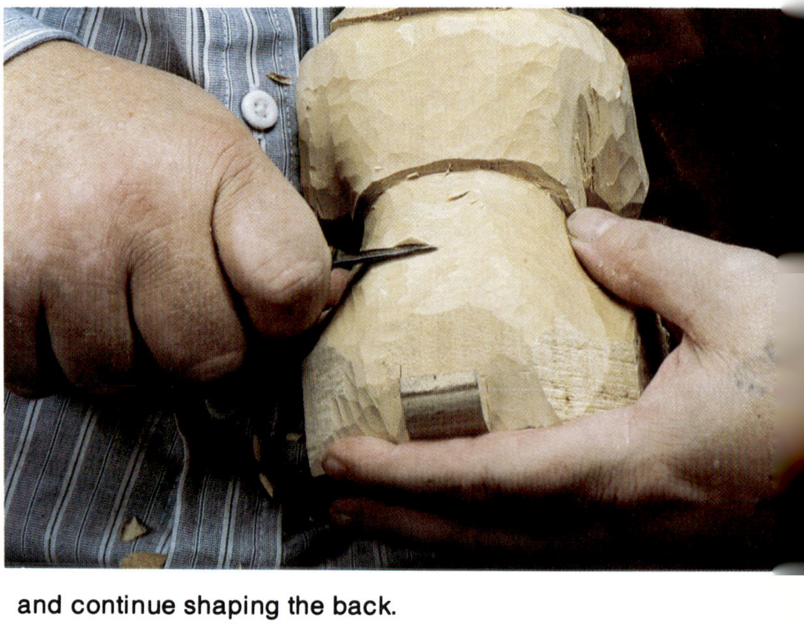

and continue shaping the back.

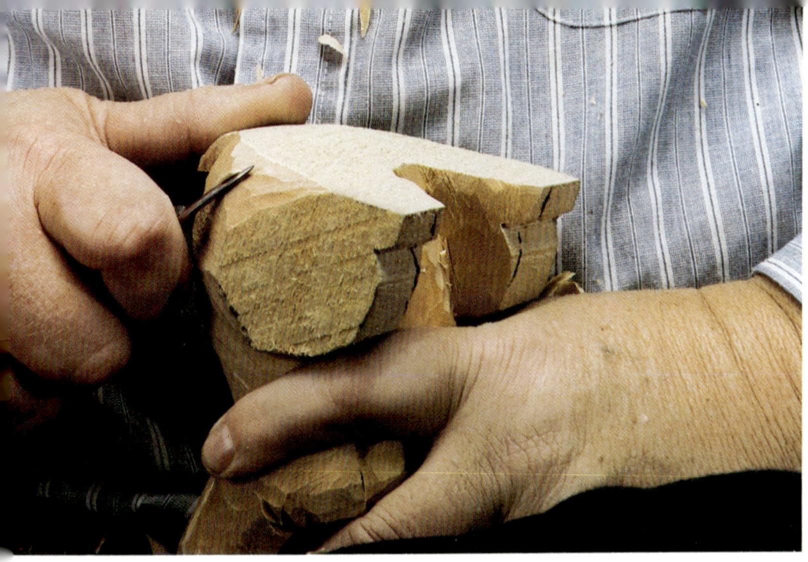

Round the edge of the base.

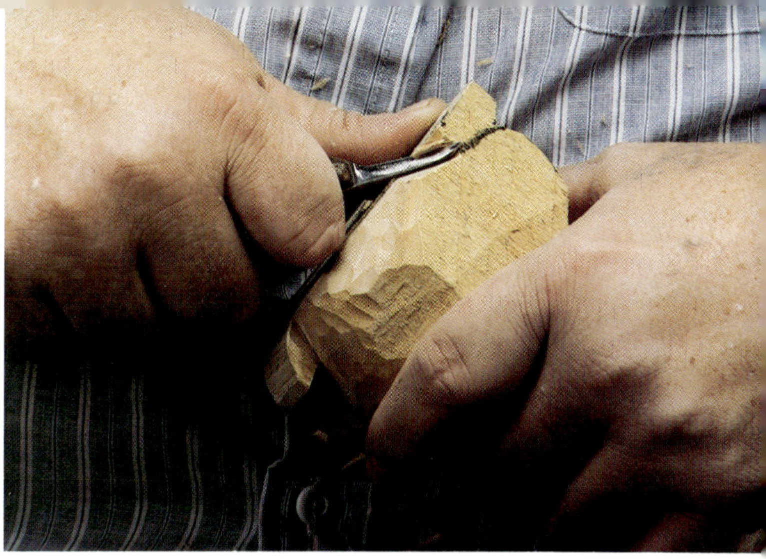

Trim the foot to size.

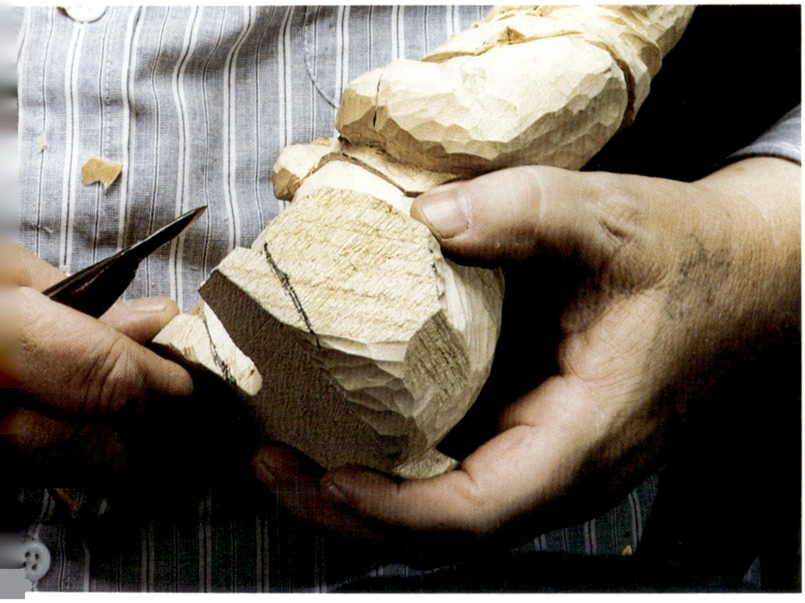

Mark the line of the foot.

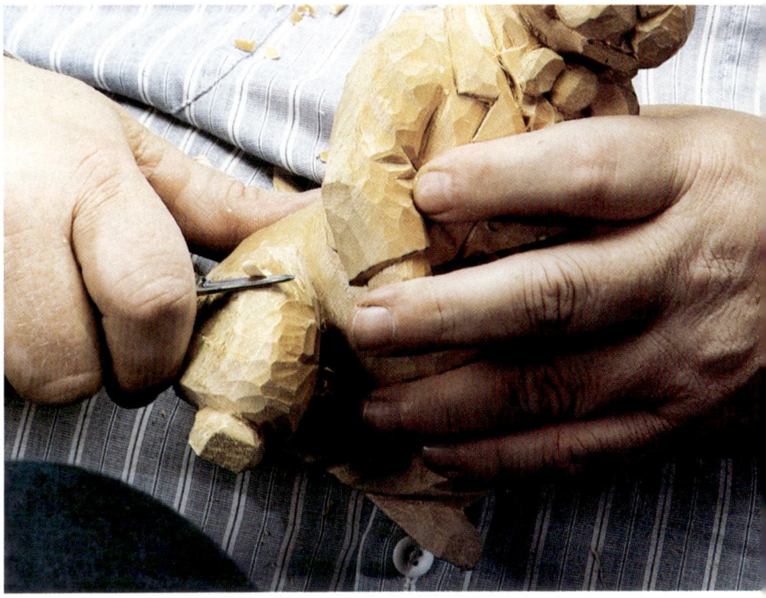

Round and shape the haunch.

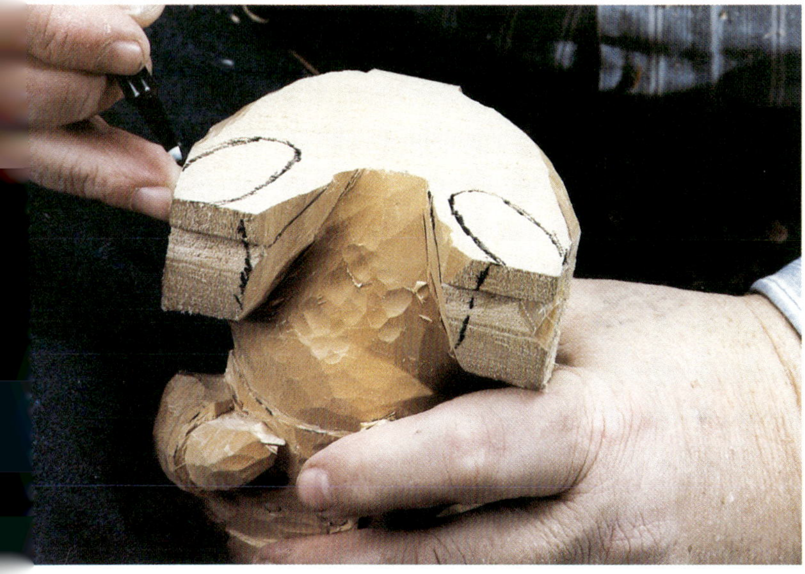

Mark the bottoms of the feet.

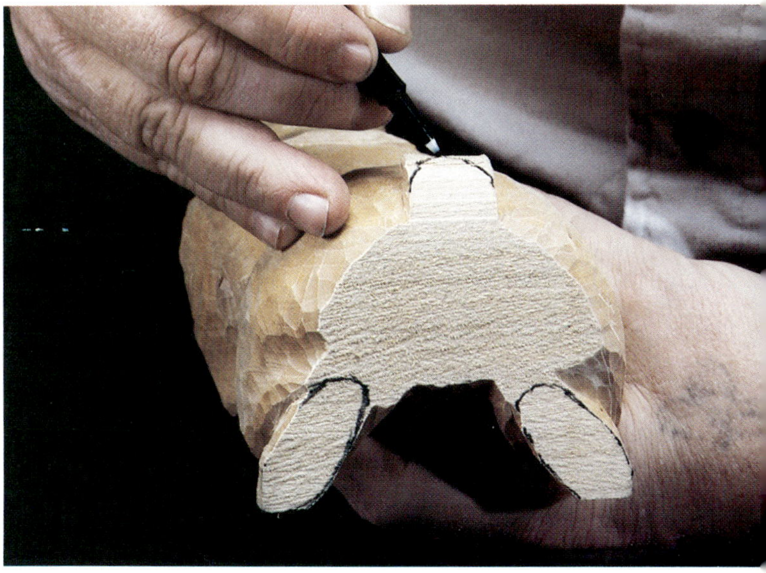

Mark the shape of the tail.

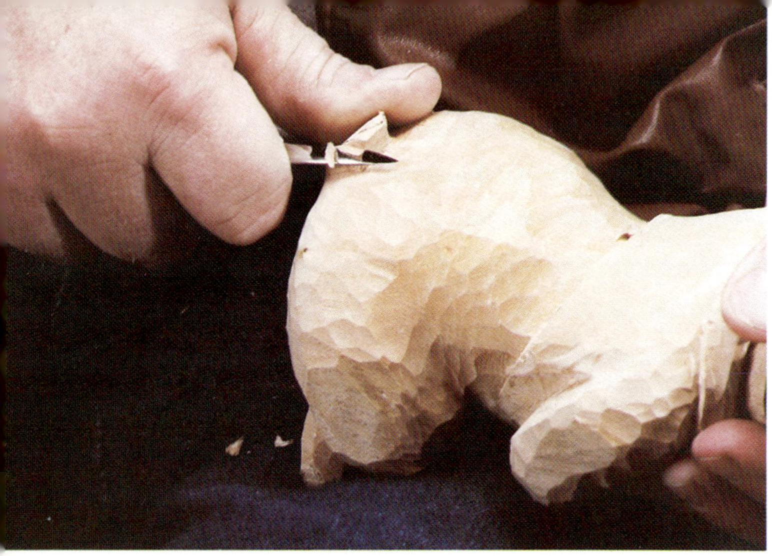

Trim from the outer edge back to the line.

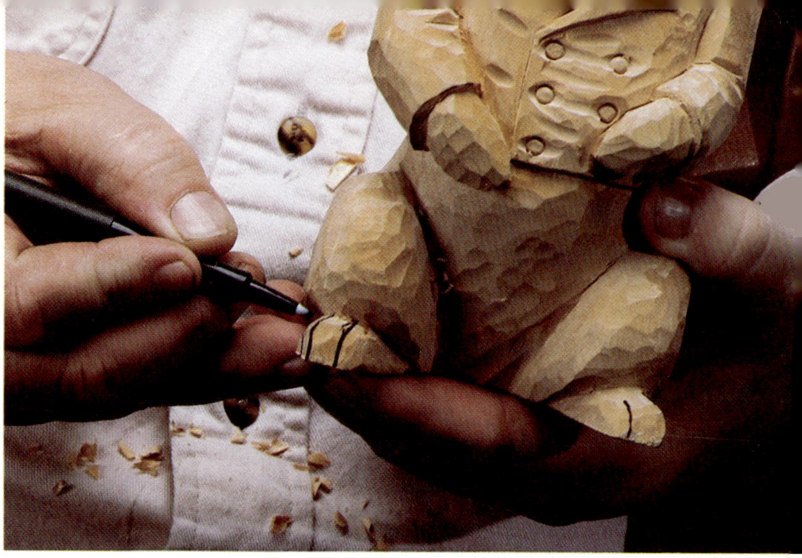

Mark the toes. Rabbits' toes are pretty long, so bring the lines back to the haunch.

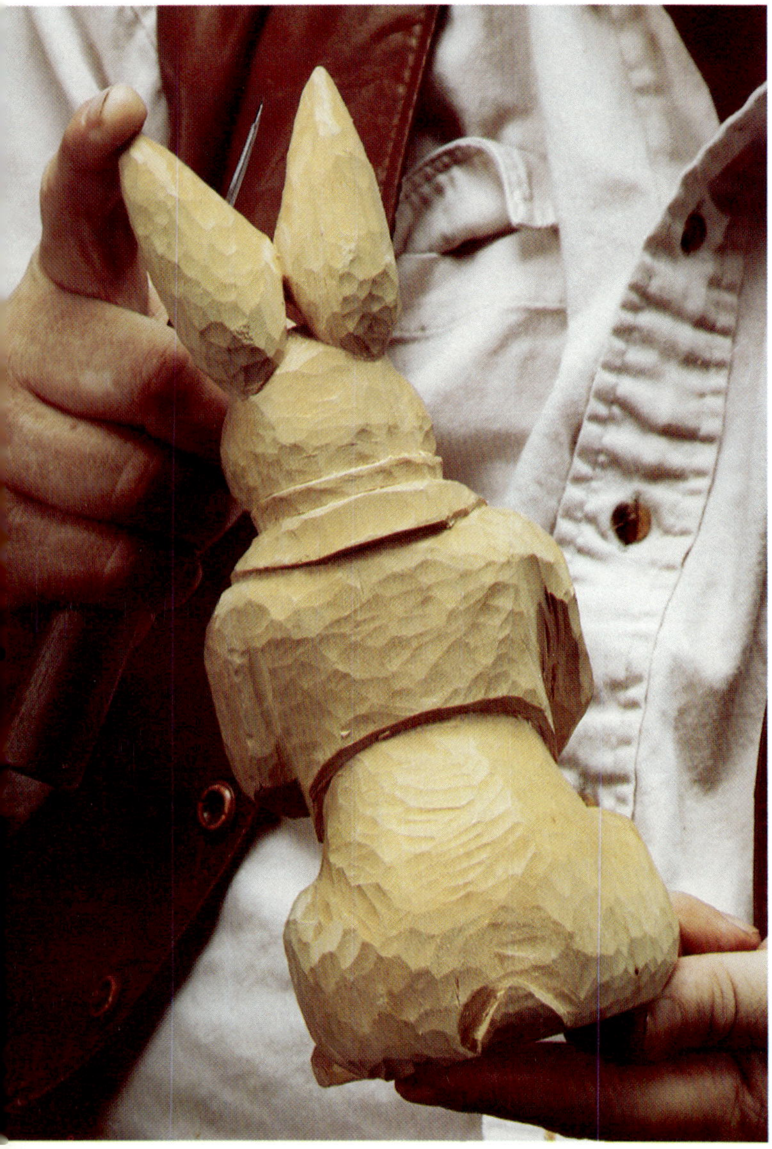

The backside of the rabbit. I sometimes use a bushy tail, but usually it looks awkward...something like a nose growing out of the wrong place. This trim, almost deer-like, tail seems to work better.

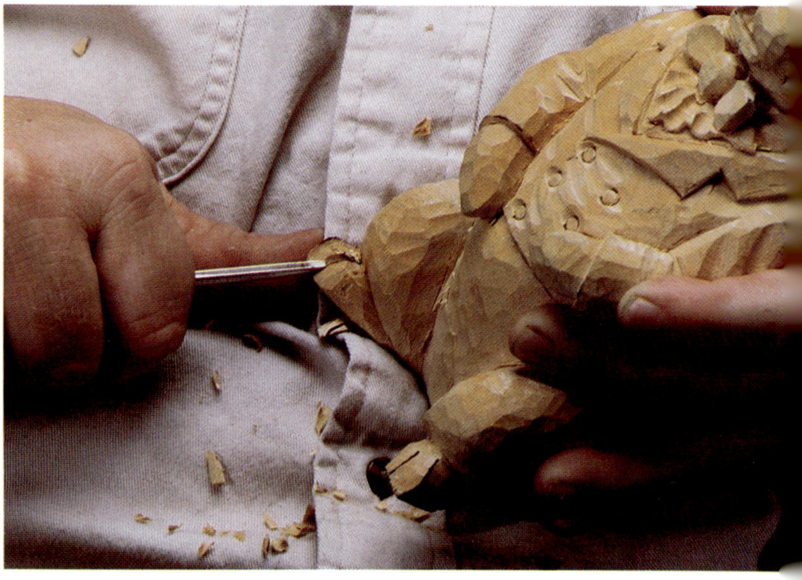

Go over the toe lines with a veiner.

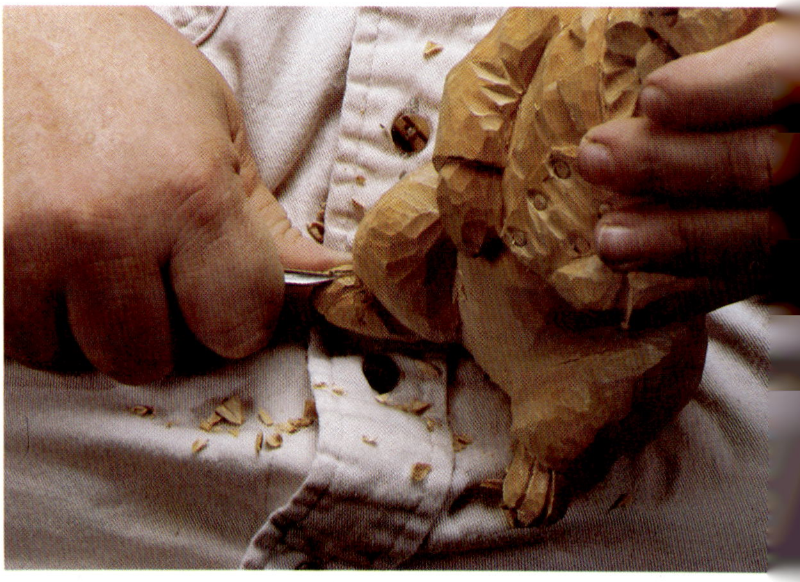

Use a knife to round off the tops of the toes.

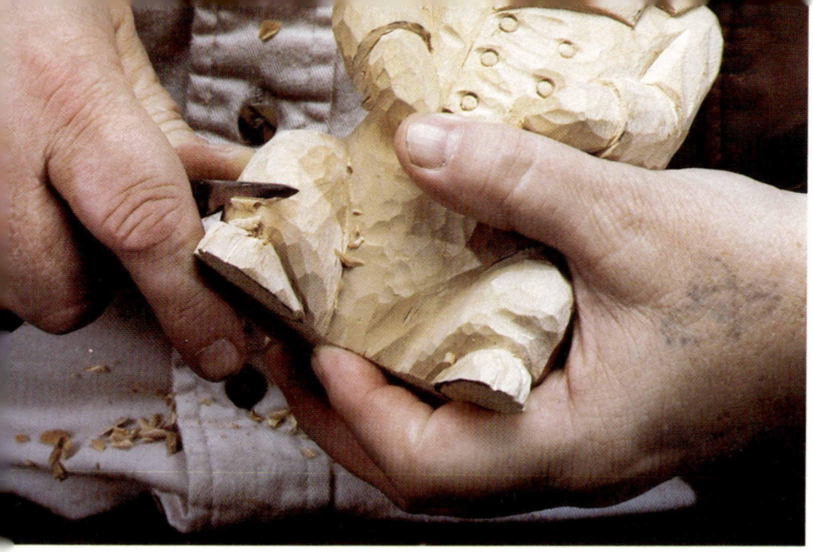

The bunny needs a little fold of skin in the leg above the foot. Use a knife to form this rounded groove.

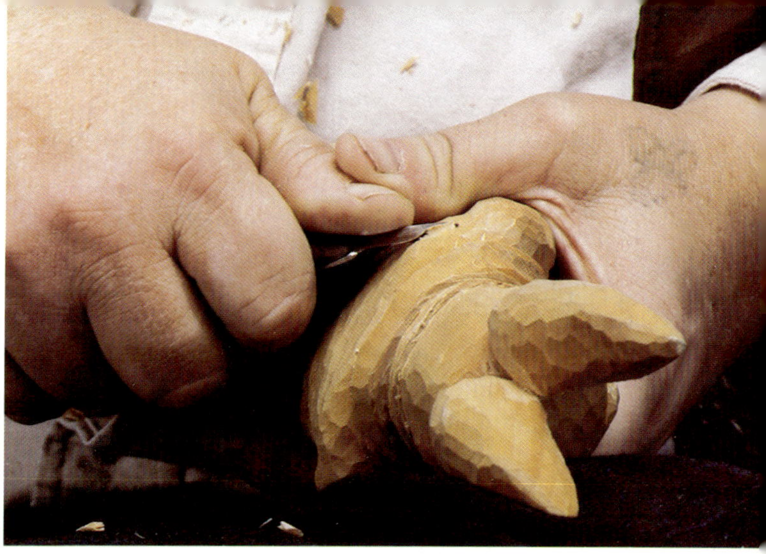

Smooth the coat and other surfaces. Notice the double-locked thumb position of my hands. This gives added leverage and pressure on the knife, while keeping good control.

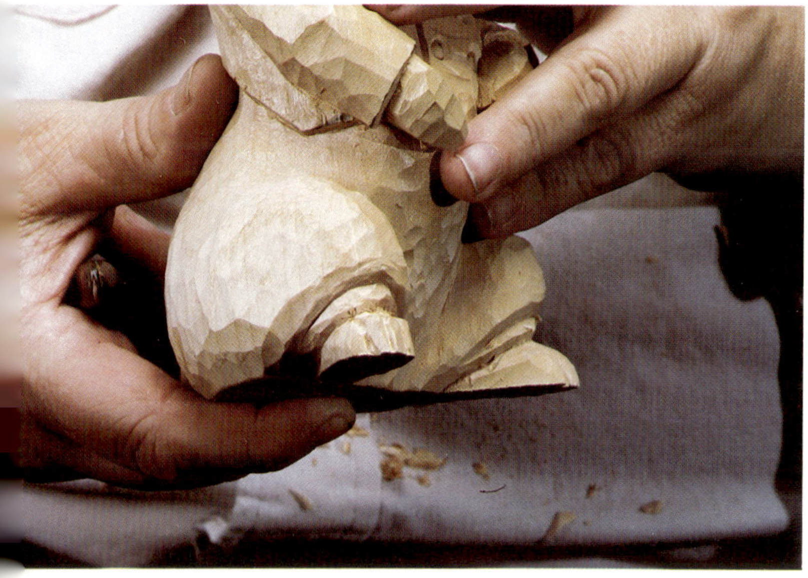

Bring the fold around the sides of the legs like this.

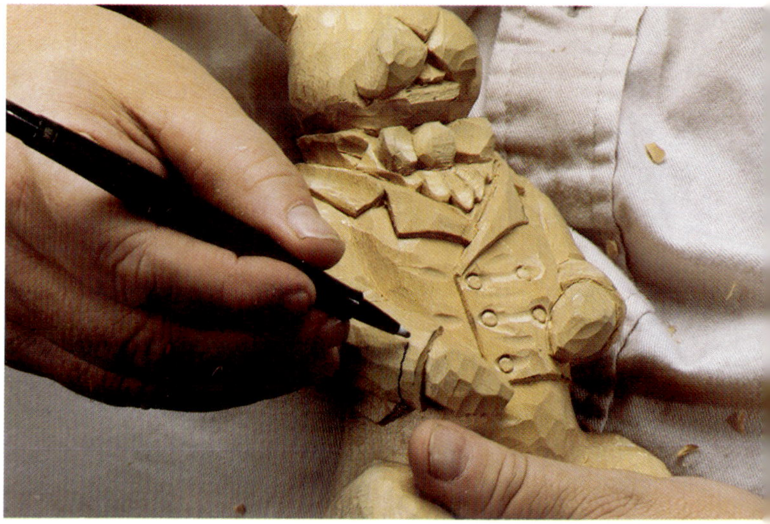

I think we need to have a little bit of the shirt sleeve showing above the hand. First mark the end of the coat sleeve.

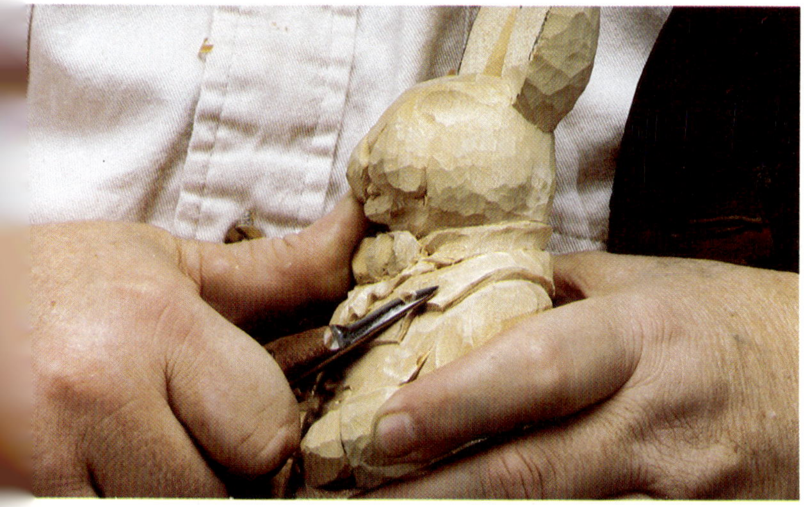

Go back over the bunny correcting things as you go. This is an important part of the work. The more you do it the better the carving will be. Here I am shaping the collar so it sits more naturally.

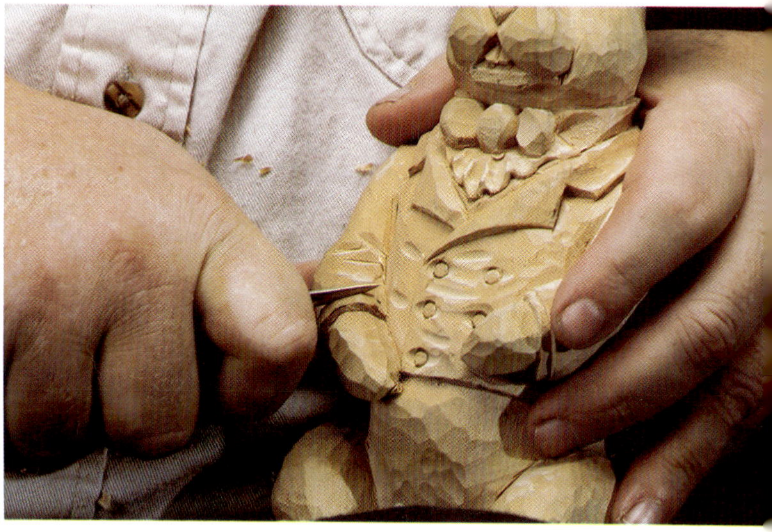

Cut a stop into the line...

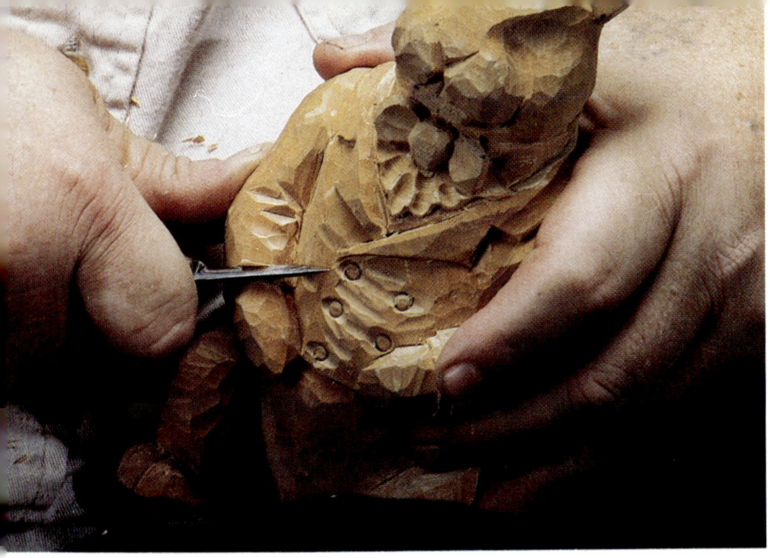

and trim back to it from the end of the shirt sleeve.

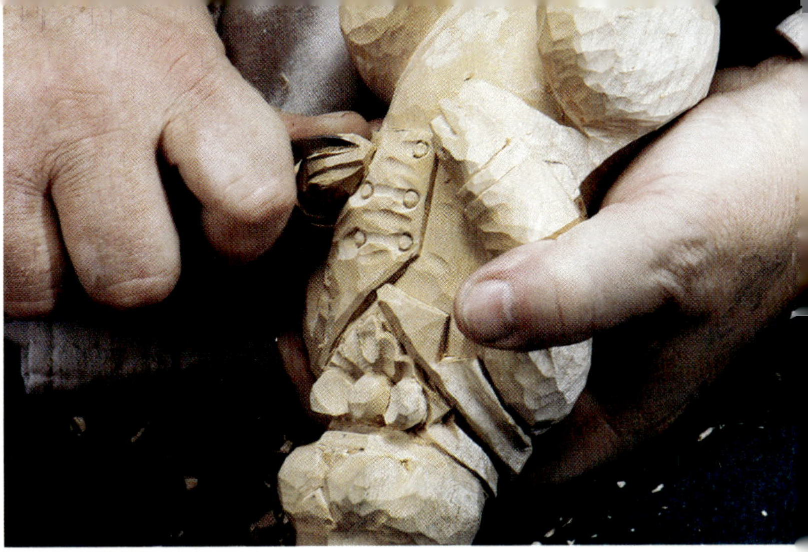

Use a knife to clean up around the fingers.

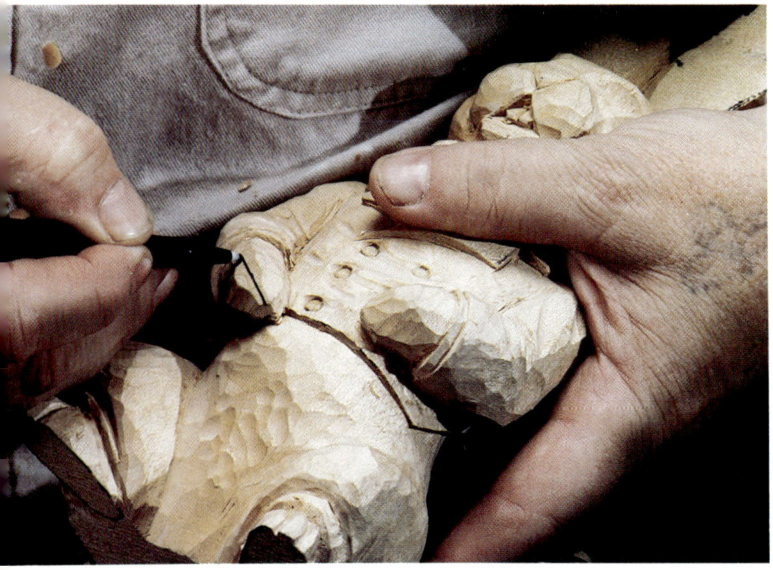

Mark in the fingers. You want to have four fingers.

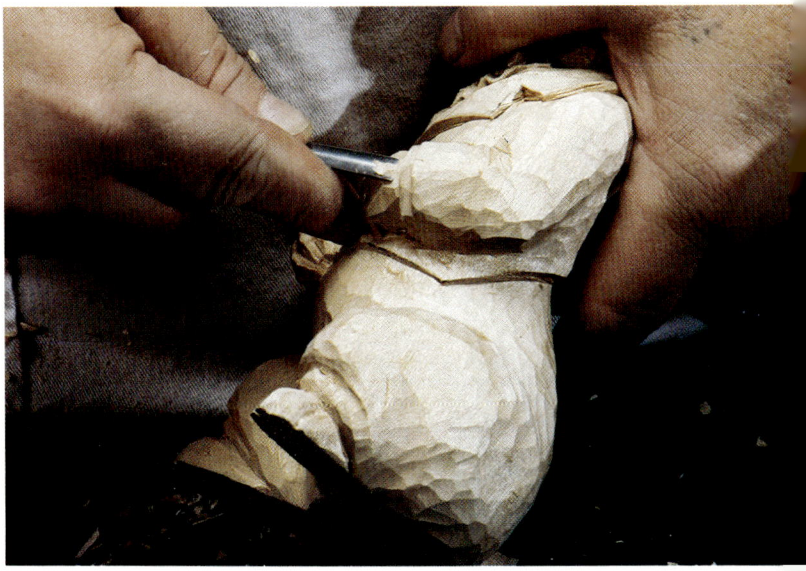

On the upper part of the hand, using a flatter gouge between the fingers brings out the boniness of the hand and makes it look more realistic.

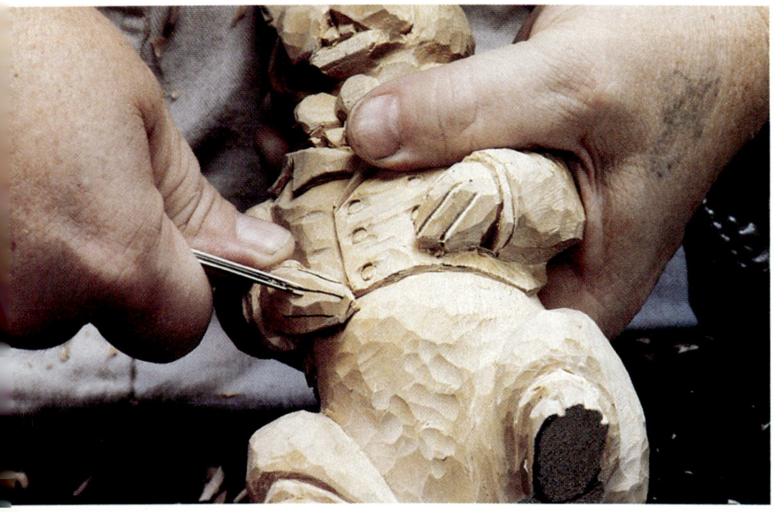

Use the veiner and follow the lines. Sometimes when going across the grain, a veiner, even when sharp, will chip at the wood. When that happens a knife should be used.

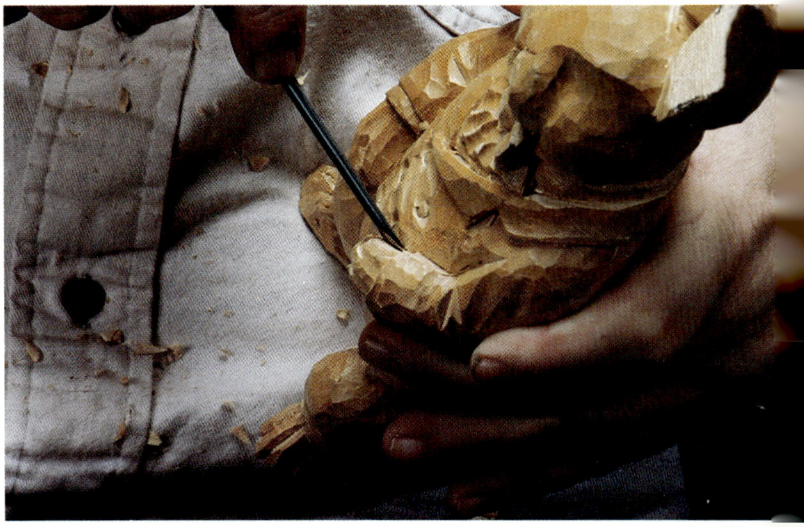

Run the same flatter gouge under the palms to make them distinct from the coat, so they don't appear to be lying flat.

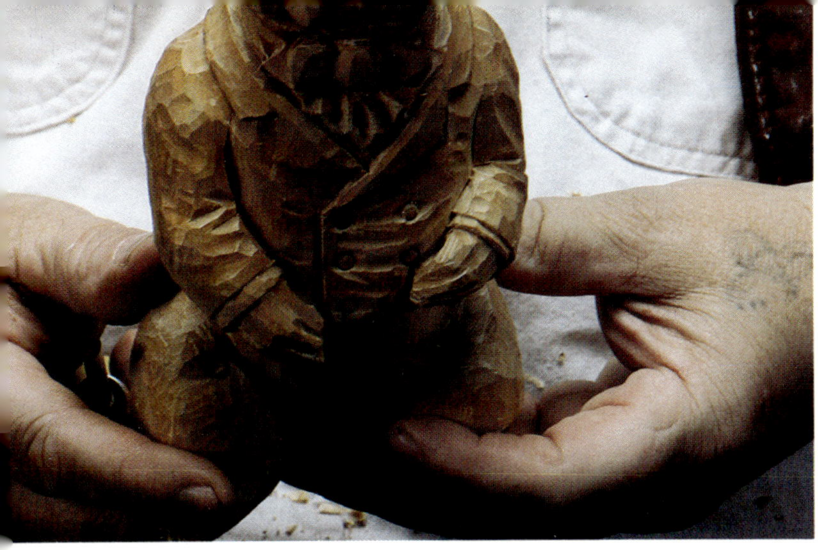

This is the effect.

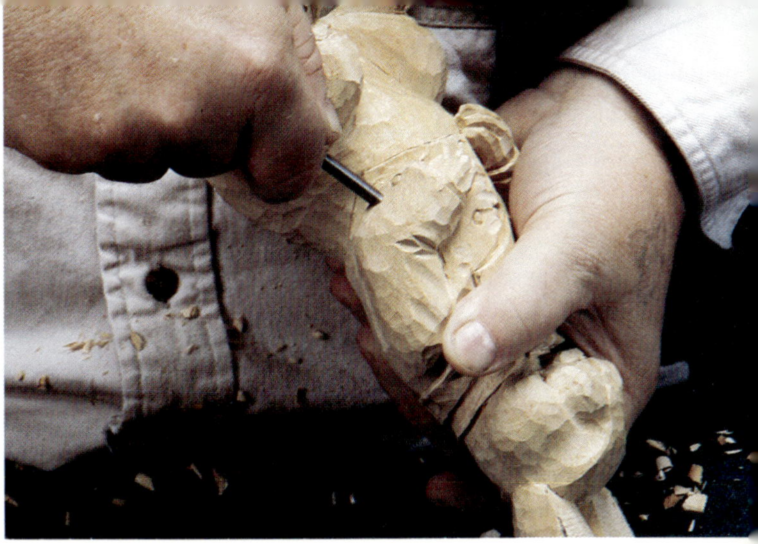

Use an eyepunch to make two buttons on each sleeve.

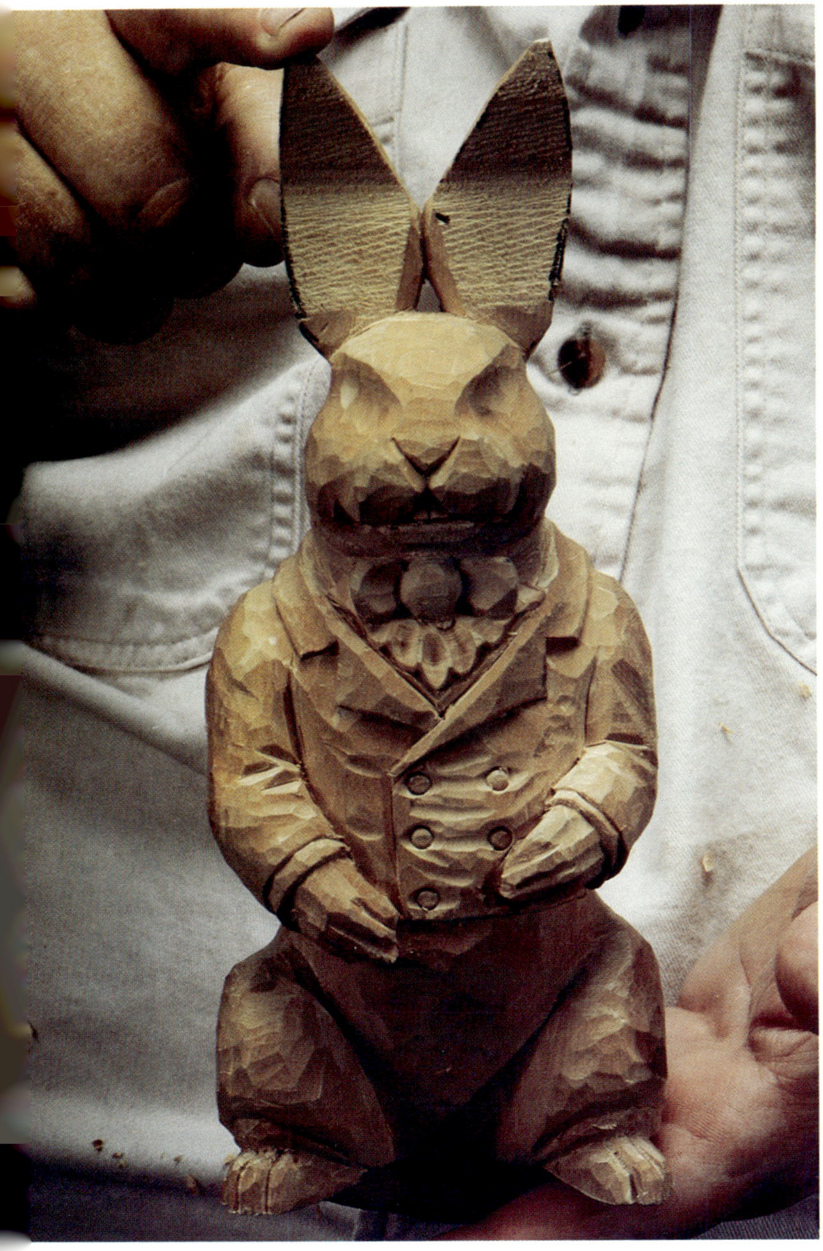

The front of the bunny so far.

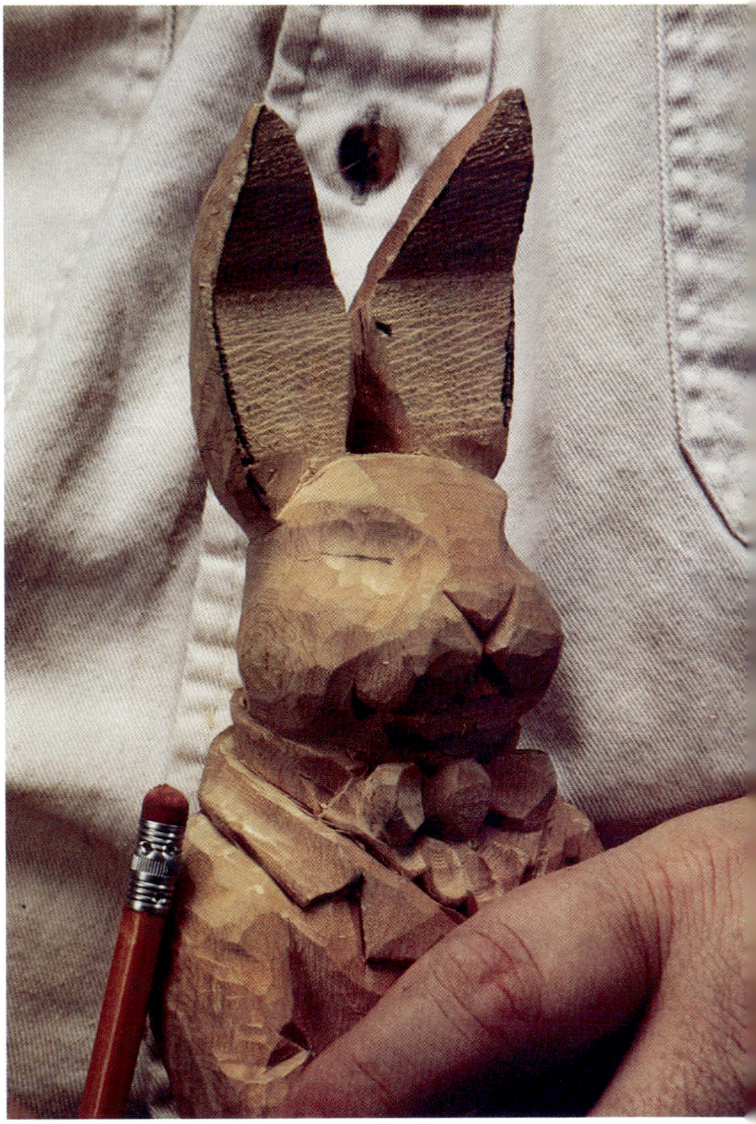

Now we move to the face. Begin with the eyes. Make sure they are level when looking straight on and even when looking down from the top. Begin on the left and draw a line on each side from just under the ear to the edge of the nose.

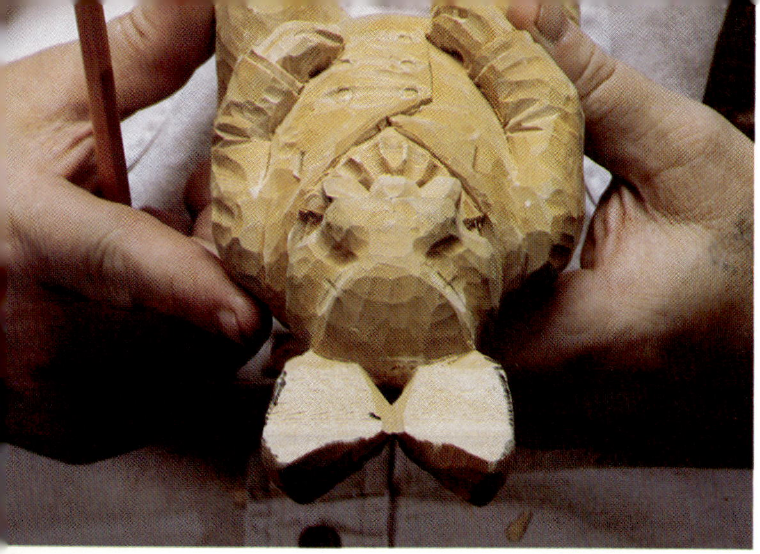

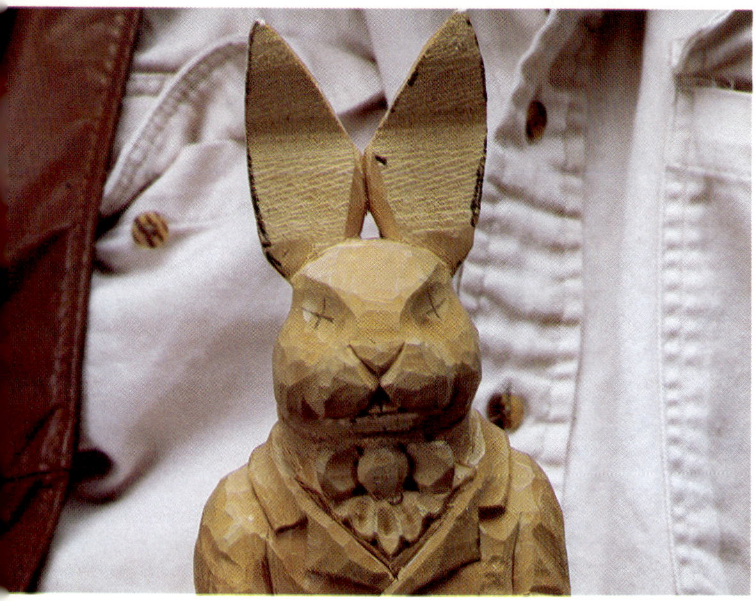

Then by looking straight down pick where the center of each eye should be and mark it.

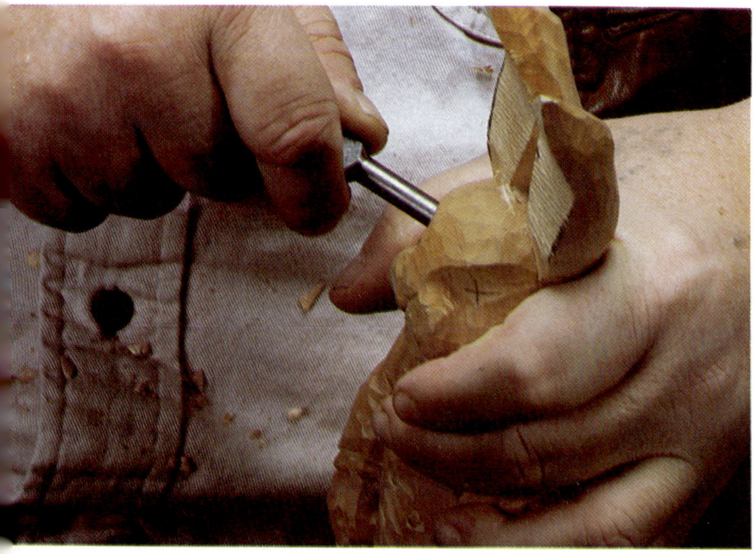

Center the eyepunch on the X you have made and make a light mark, first on one side, then the other. If it is not quite right you can erase the line and do it again.

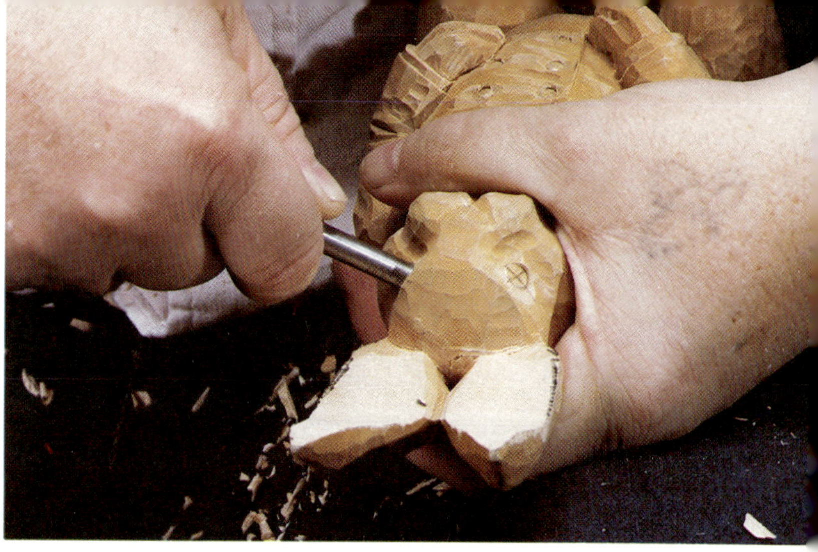

If everything checks out, go back and push and turn the eyepunch to form the iris.

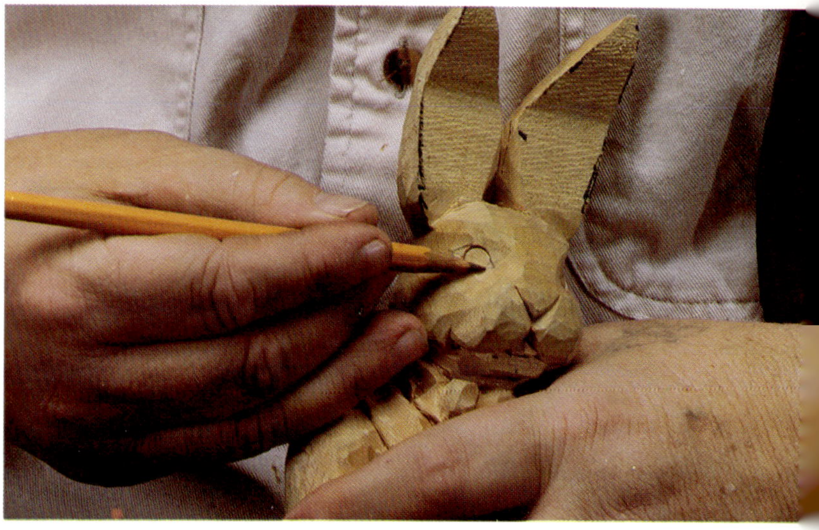

Finishing the eye of the rabbit is tricky. If the lines at the front of the eyes go up the rabbit will take on a mean look. Bring the line down like this...

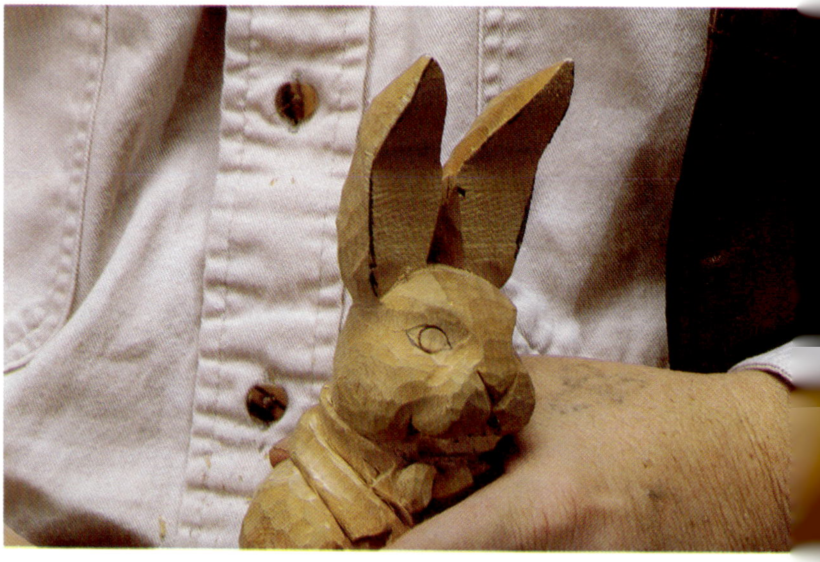

then draw in the rest of the eye. A rabbit is not beady-eyed, but has large warm eyes.

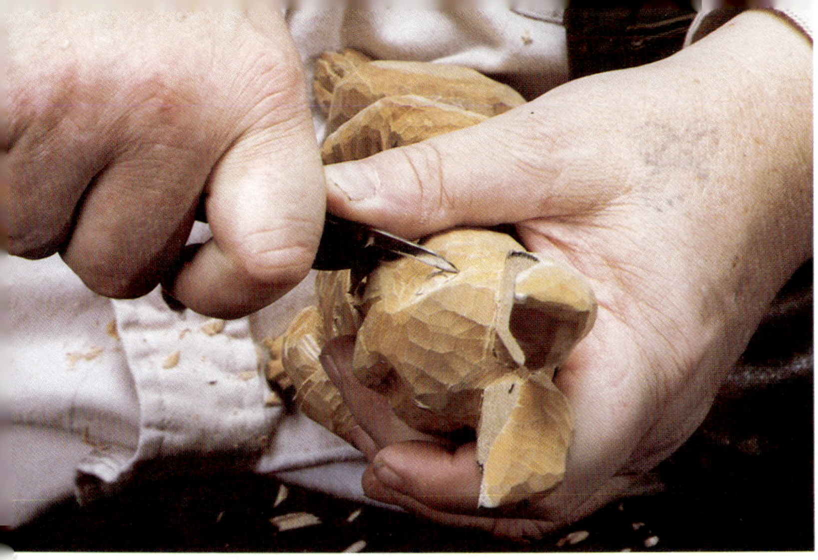

Cut two stops along the triangle at the back of the eye...

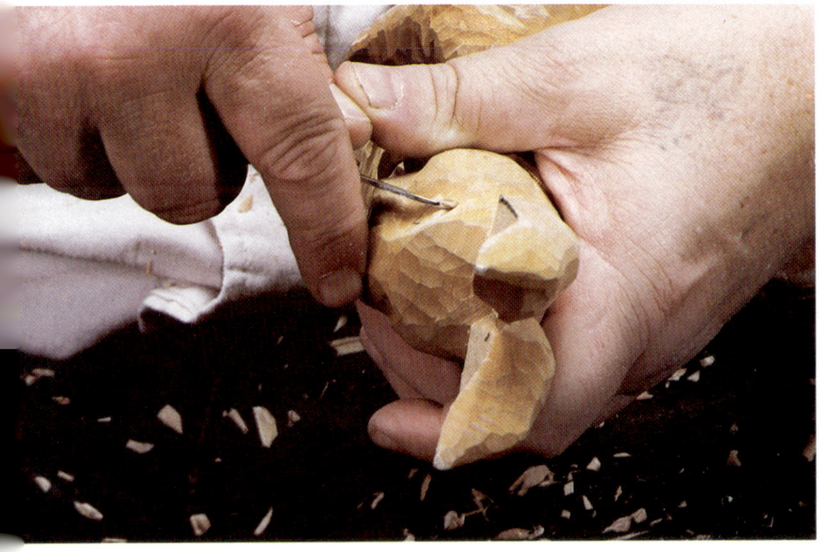

and come back into the stops with your knife angled away from the iris. This gives a rounded shape to the eyeball and gives the illusion of the eye being bigger.

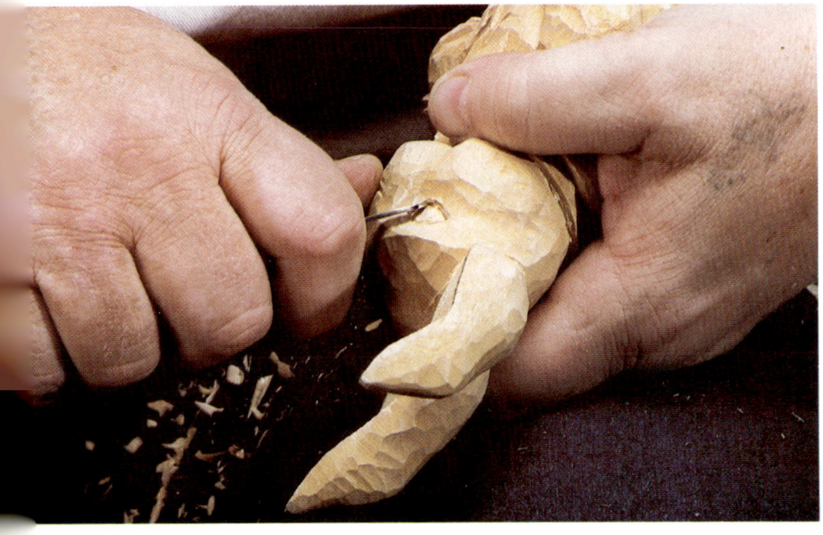

Do the same at the front of the eye, then go around the eyeball with your knife angled away, to give it its rounded shape.

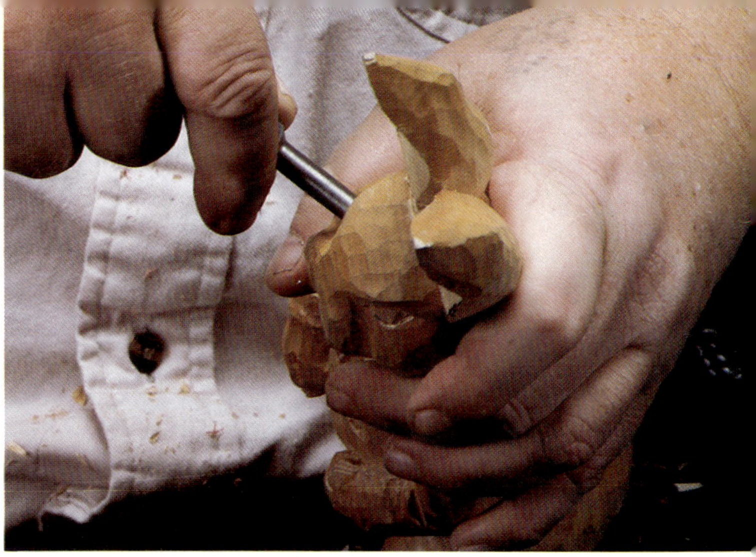

After rounding the eyeball, go back with the eyepunch and define the iris again.

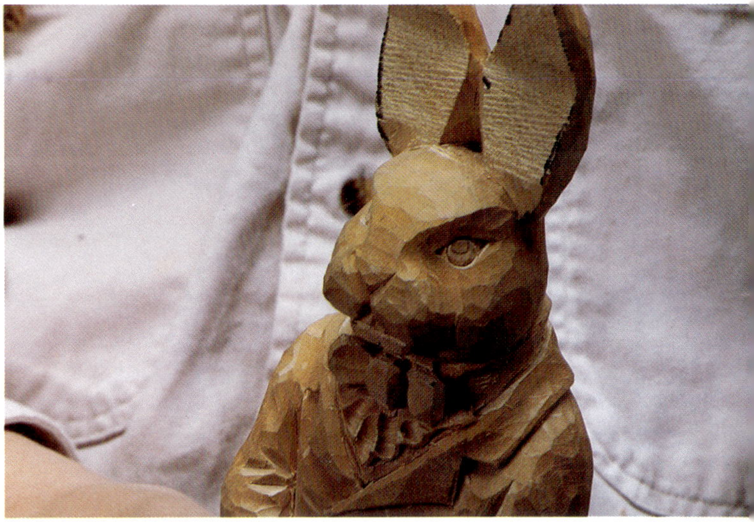

Draw in the position of the pupil. The "looking-up" position gives an innocent look and is a natural position for carving.

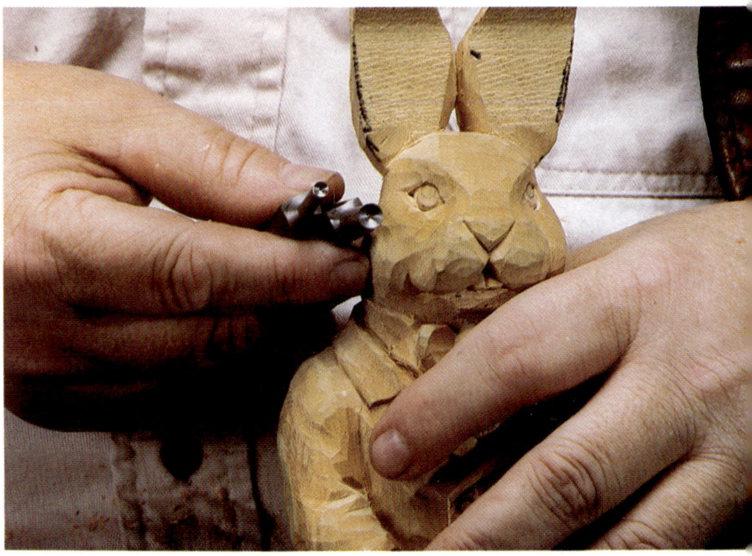

You want the pupil to be considerably smaller than the iris.

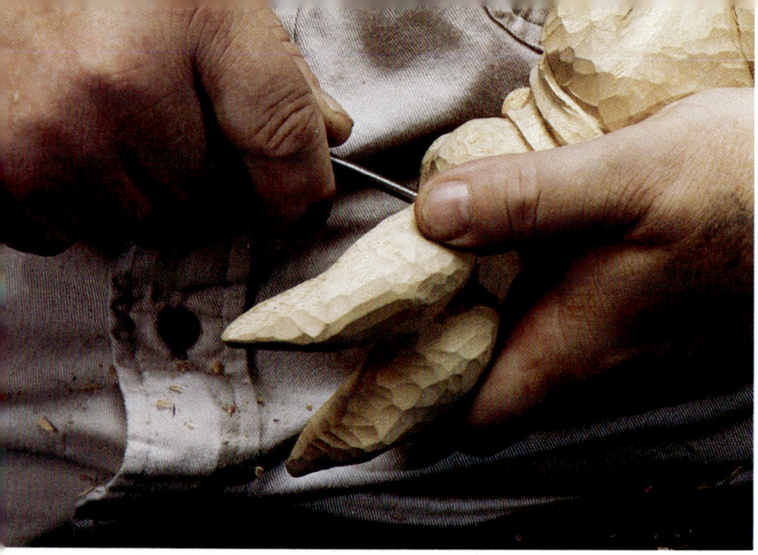

Use the eyepunch in the same way you did for the iris.

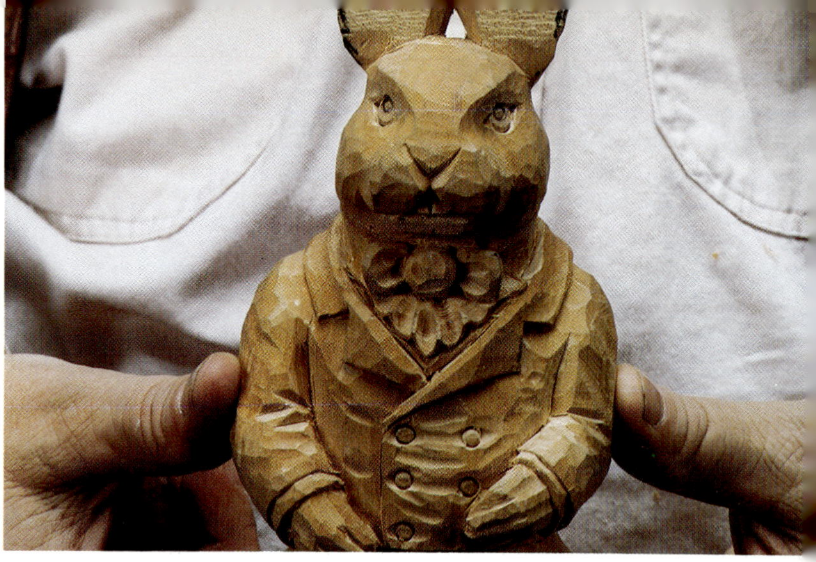

The spruced up tie.

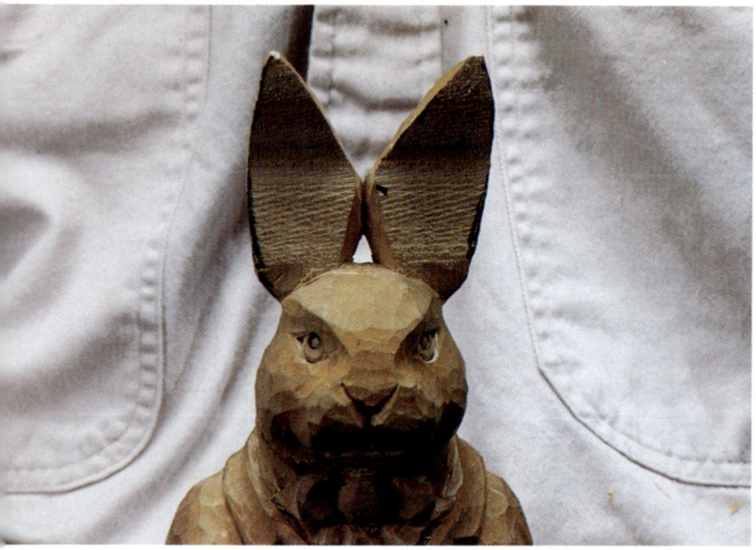

The finished eyes.

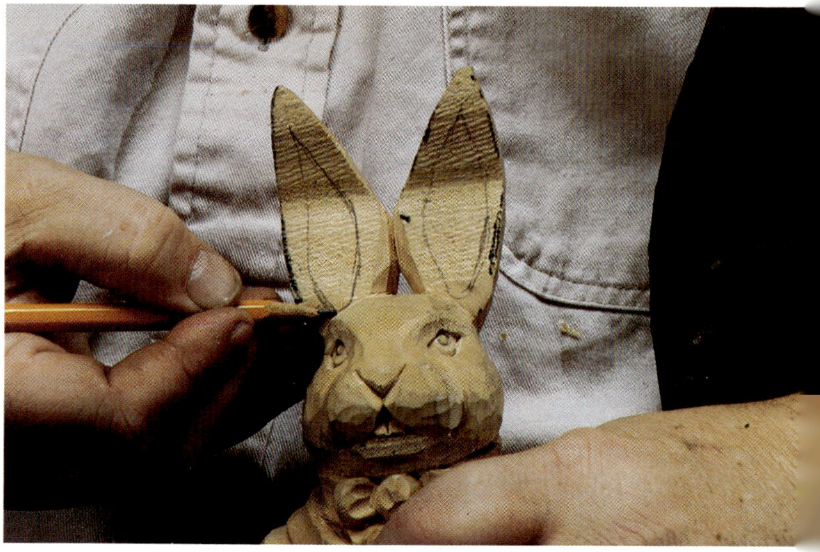

Draw in the inside of the ears.

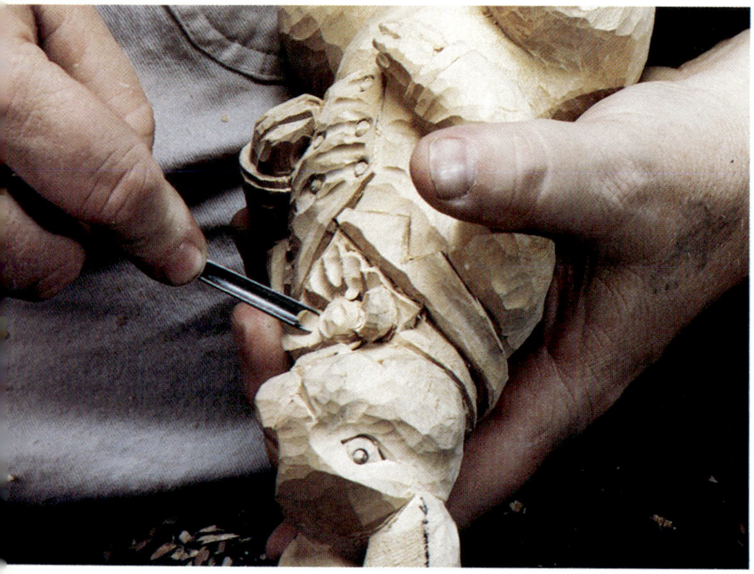

Another detail we can add is some folds in the tie. Use a half round gouge and go into the knot of the tie from the bow.

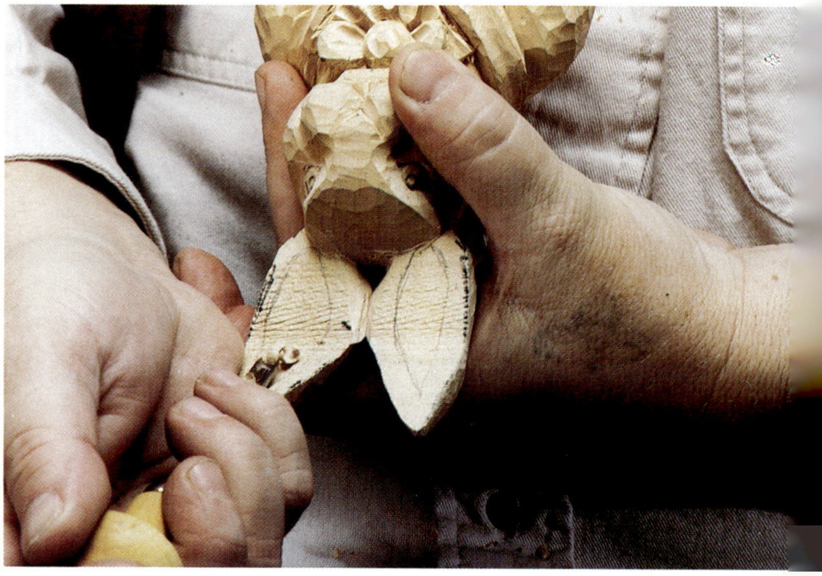

Use a half-round gouge to remove the material from the ear. A knife could be used, but this is one of the hardest spots to use a knife and many mistakes can be made.

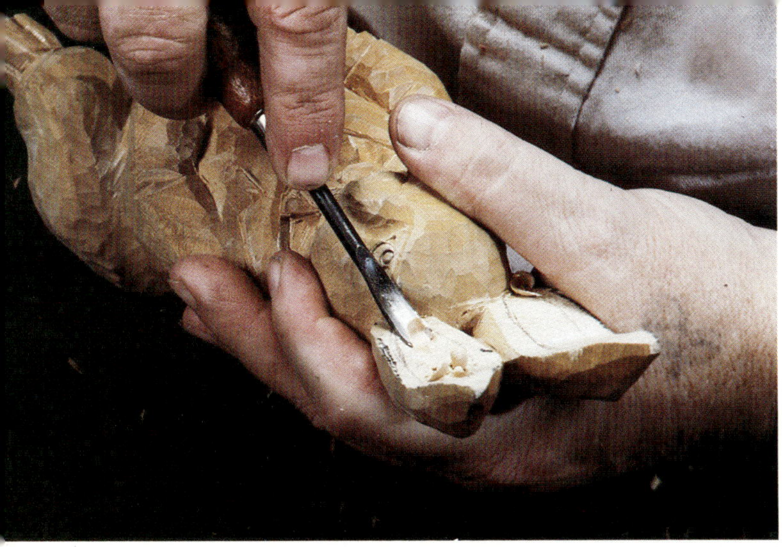

Against the head, a spoon chisel comes in handy. It is one of those tools that makes you wonder why you have it in your toolbox. But when you need it, it's the only tool that can do the job.

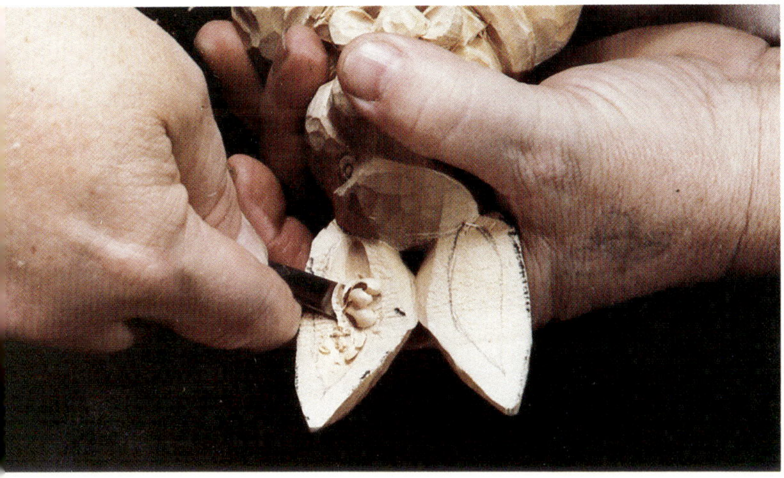

At the center of the ear use a flatter gouge and come from one side...

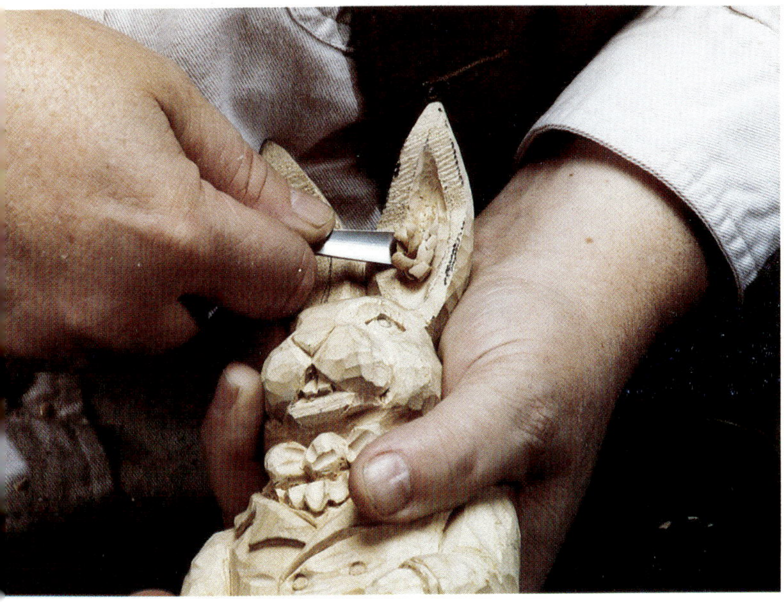

then the other.

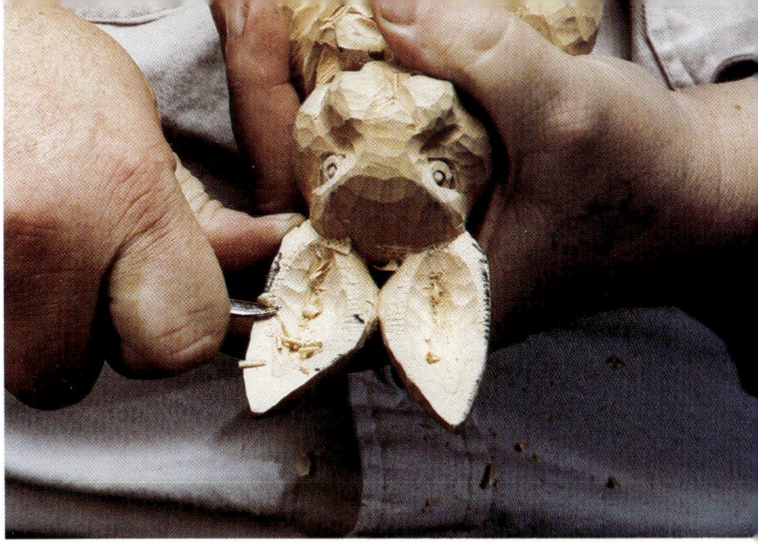

Clean up the saw and pencil marks with a knife. About the worst thing you can do on a wood carving is leave a saw mark, although I do it sometimes and so does everybody else. Check and recheck the piece for anything you may have missed.

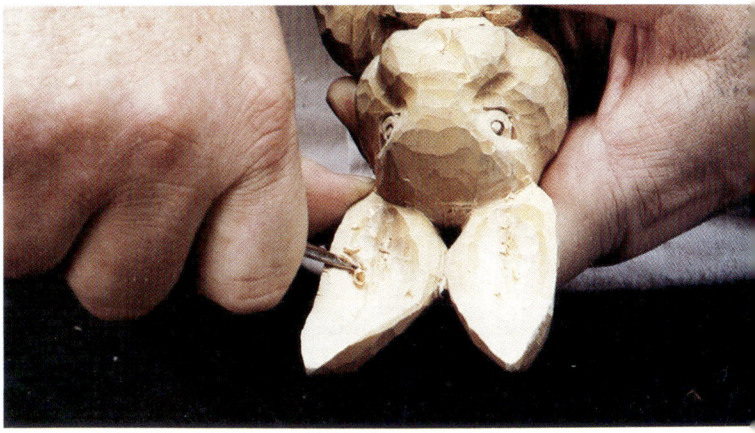

Round off the edges of the ears, particularly on the inside. The outside edge can stay fairly sharp.

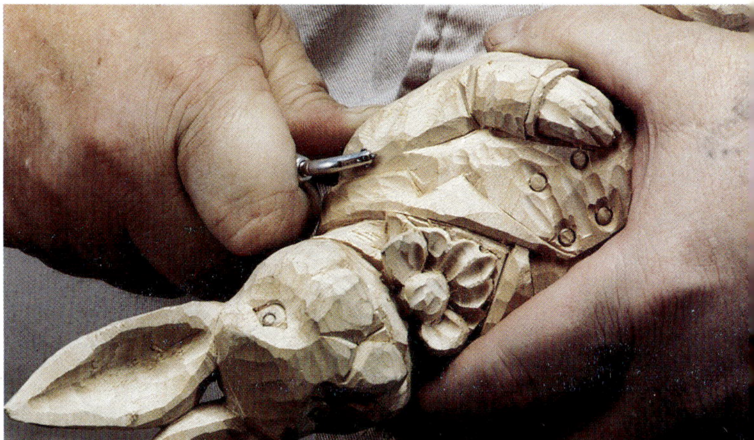

The stitches of the jacket are formed with a tracing wheel. The set I use has three sizes. Use the wheel to make seams around cuffs, shoulders, lapels, collars, and any other place where they should be. This little detail makes a big difference in the character of the carving.

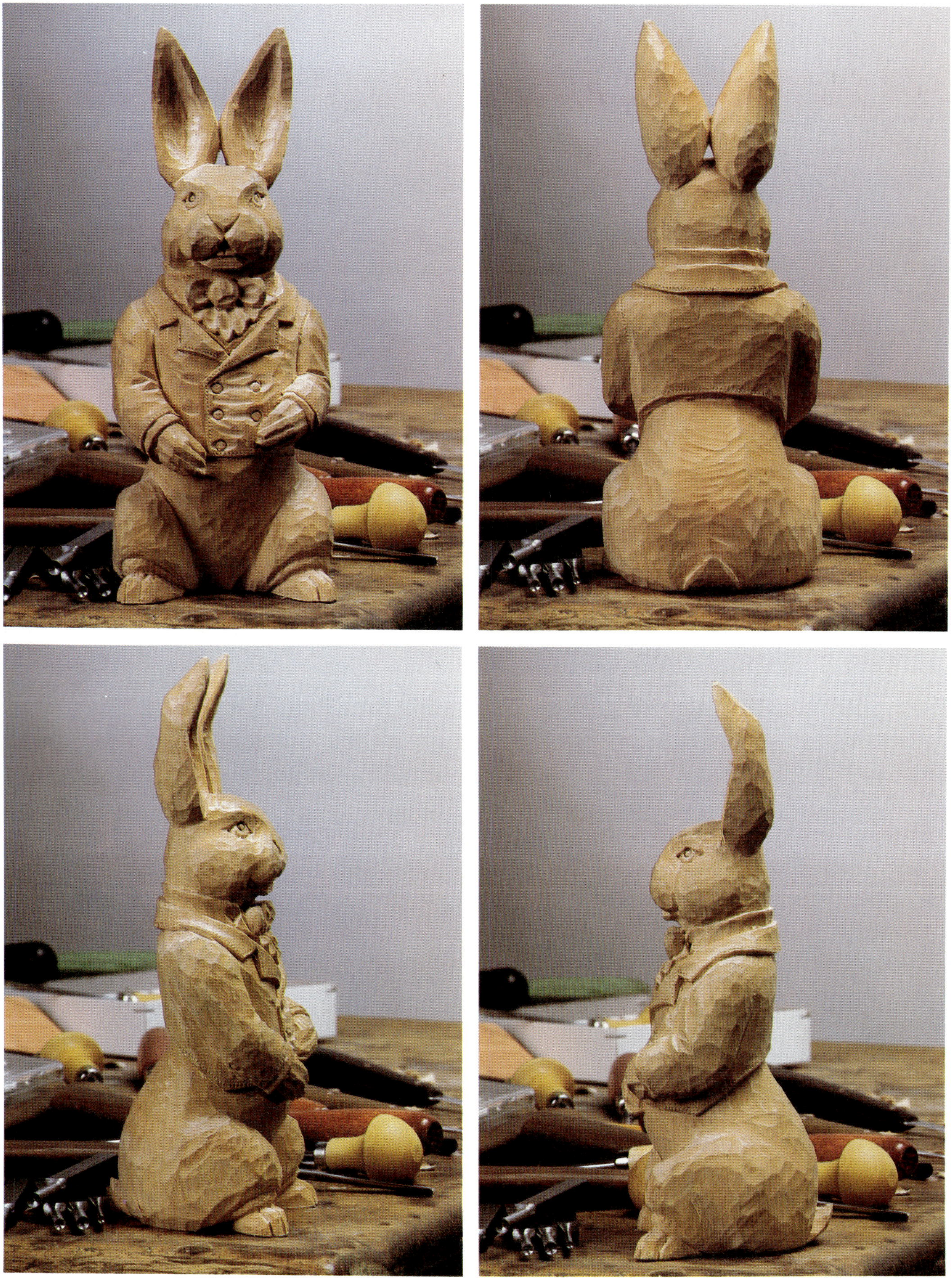

The finished Easter Bunny carving.

Burning the Decorated Easter Eggs

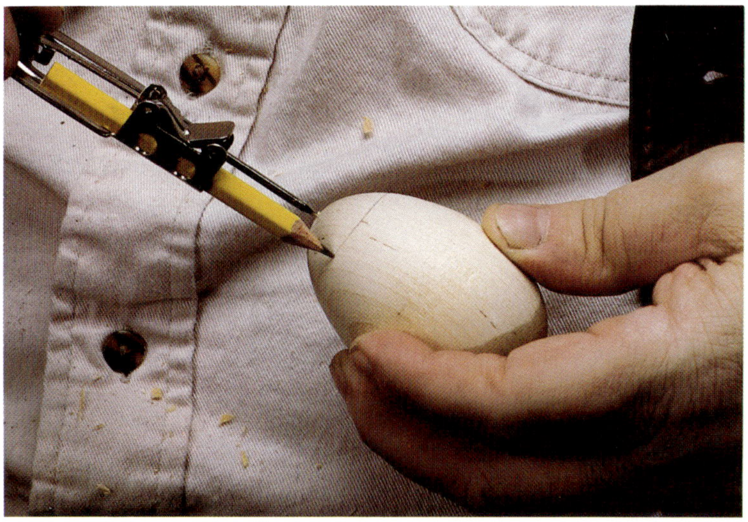

To go with the bunny we will decorate a few wooden eggs. The egg blanks are maple and readily available at most craft stores. They are nice things to work with, and I sometimes carve faces on them. Use a simple compass to mark the egg. Place its point in the lathe mark on the egg, and draw a ring around the egg at each end, or wherever else you please

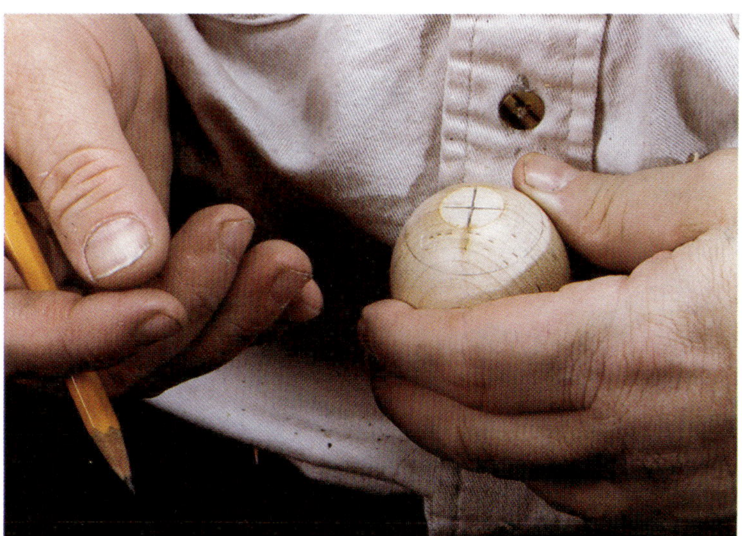

Draw a cross in the circle at one end...

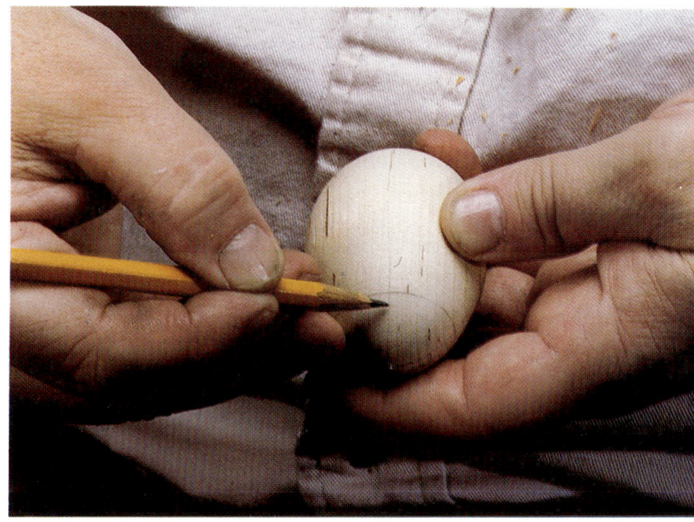

and carry the lines to the other end. Don't worry about little wobbles; they give that hand-crafted look.

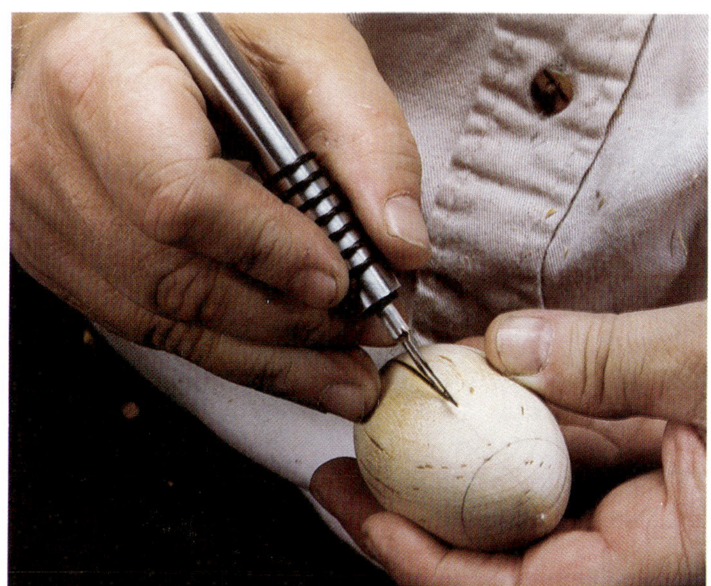

The lines you have drawn give you reference points for the freehand work that follows. I usually begin work with the burner at this point, though you may feel more comfortable drawing in your design first.

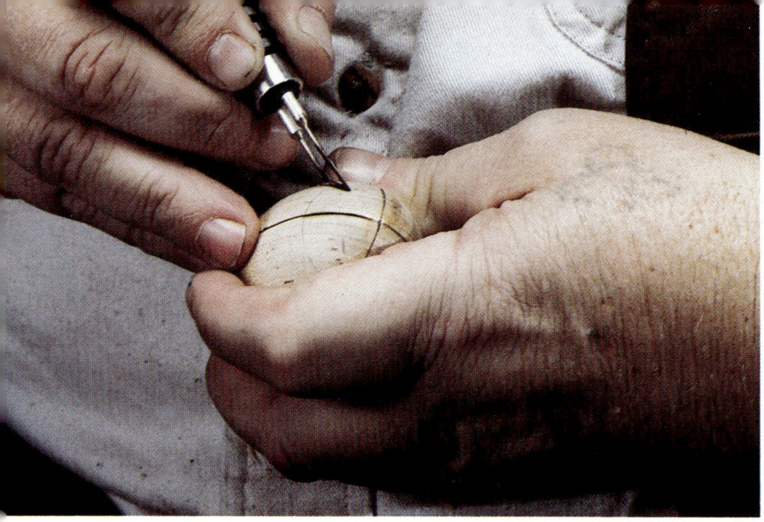

Go over the guidelines with the burner. One of the reasons a burner works so well on these eggs is that it keeps the paint from migrating from one area to another much better than a pencil mark or a carved line would. When the guidelines are burned you can begin your freehand design. I'm going to add lines to make eight lengthwise sections.

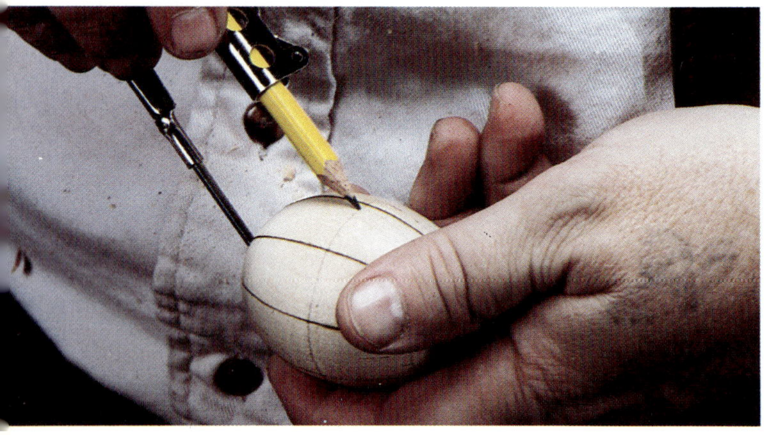

I again will use the compass to draw a center line around the mid-section of the egg.

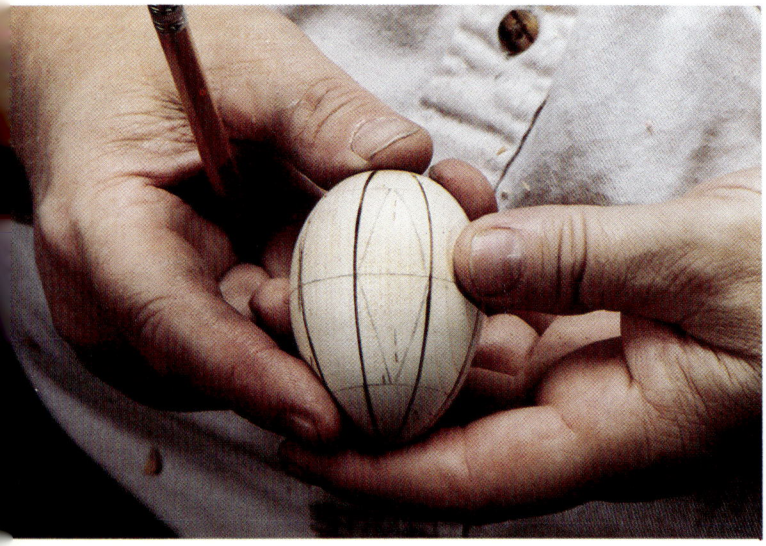

In each section, between the end circles, I'll draw a diamond.

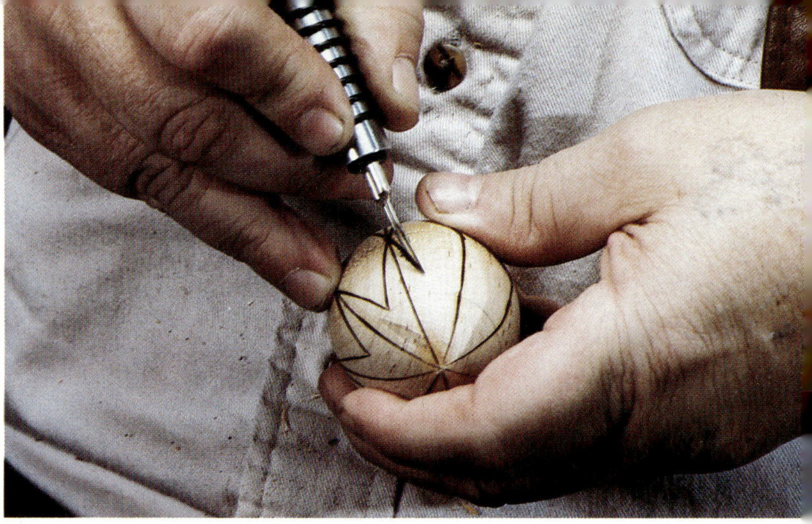

Burn in the pattern.

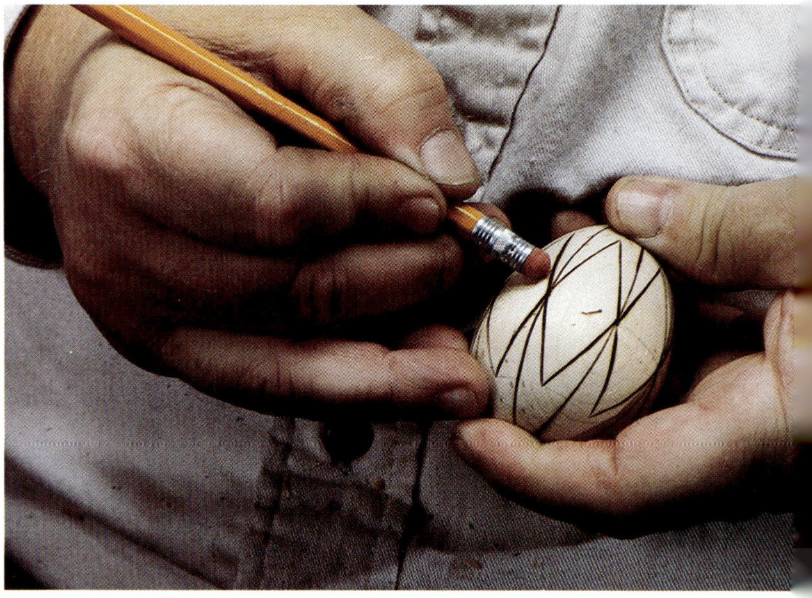

Erase the pencil lines you used as guides.

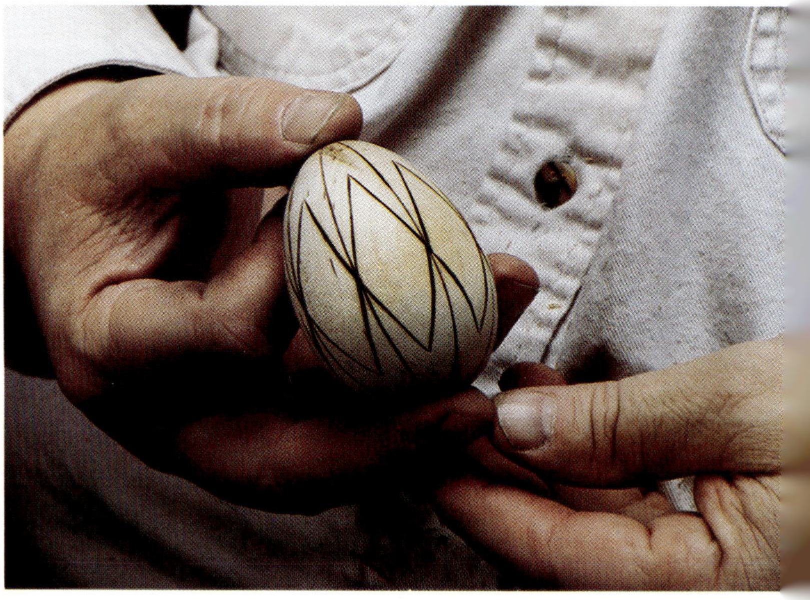

The finished pattern ready for painting.

Painting the Easter Bunny and His Eggs

I use Winsor and Newton Alkyd tube paints for wood carving. These are thinned with pure turpentine to a consistency that is soaked into the carving, giving subtle colors. What I look for is a watery mixture, almost like a wash. In this way the turpentine will carry the pigment into the wood, giving the stained look I like. It has always been my theory that if you are going to cover the wood, why use wood in the first place. It should be noted that with white, the concentration of pigment should be a little stronger.

I mix my paints in glass juice bottles, putting in a bit of paint and adding turpentine. I don't use exact measurements. Instead I use trial and error, adding a bit of paint or a bit of turpentine until I get the thickness I want.

The juice bottles are handy for holding your paints. They are reclosable, easy to shake, and have the added advantage of leaving a concentrated amount of color on the inside of the lid and the sides of the bottle which can be used when more intense color is needed.

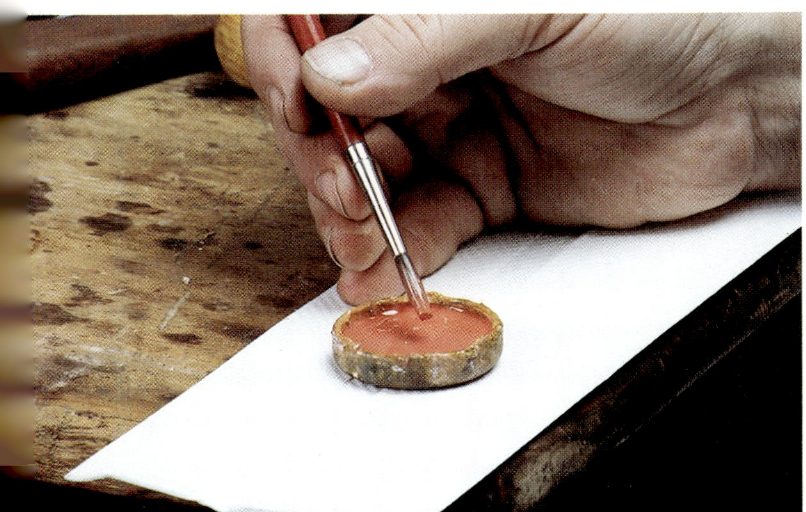

A flesh color is first. It goes around the mouth, nose, and eyes, in the ears and other places where the skin may show through on the bunny. Pour some in the cap and mix it with the brush.

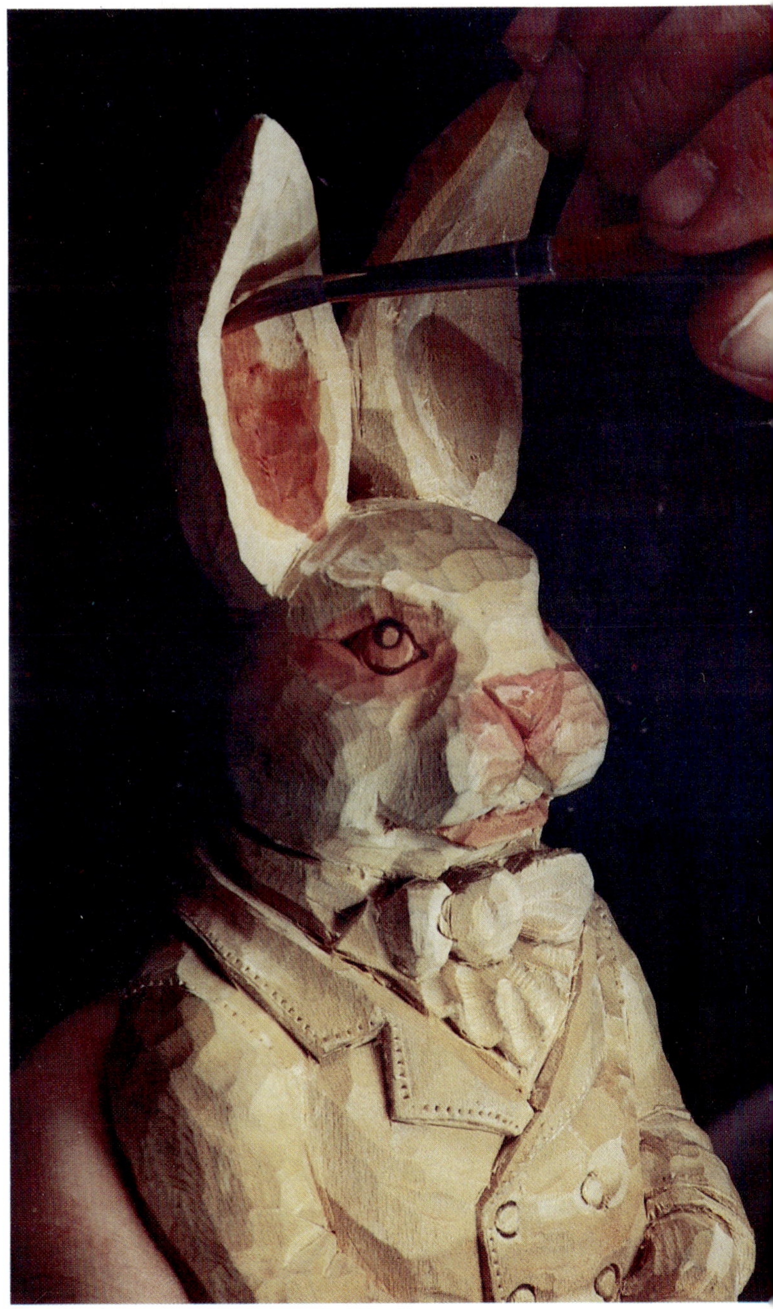

You don't have to be too careful with this color because you are going to go back over it with white.

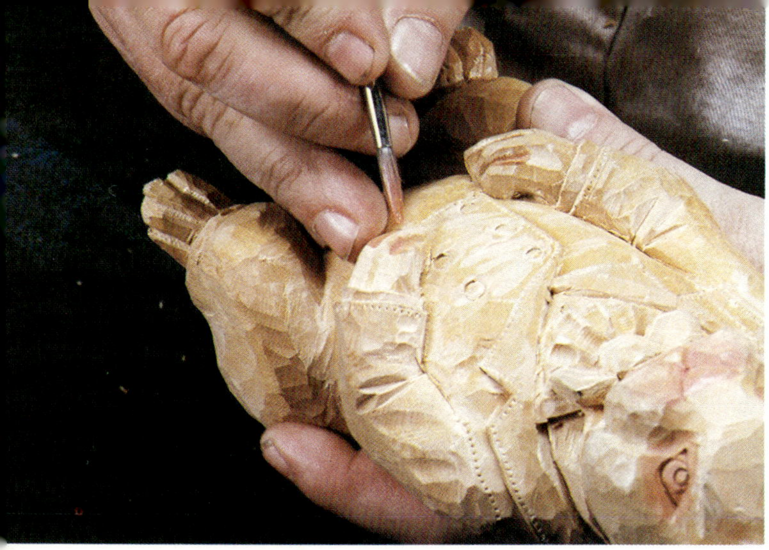

Apply the flesh color between the fingers and the toes.

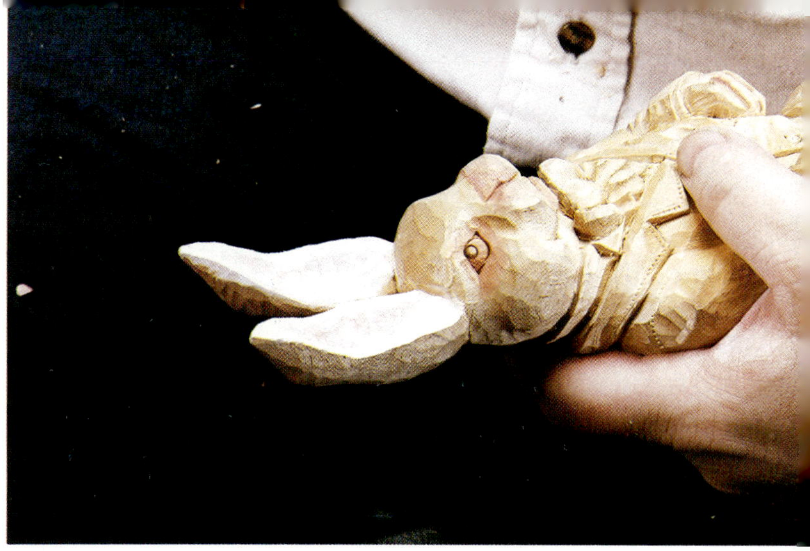

Apply the white to the ears, covering the pink.

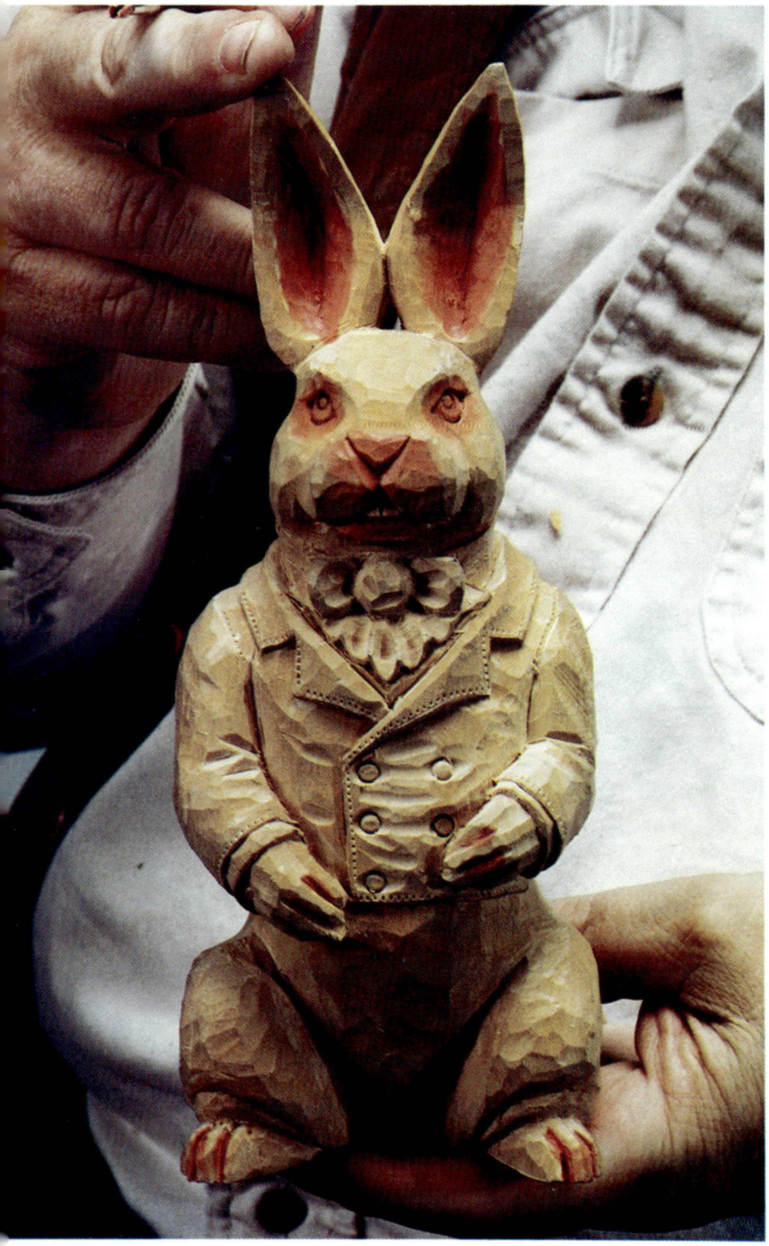

The flesh tones applied.

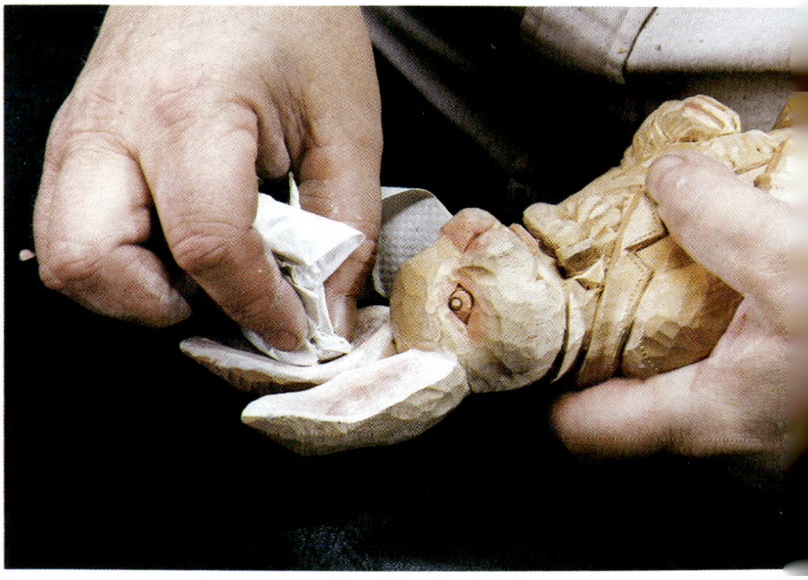

Then wipe away some of the white to be sure the pink shows through.

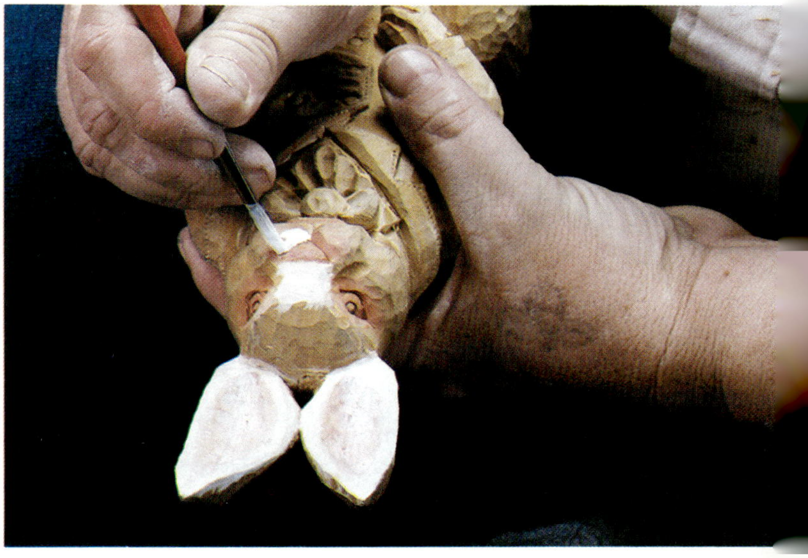

I want to leave the full color on the nose and lips, and paint around them with the white.

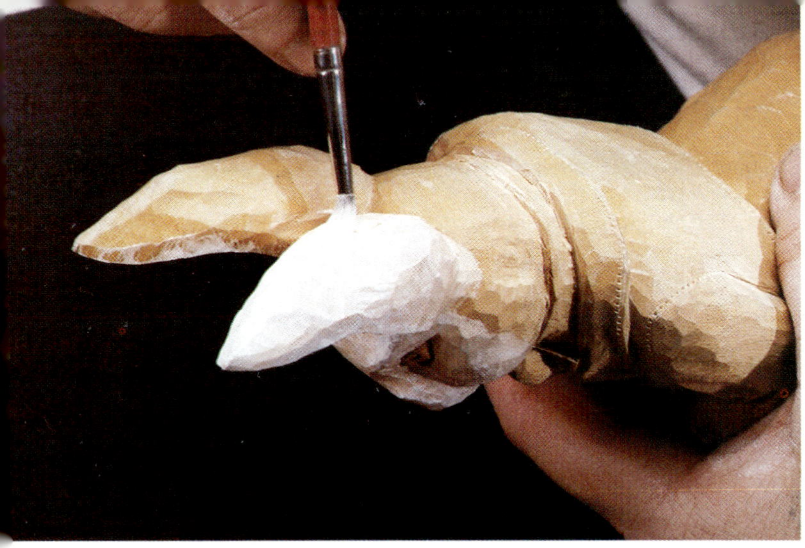

Continue to paint the head. With white paint you will always miss places. Many of these will not appear until the paint starts to dry, and you will need to go back over the piece.

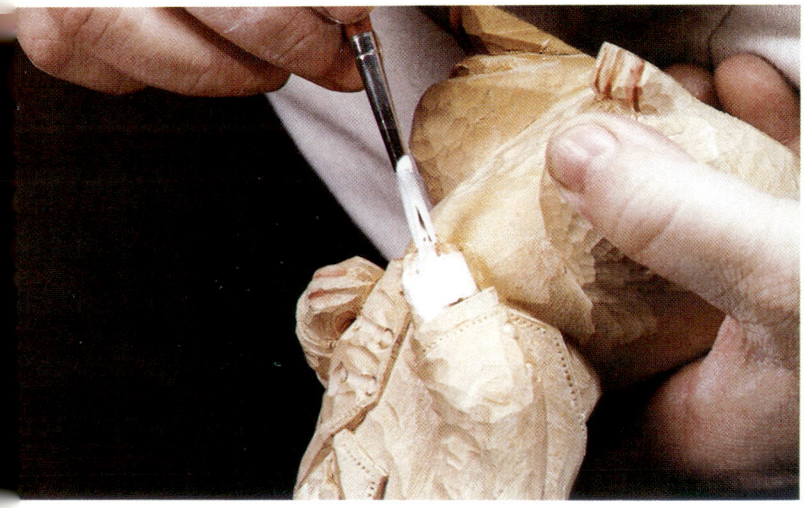

Paint the hands...

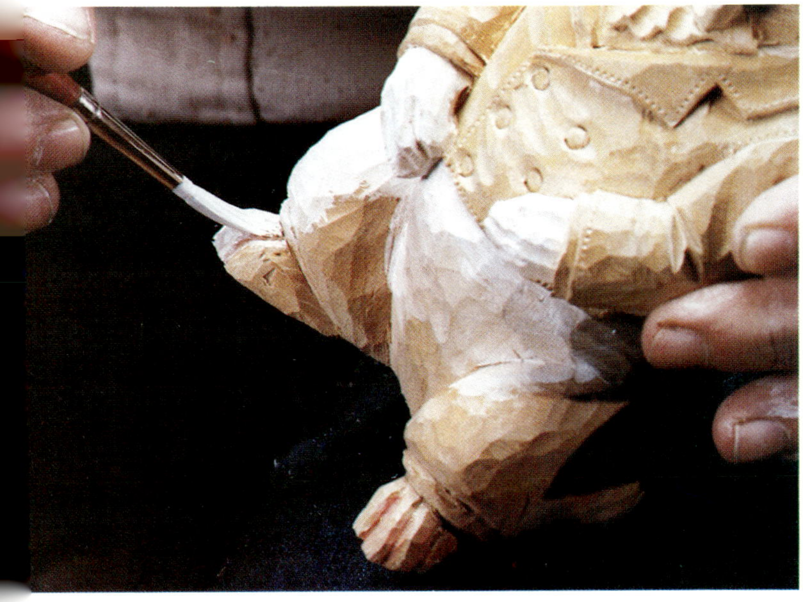

bottom and feet.

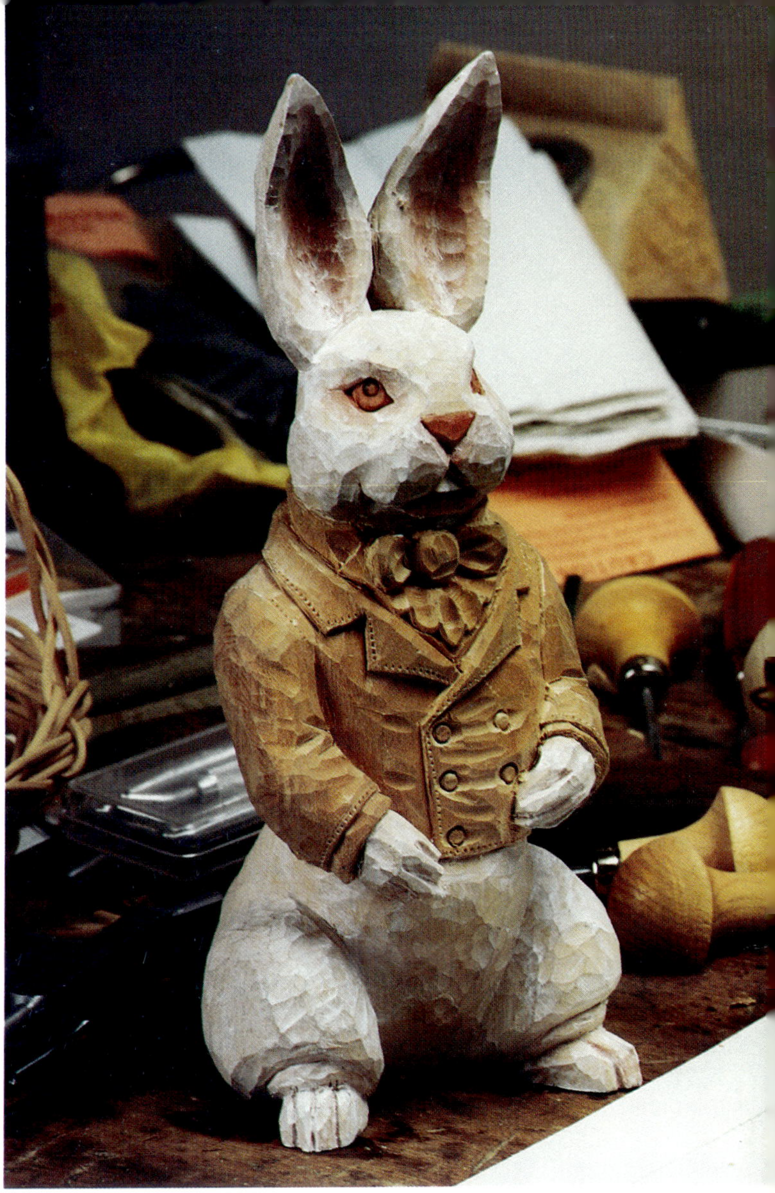

The white is finished.

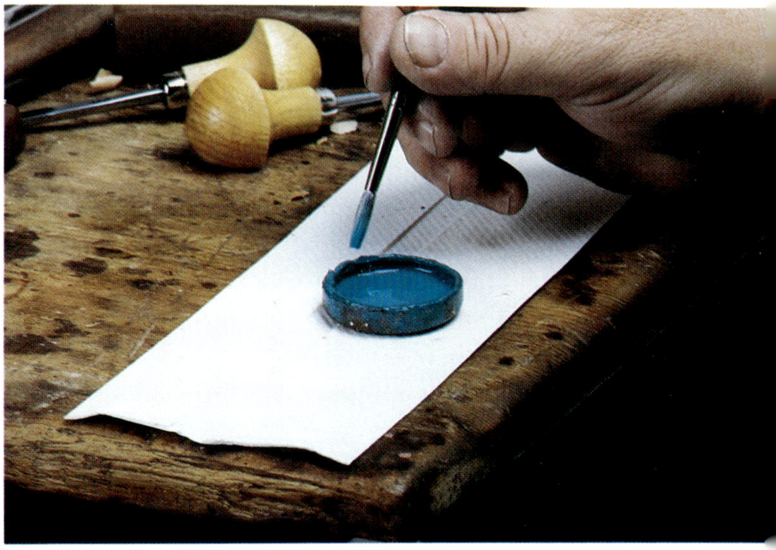

For the jacket we'll use Alizarin Crimson, a red tone, with a light blue (Cerulean Blue Hue) shirt. Begin with the shirt in blue.

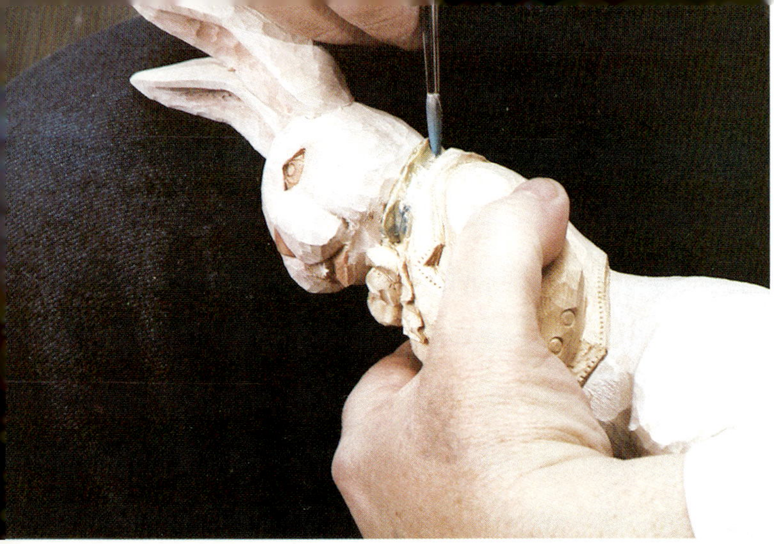

Do the collar first...

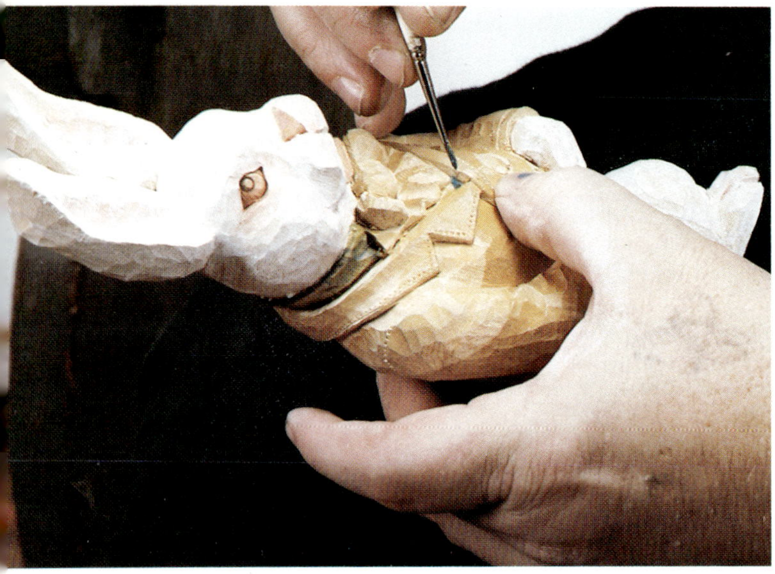

and continue around the ruffle, using a very fine brush.

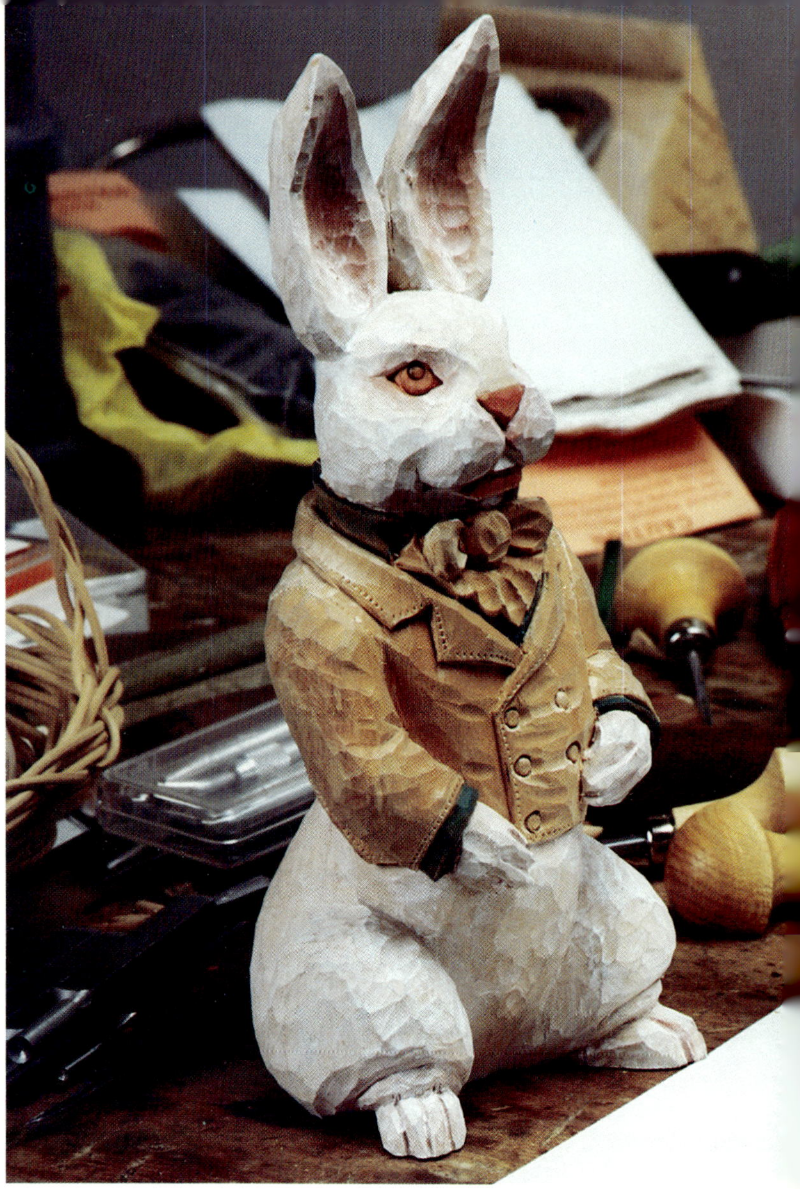

The finished blue.

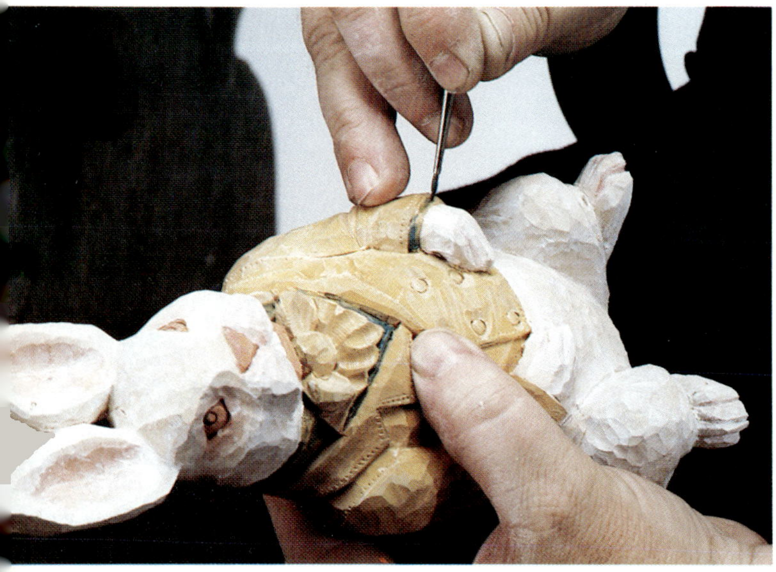

Finally paint the shirt cuffs as they come below the jacket sleeves.

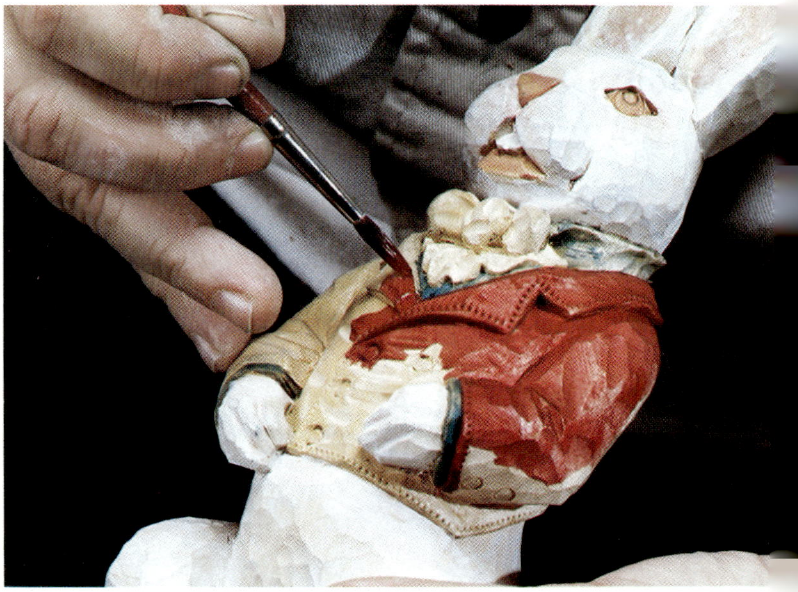

Apply the red to the jacket.

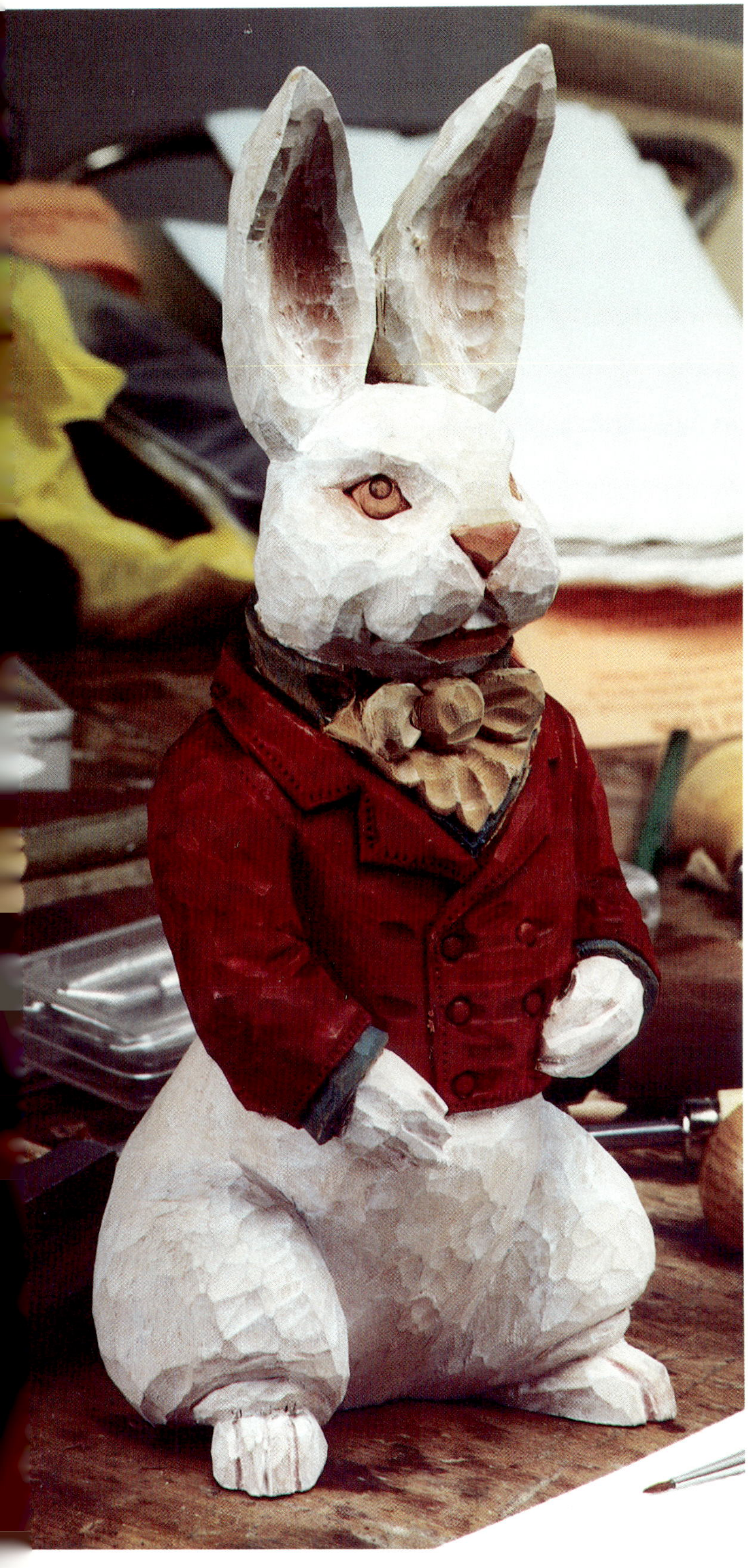

The finished red.

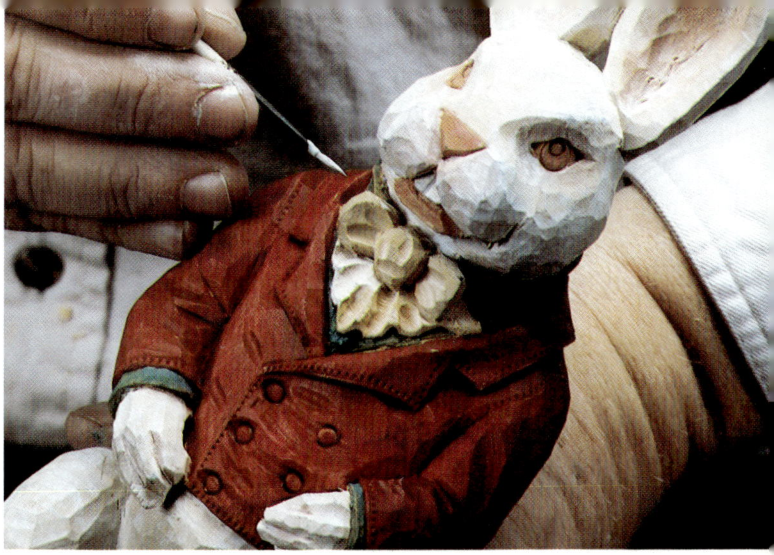

The ruffles should look good in white.

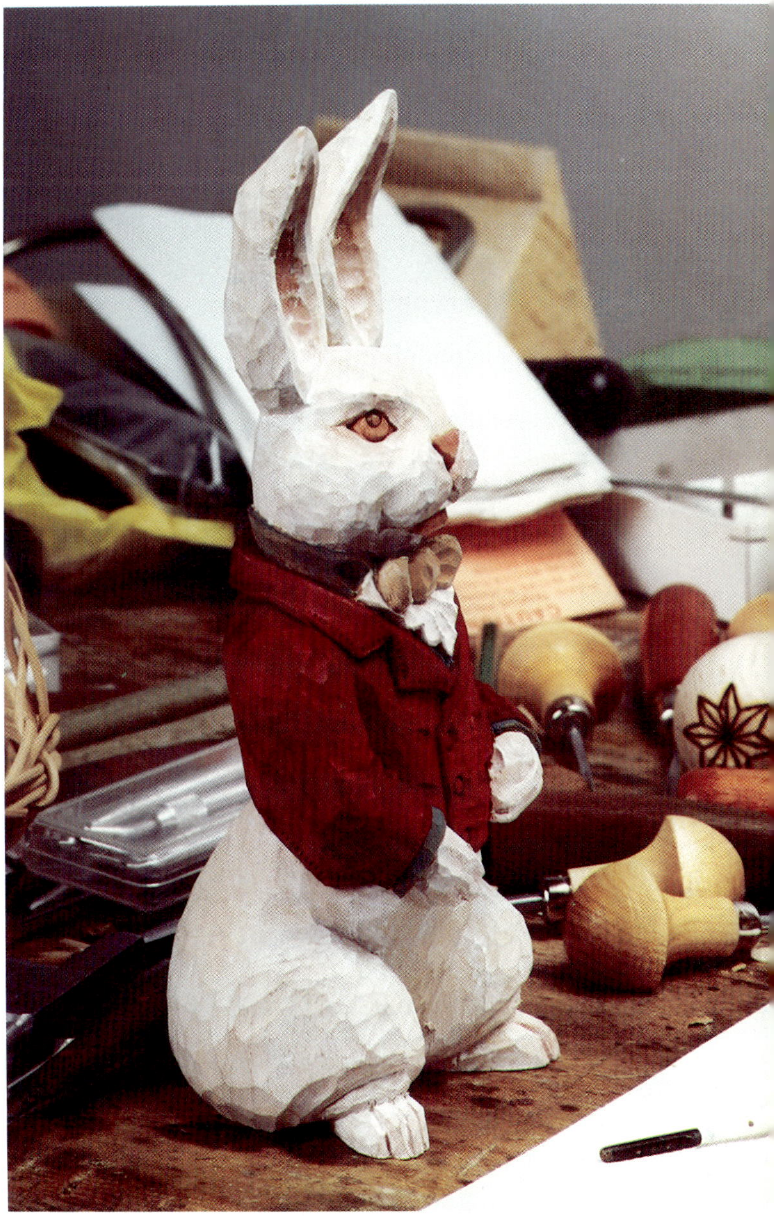

Having gone this far, it's time to consider the tie. To me it seems to be saying "Paint me red!"...so I will.

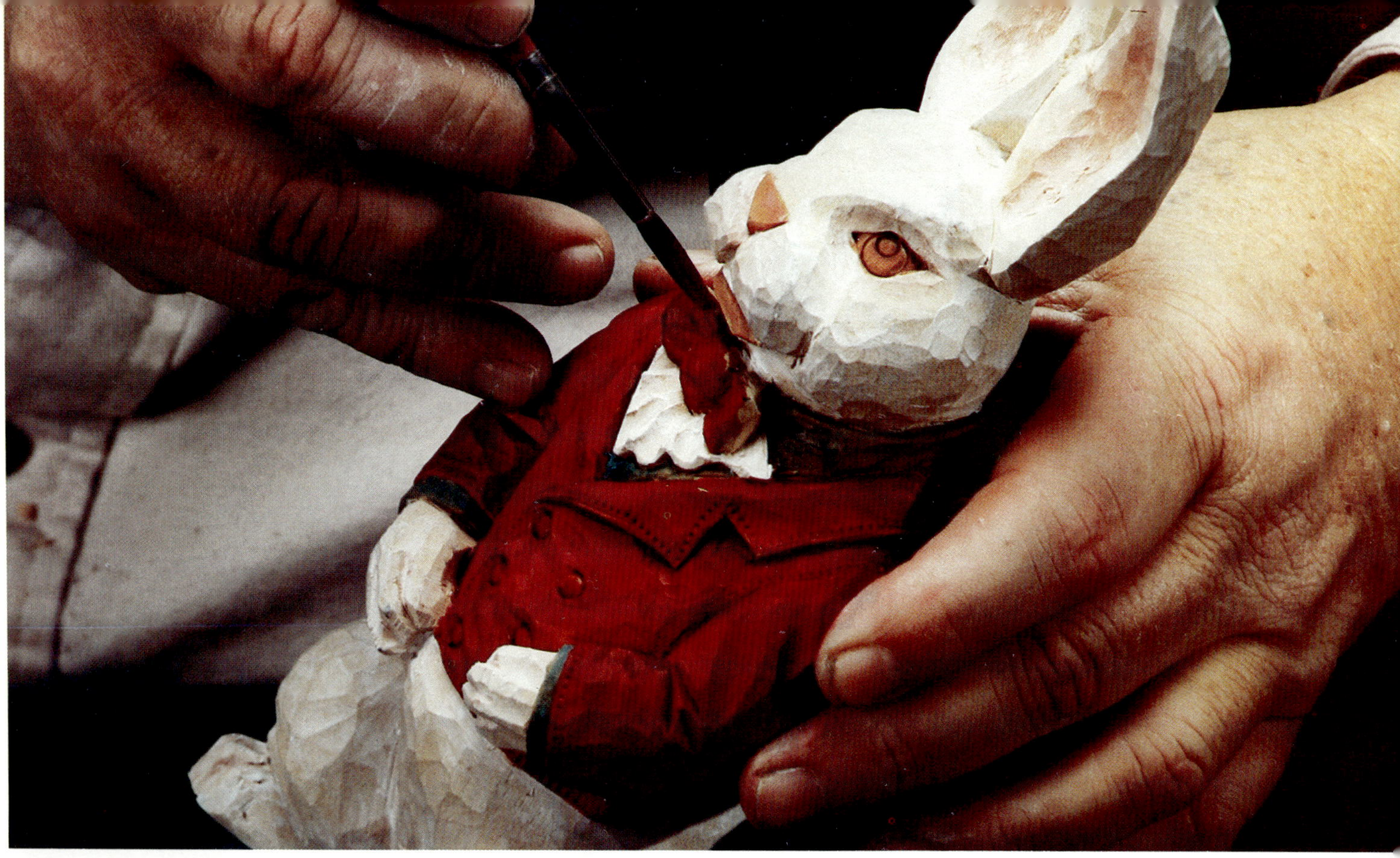

The red tie.

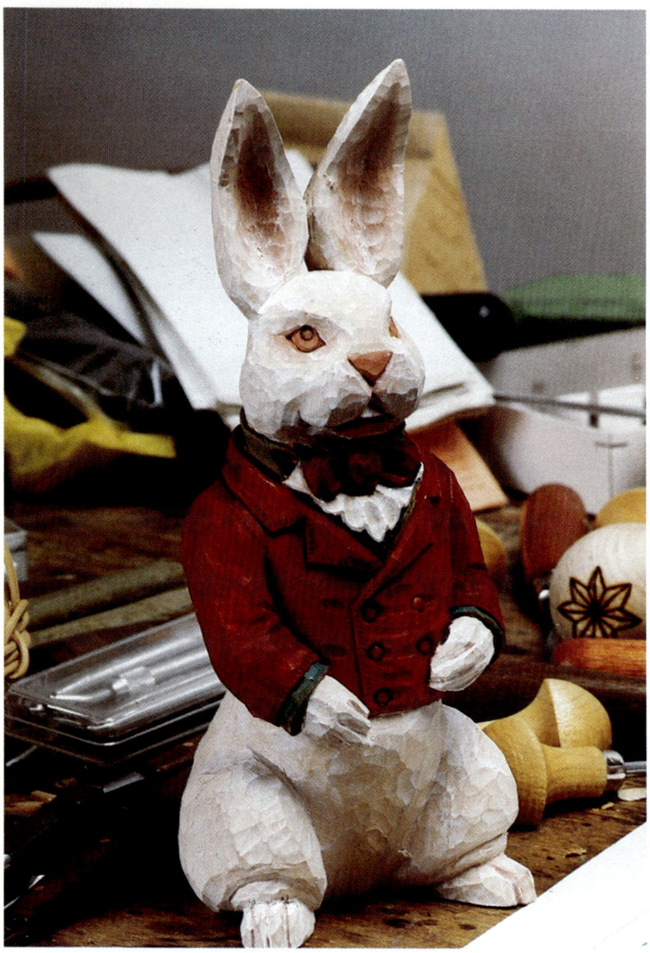

Now the bunny is ready for some final touches...

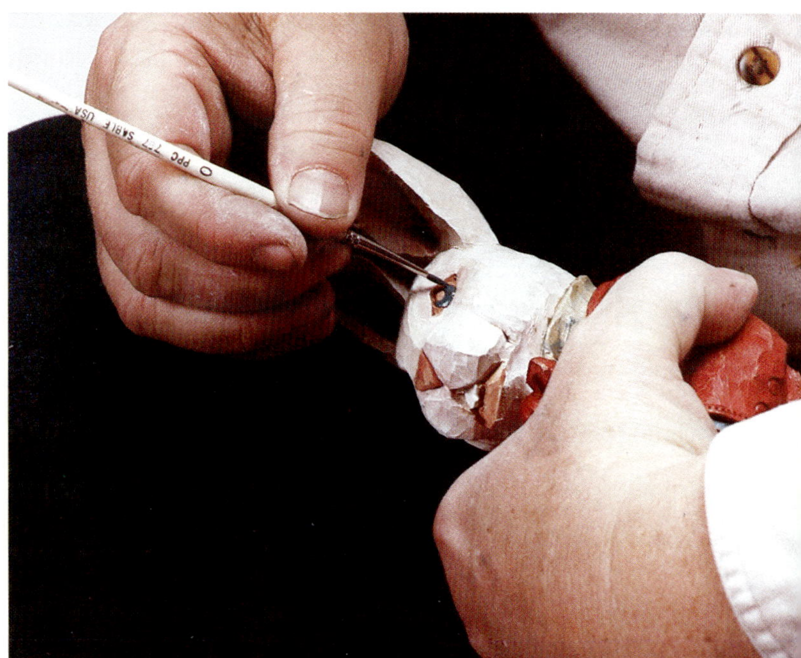

like blue on the iris. Follow the lines of the eye punch.

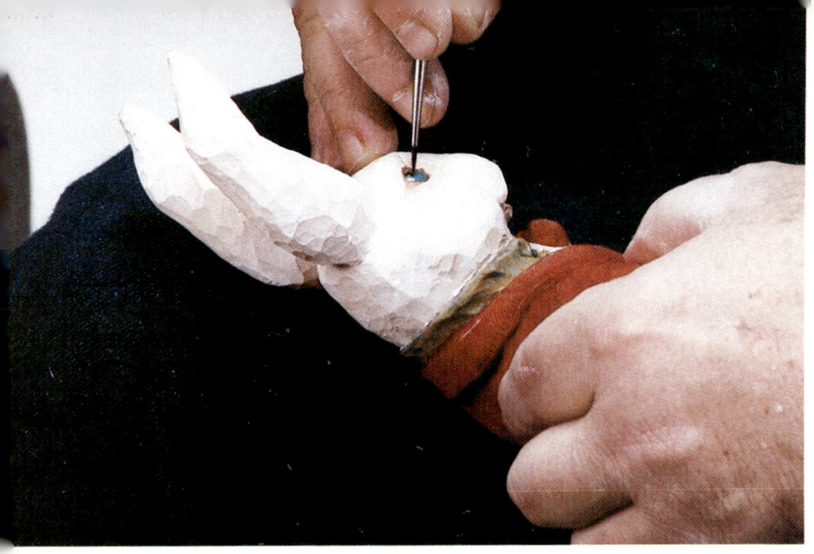

Paint the pupil of the eye black. Again, follow the lines of the eye punch.

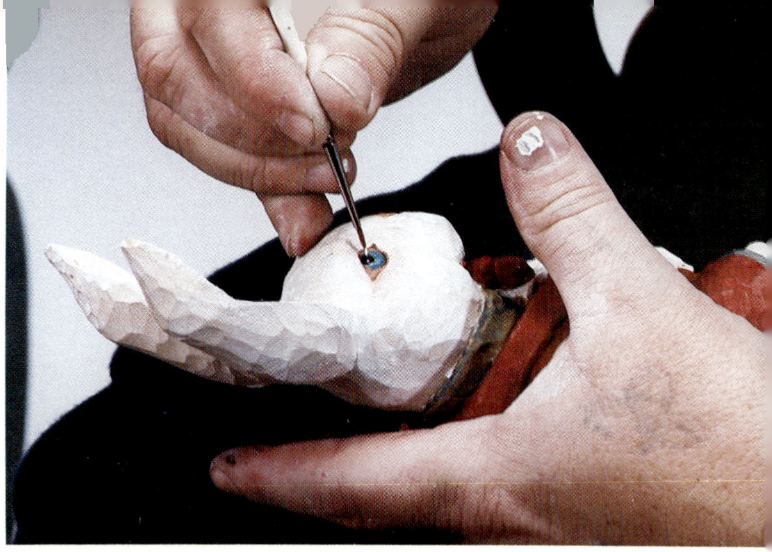

Add a little white glint. Two little spots of white should do it. For these small areas, I use my thumb nail as a palette. This allows me to get just the speck of paint I want on my brush.

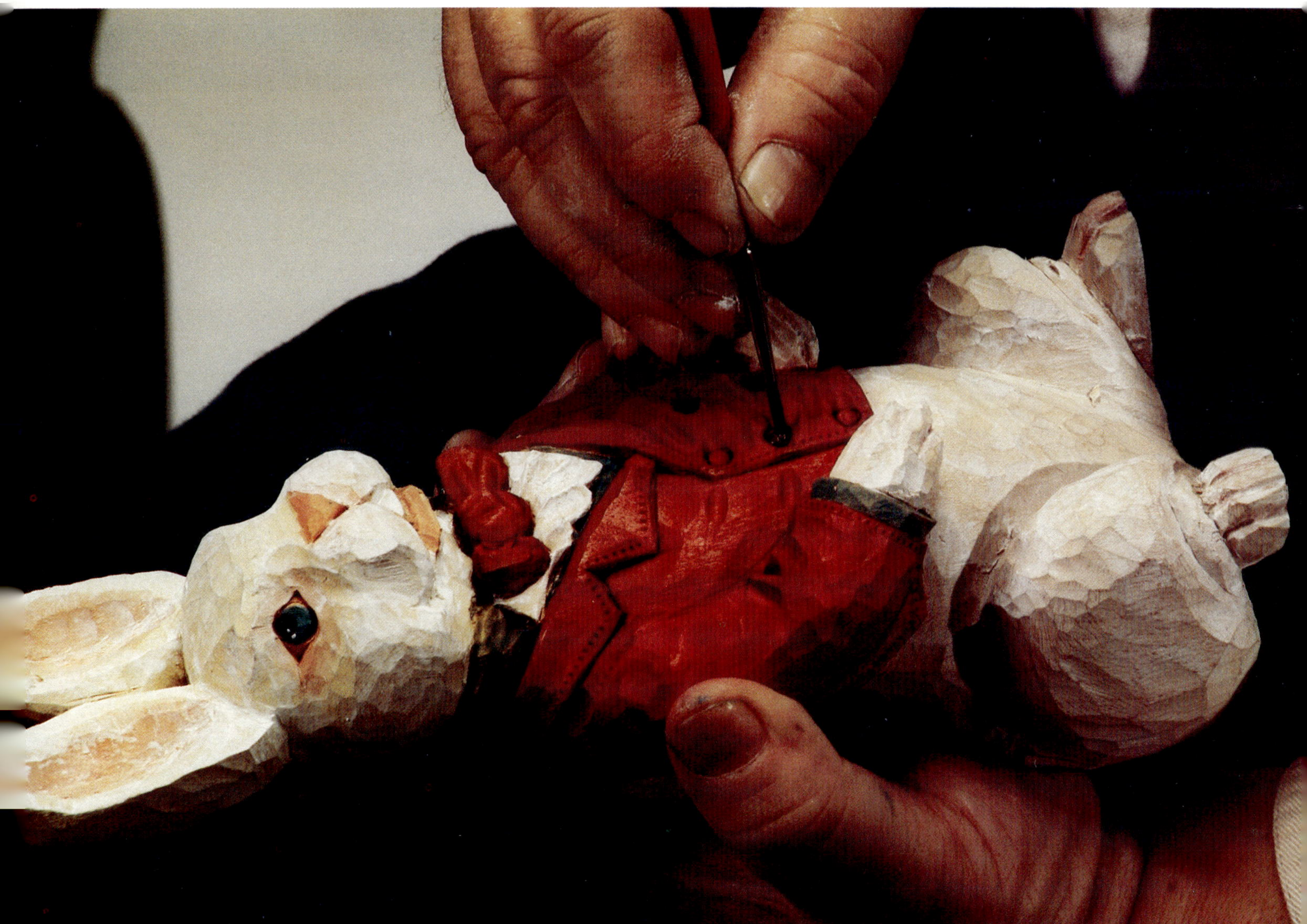

Finally, add a little paint to the buttons. I will use burnt umber.

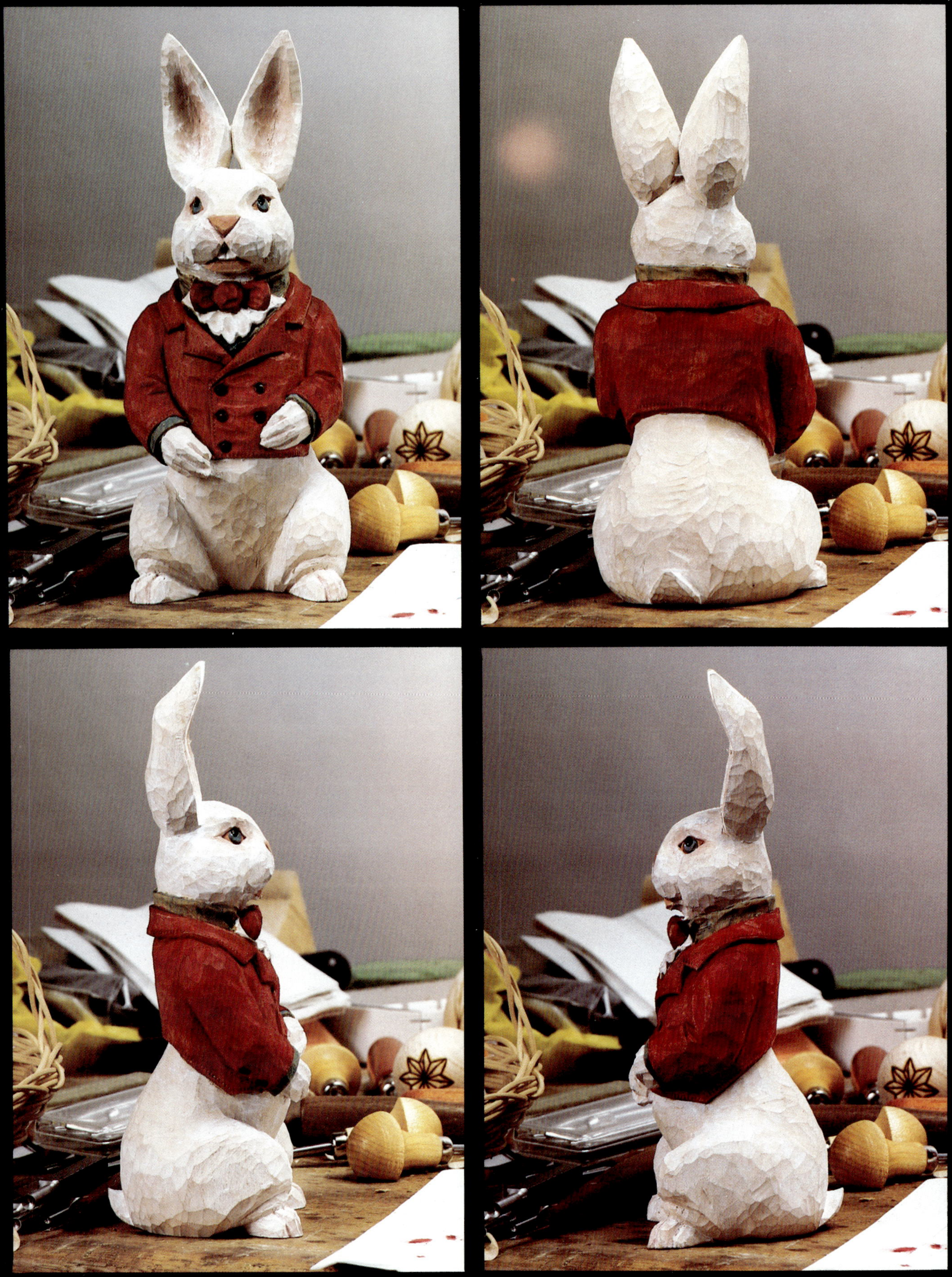

The finished rabbit.

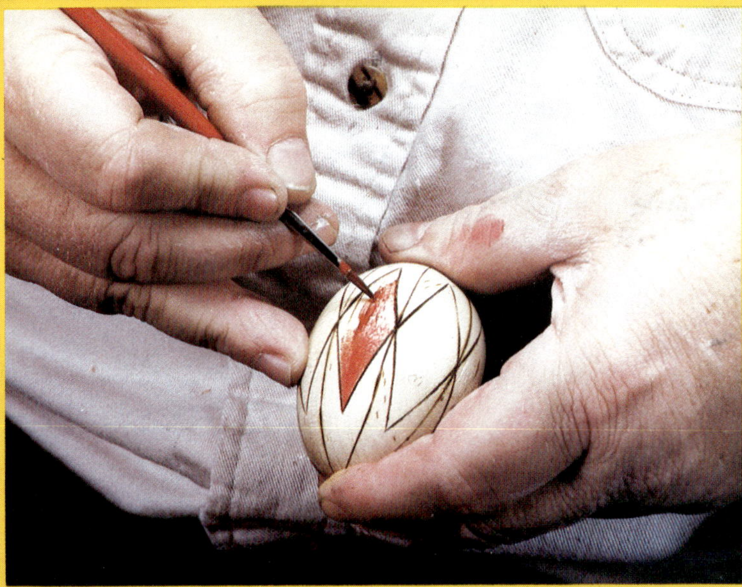

The first step in painting the egg is to decide what the color plan will be. If you don't take the time to figure it out in advance, you are likely to find yourself painted into a corner. I'm going to start with red in some of the diamonds.

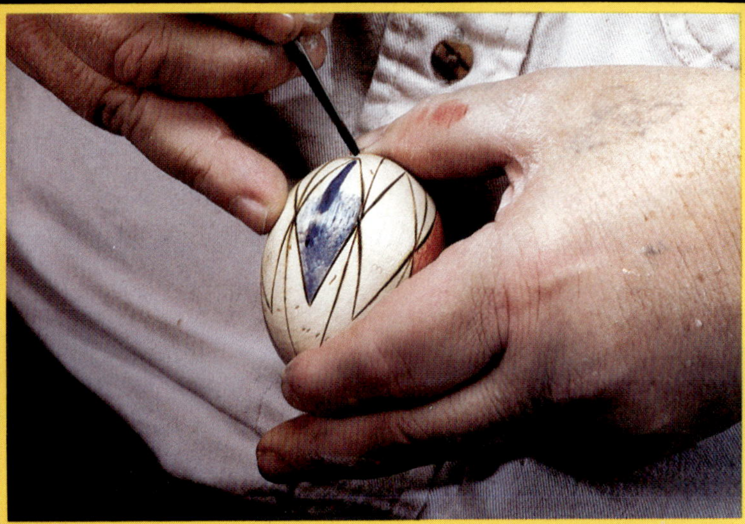

Next we'll add an ultramarine blue to some other diamonds...

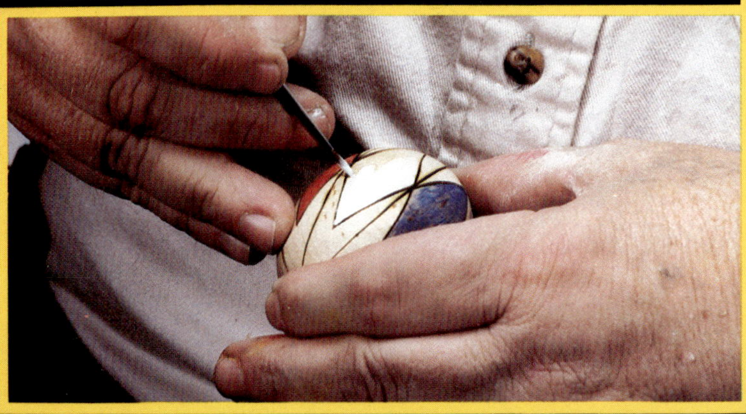

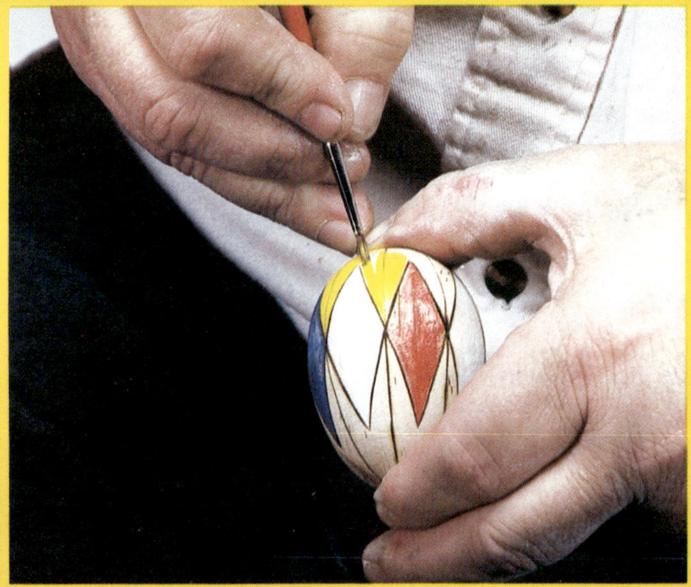

Finally, I'll paint the top and bottom in yellow.

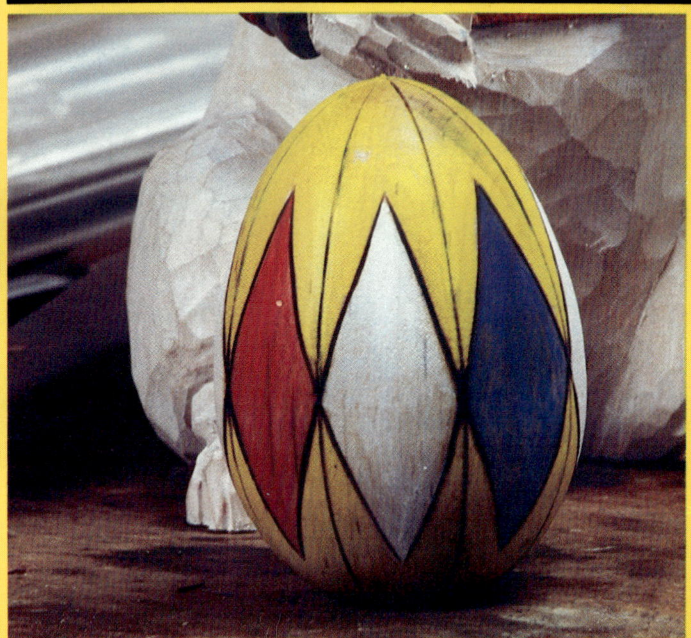

The painted egg.

The Bunny Gallery

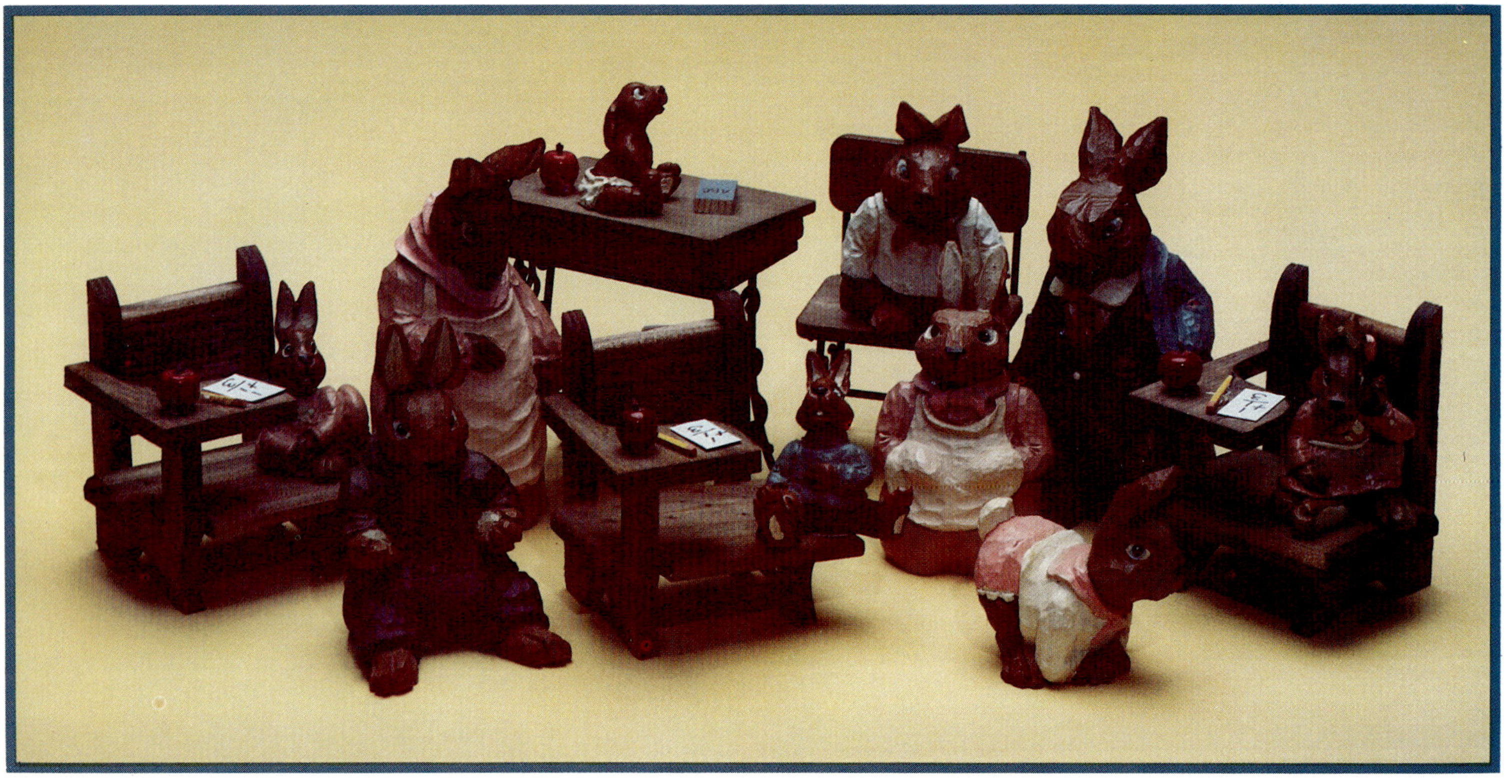

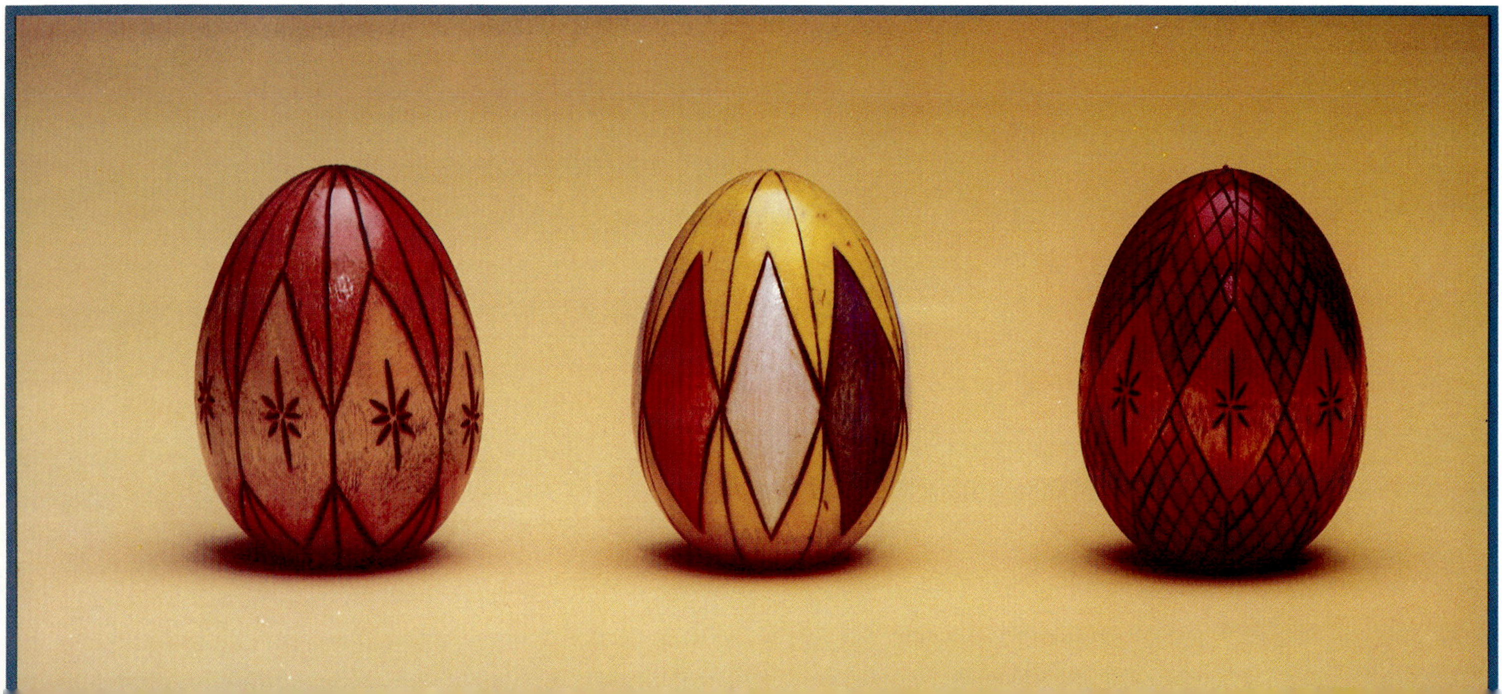

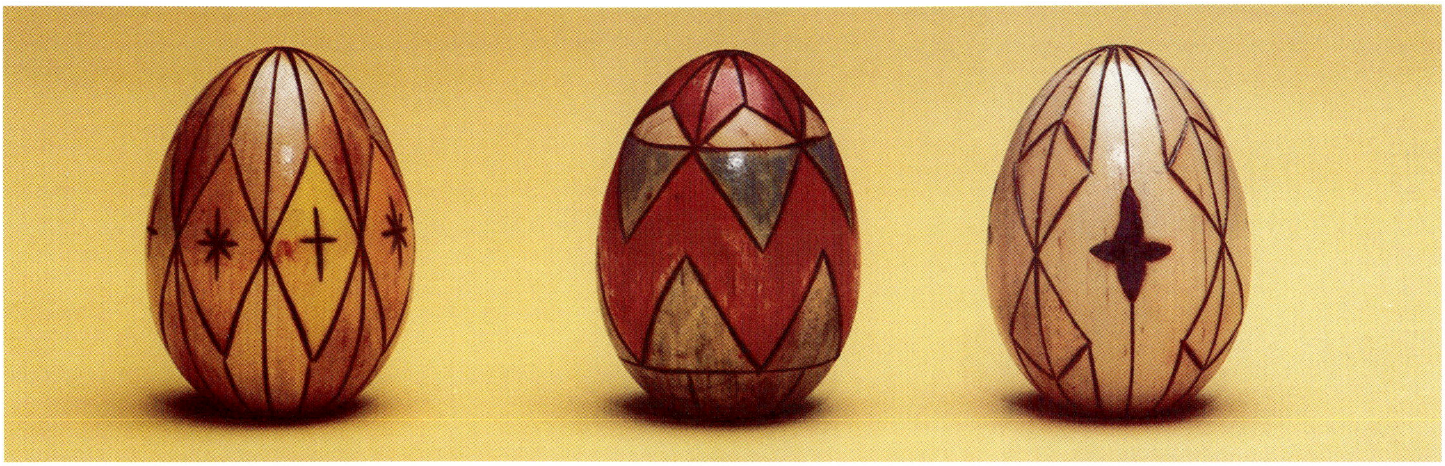

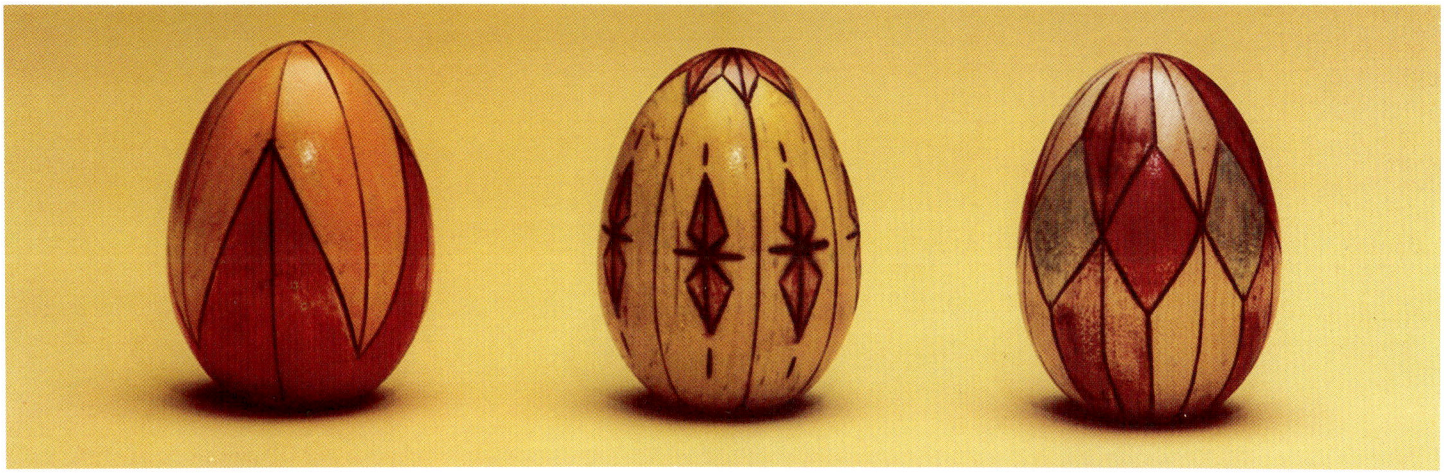

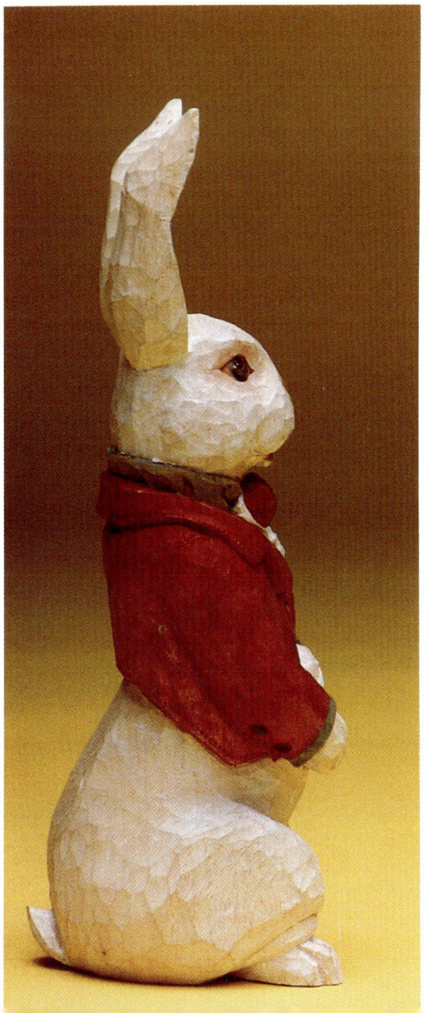

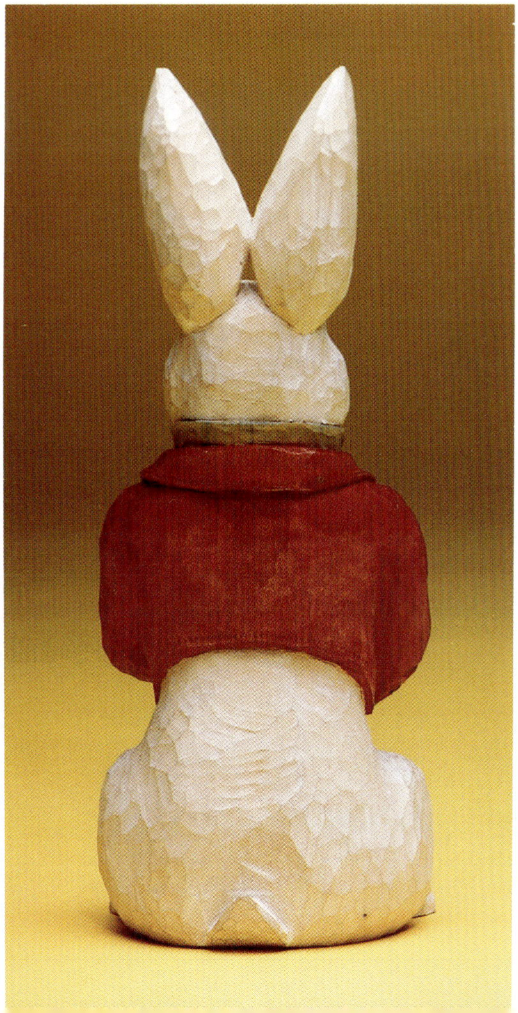

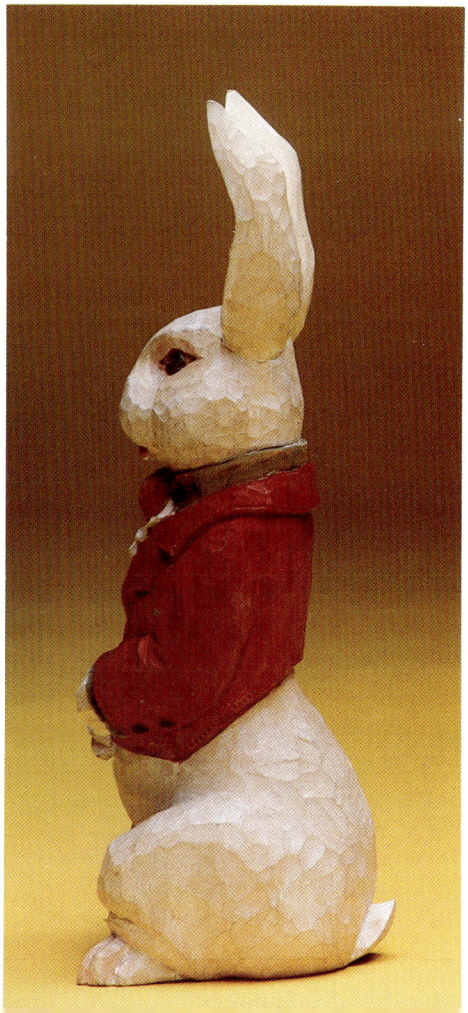

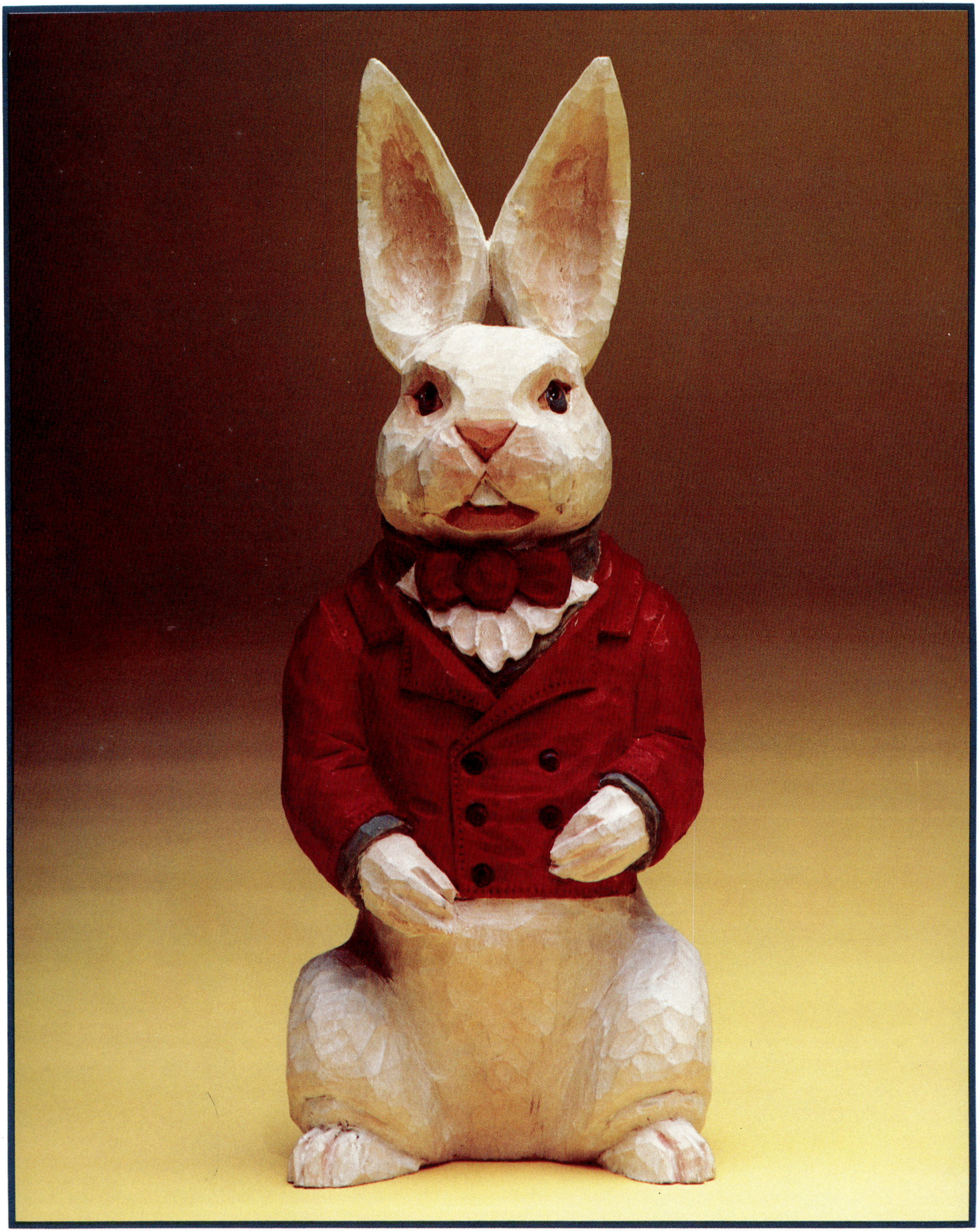

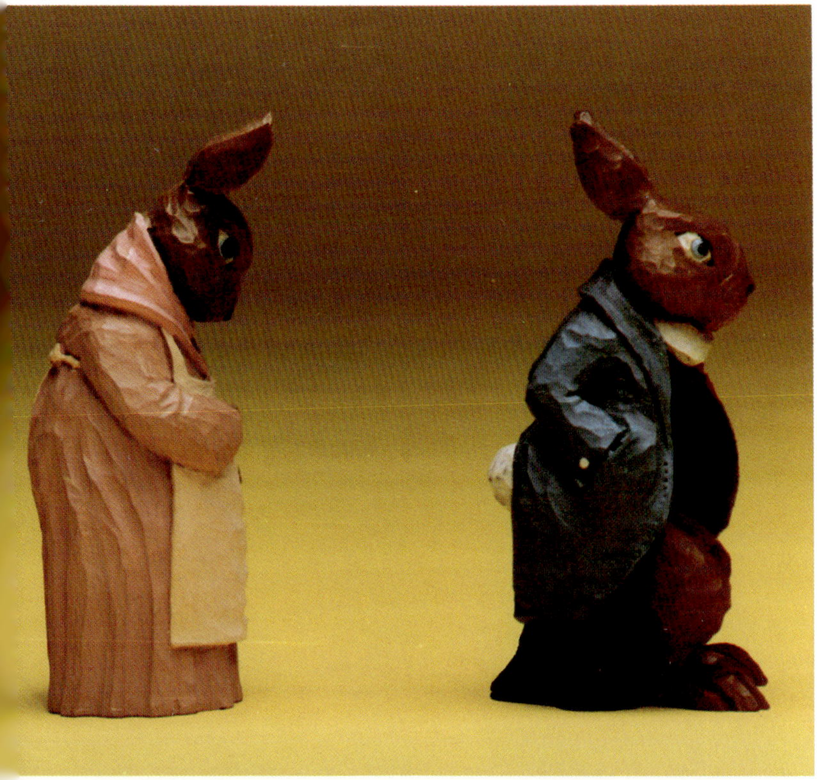

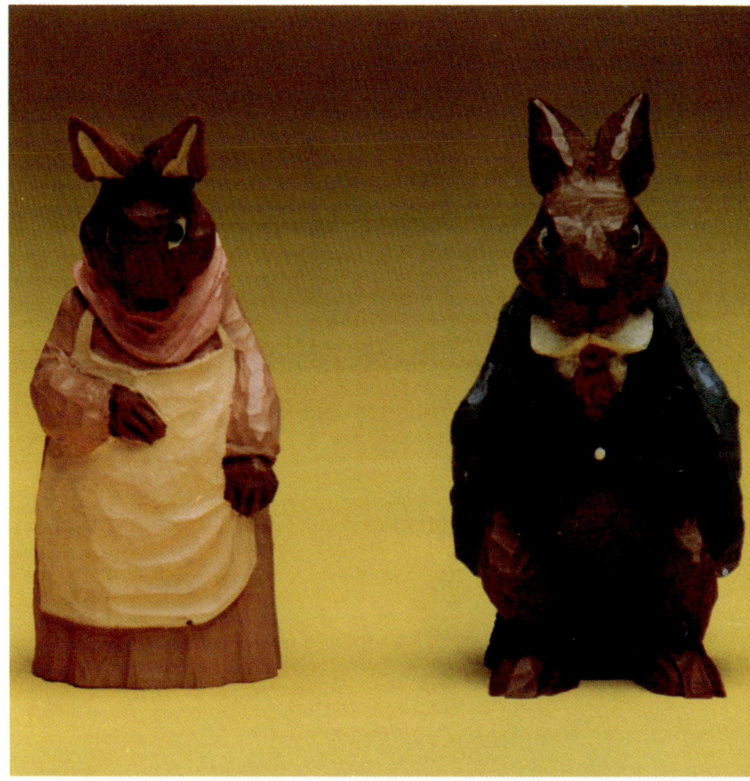

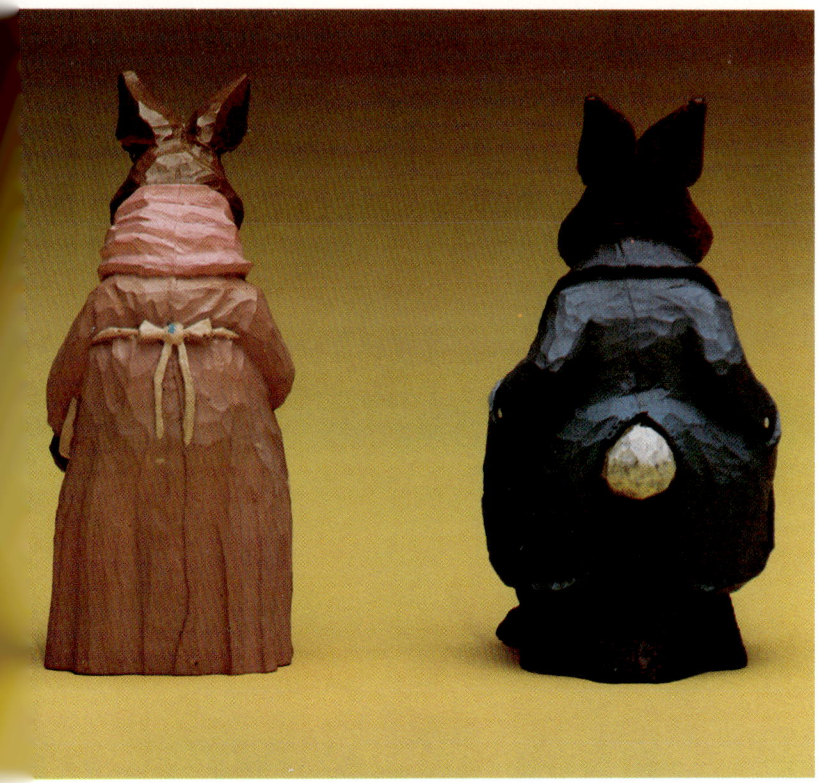

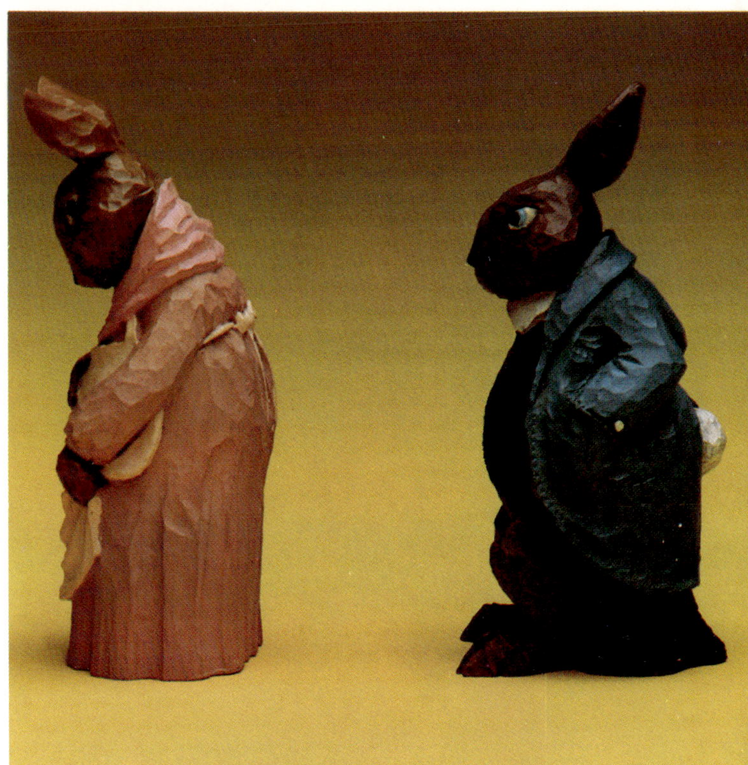

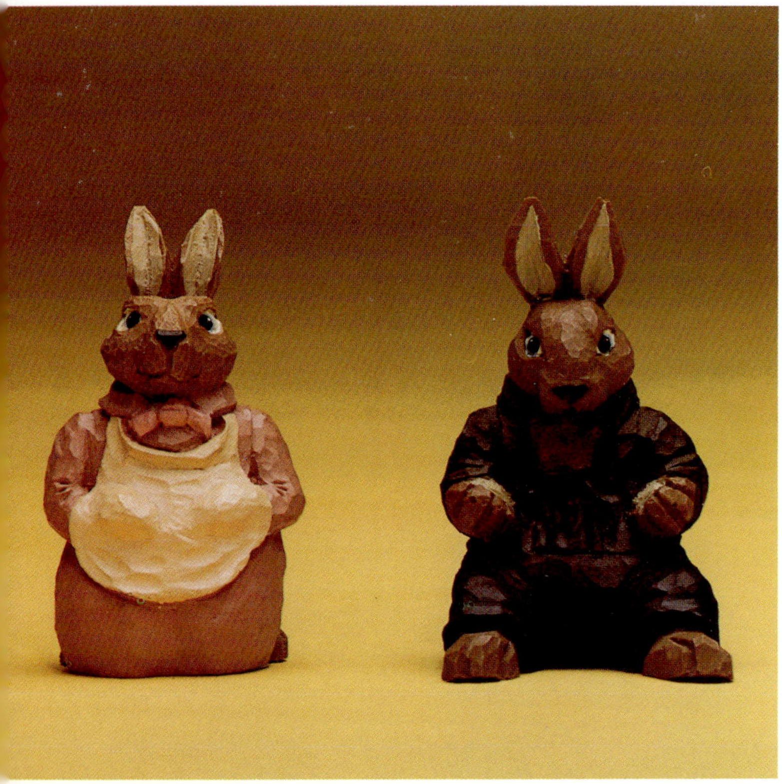
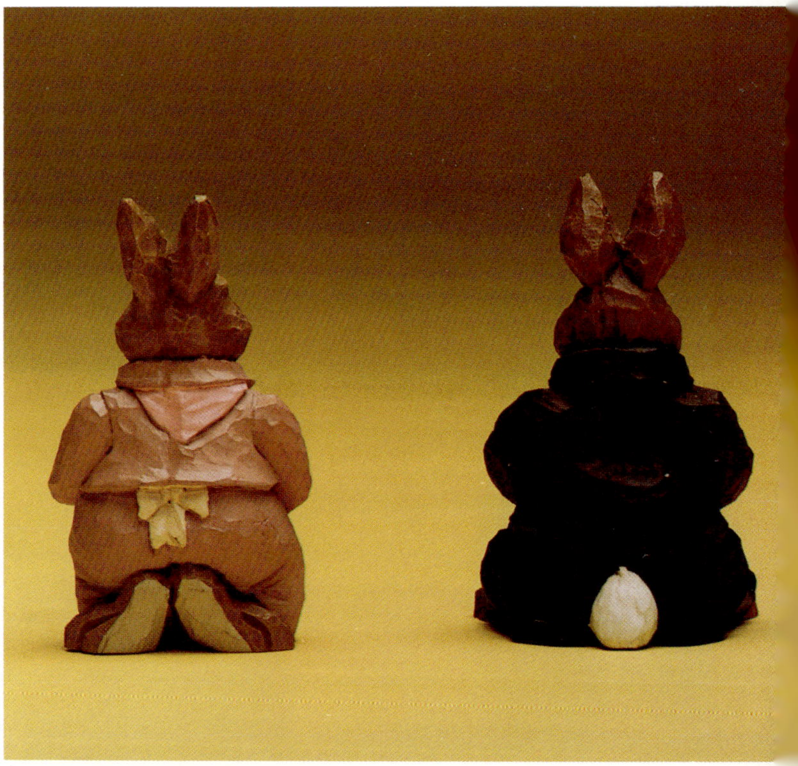
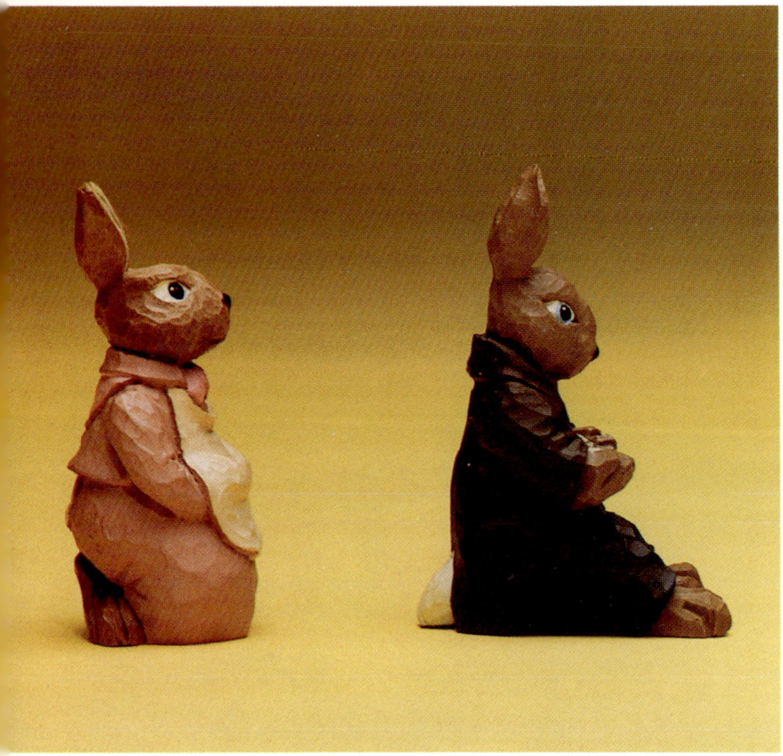
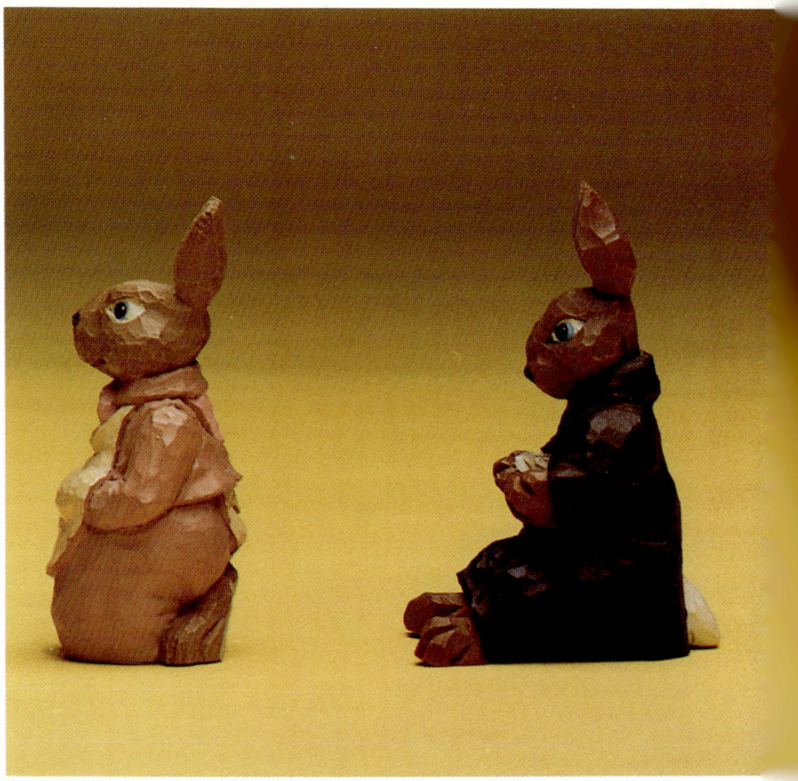

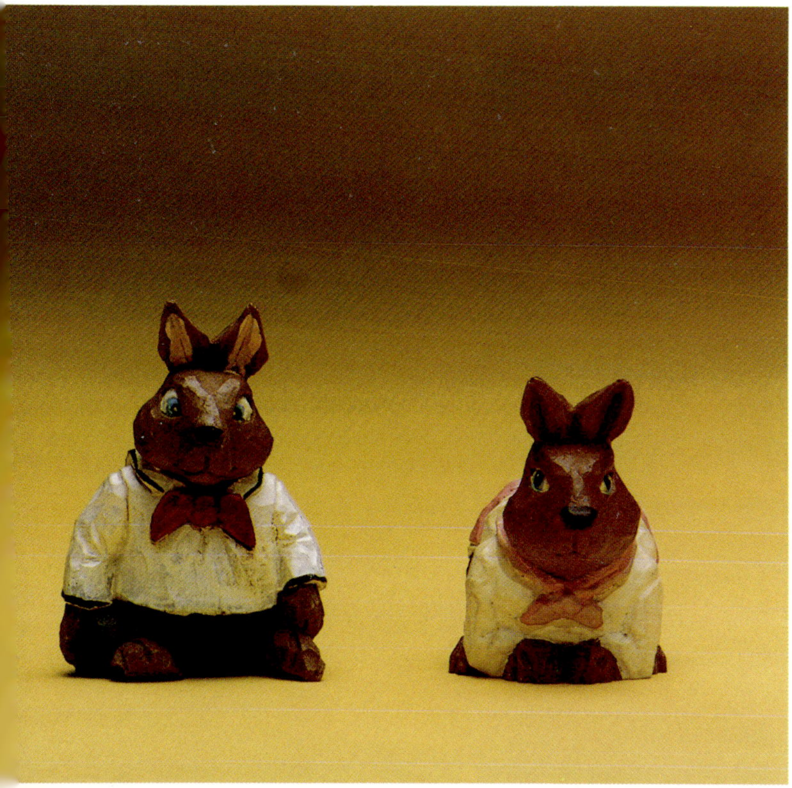
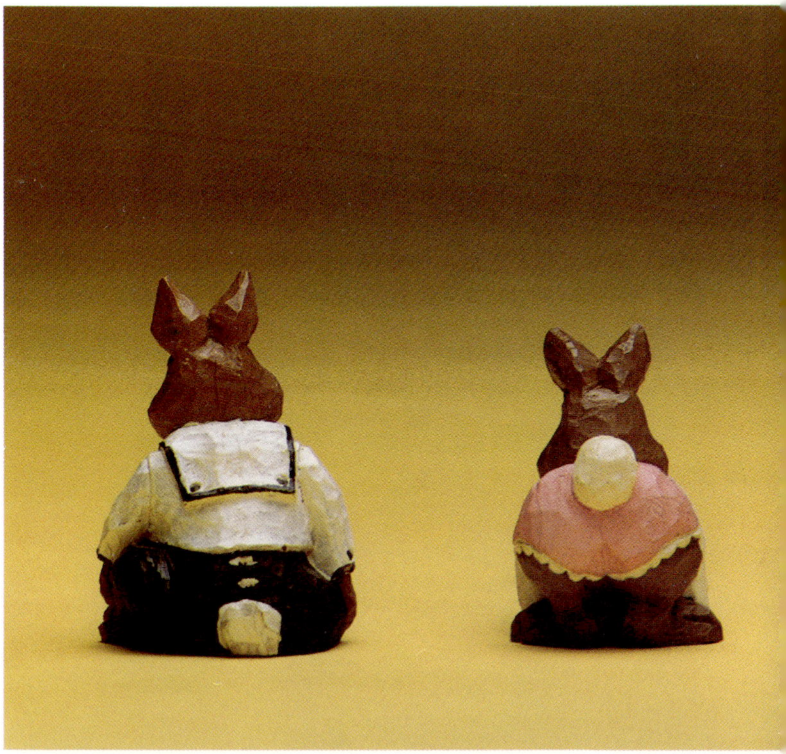
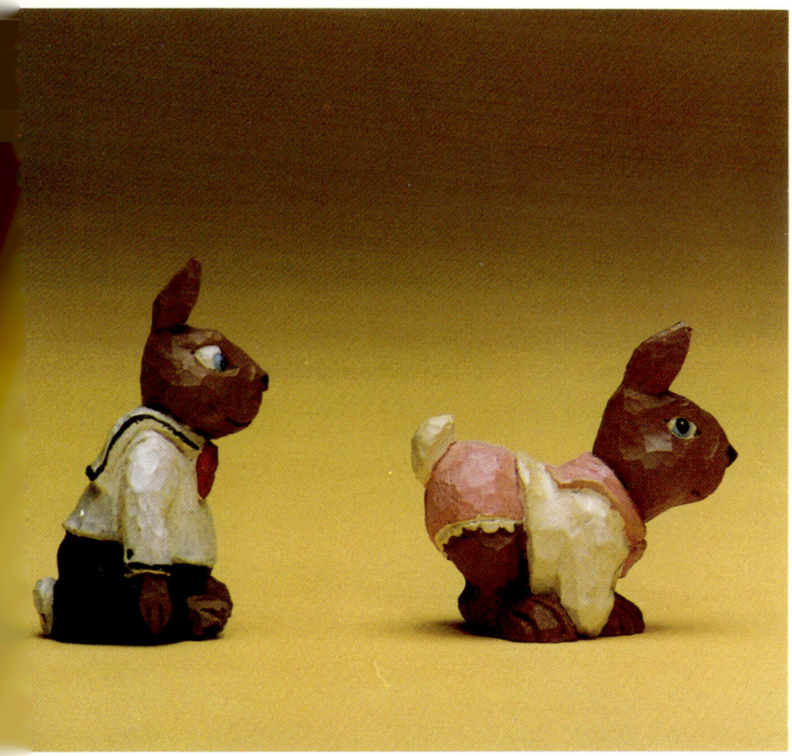
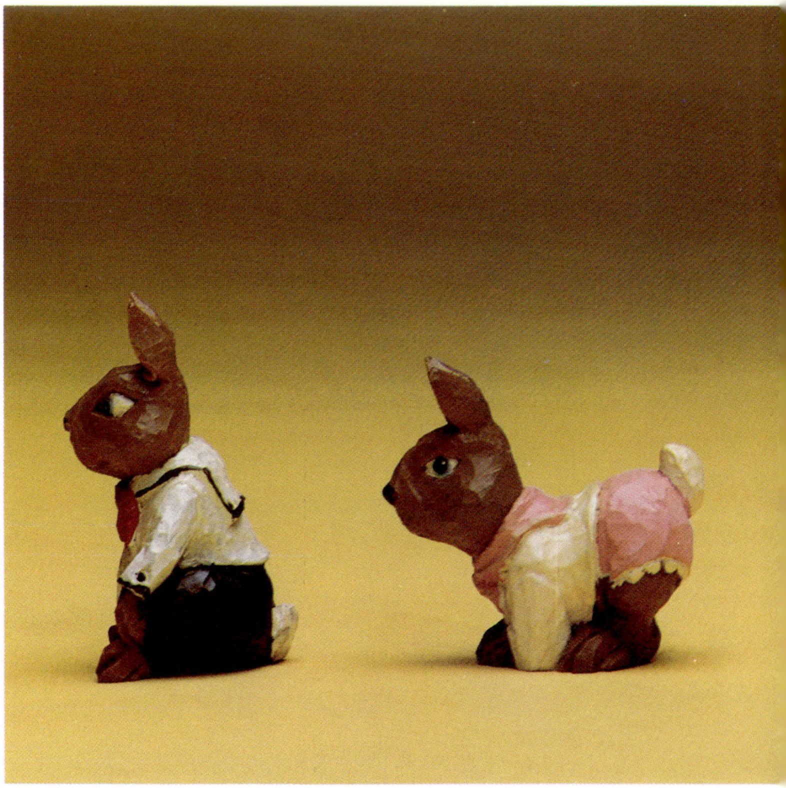

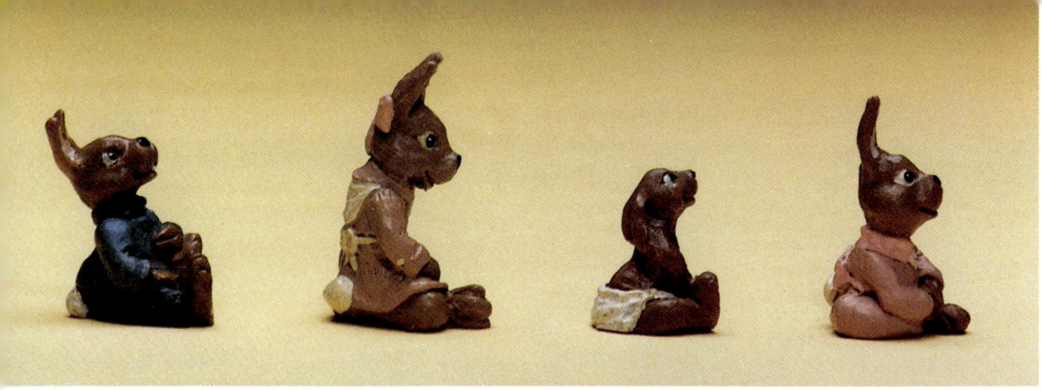
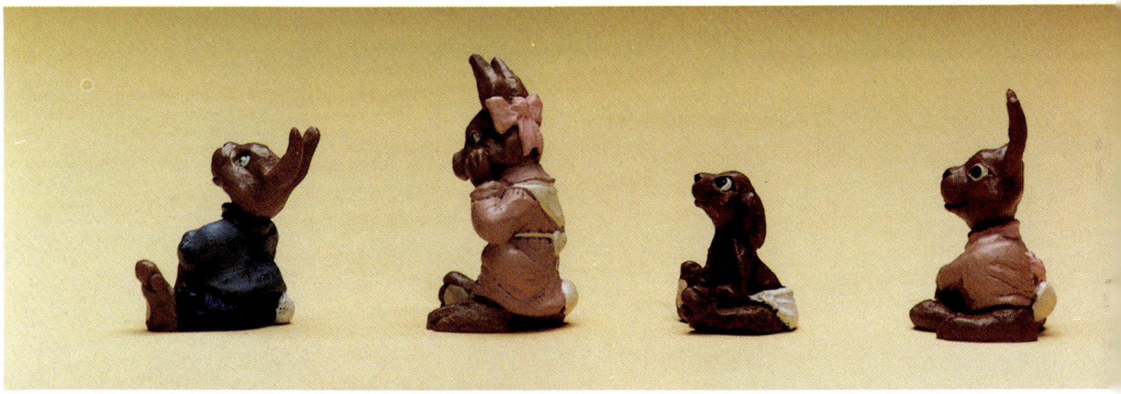
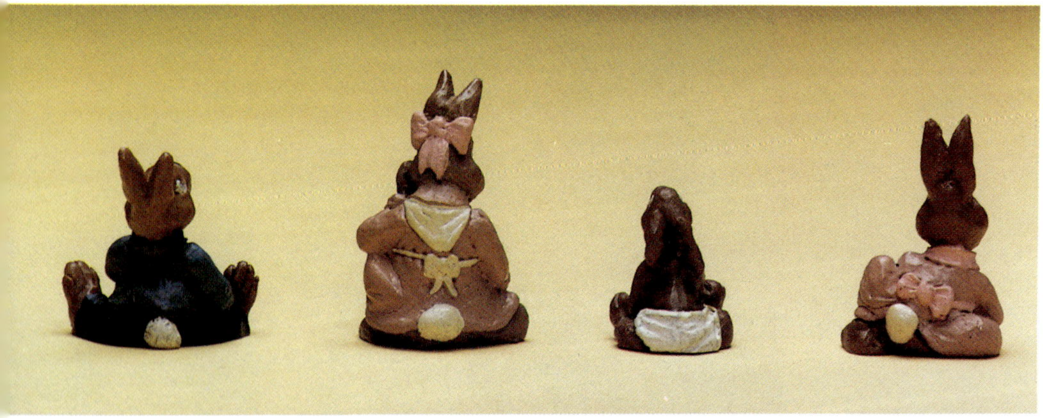
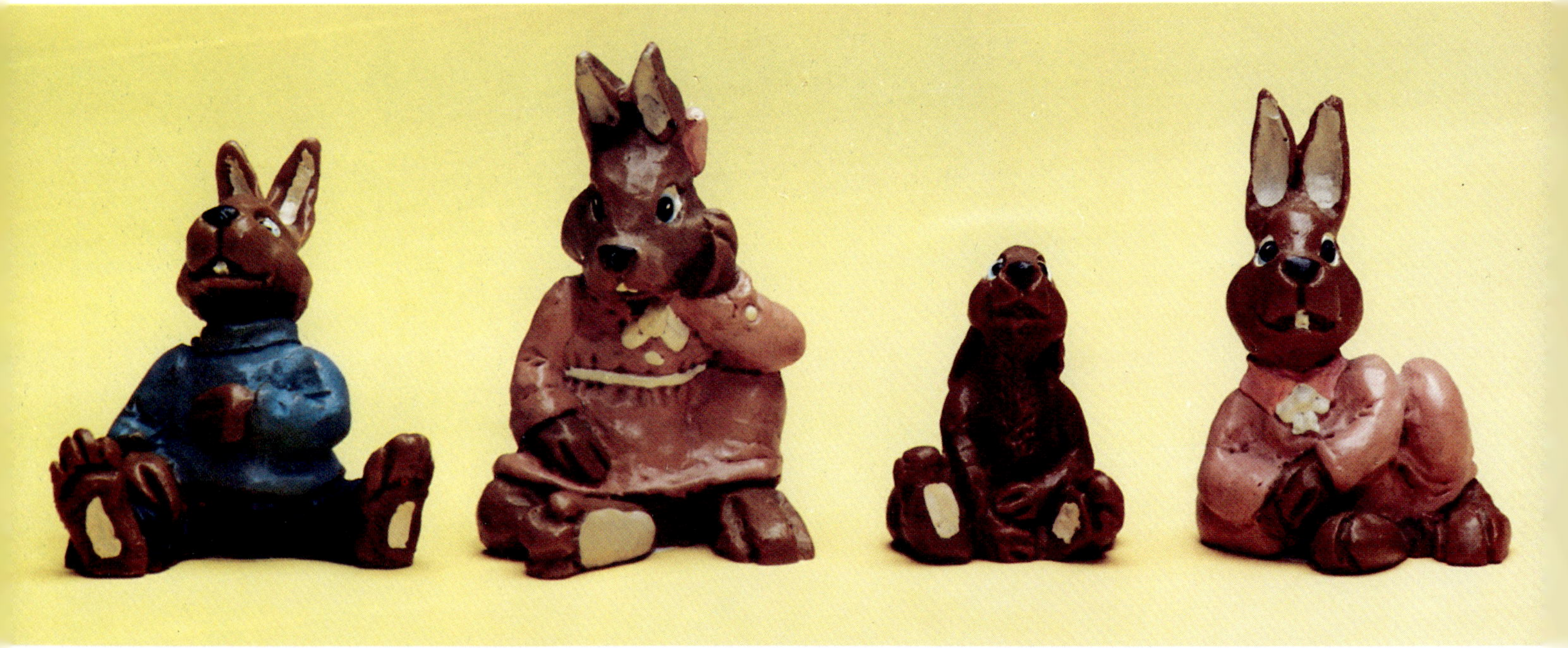